# LIVE LIKE A GUIDE DOG

TYNDALE
MOMENTUM®

*A Tyndale nonfiction imprint*

**Michael Hingson
& Keri Wyatt Kent**

# Live Like a
# Guide Dog

true stories from a blind man and his dogs
about being brave, overcoming adversity,
and moving forward in faith

Visit Tyndale online at tyndale.com.

Visit Tyndale Momentum online at tyndalemomentum.com.

Visit the respective authors at michaelhingson.com and keriwyattkent.com.

*Tyndale*, Tyndale's quill logo, *Tyndale Momentum*, and the Tyndale Momentum logo are registered trademarks of Tyndale House Ministries. Tyndale Momentum is a nonfiction imprint of Tyndale House Publishers, Carol Stream, Illinois.

*Live like a Guide Dog: True Stories from a Blind Man and His Dogs about Being Brave, Overcoming Adversity, and Moving Forward in Faith*

Designed by Dean H. Renninger

Published in association with the literary agency of The Steve Laube Agency.

For information about special discounts for bulk purchases, please contact Tyndale House Publishers at csresponse@tyndale.com, or call 1-855-277-9400.

**Library of Congress Cataloging-in-Publication Data**

A catalog record for this book is available from the Library of Congress.

ISBN 978-1-4964-7655-5 HC
ISBN 978-1-4964-8973-9 SC

Printed in the United States of America

| 30 | 29 | 28 | 27 | 26 | 25 | 24 |
|----|----|----|----|----|----|----|
| 7  | 6  | 5  | 4  | 3  | 2  | 1  |

*This book is dedicated to Karen Hingson—*
*who has taught me to live and love courageously.*
*Karen, you really are my guiding light, my grounding*
*influence, and my solid foundation. All this is for you.*

*I also must give special mention to my eight guide dogs,*
*Fantasia, and every guide dog organization whose*
*people have put their efforts into training the best*
*guides possible. Thanks for everything and for showing*
*us all how to move forward in managing our fears.*

# Contents

# Preface

**FOR MORE THAN TWO DECADES,** my guide dogs and I have been traveling the world, speaking to audiences about trust and teamwork, ethics, diversity, and inclusion and, of course, telling my 9/11 survival story. Escaping Tower One on that fateful day taught me a lot about how to turn fear into courage. That is the premise of this book.

If you experience fear, you're not alone. Everyone feels afraid at various times in their life because it is a normal human response, like sweating when you're hot or bleeding when you're cut. But because of my experiences, and my rather unique upbringing, I've learned how to leverage my fear and use it to empower me to control that fear and be brave. Additionally, I've discovered the value of awareness and preparation, trust and teamwork, empathy and faith.

While my parents instilled these values in me, I also watched my dogs demonstrate these character qualities too—all of which are essential to being brave. Some guide dog experiences showed me that even these loving creatures could exhibit fear and simply not overcome it. All of my dogs were loving and loyal. But each of them exhibited certain strengths, and together we learned lessons about how to be brave.

Over the years, I've navigated a world designed for sighted people. Since childhood, I've been mainstreamed into that world, although that world did not always easily accept my participation. I've needed courage to make my way and to fight against discrimination and condescension that wanted to prevent me from thriving. I realize that most people know little about blindness even though they think they are experts. I hope that you will come to see that there really is more to the world than eyesight to support us.

My book, *Thunder Dog*, showed how teamwork, trust, and faith in God helped my guide dog and me survive the horrifying event in New York City on 9/11. Readers and audiences I spoke to were inspired by our story, but they weren't instructed in how to be brave themselves. I hadn't really given my audiences a strategy for managing fear and turning it into courage. This book seeks to remedy that.

During the pandemic, I realized that all around me people were being blinded by fear. They let their fear keep them stuck, cowering, and afraid. Now, more than ever, people need to know how to take fear and turn it around, to leverage and use it to live more freely.

In writing this book, with the help of Keri Wyatt Kent, I wanted to make it clear that I do know fear. It may not seem as if I showed much fear during my life. Not true. I had wonderful and thoughtful parents who gave me the framework for developing tools that helped me focus and not let fear blind me. By allowing me to try things, to explore and expand my world, by insisting that I had the opportunity to learn, play, and work alongside sighted people, they showed me how to be brave and thrive even in the face of seemingly insurmountable odds.

If I have learned anything during my seventy-plus years of life so far, it is that fear and being afraid should be a positive thing that helps us deal with any situation that befalls us. The issue is whether we let our fears overtake us or whether we learn to use our natural fear reactions to better focus and concentrate to make better decisions. In other words, to turn our fear into courage and a positive and powerful tool we can use anytime.

Dogs do this. Especially when guarding or assisting their humans, they will be quite brave, even in the face of scary circumstances. But often their courage is developed by training. The good news is that you can train yourself to control your fears as well.

Yes, faith and belief in God fuels my courage. God always talks with and to us. The question is whether we learn to listen. Since July 1964 I have had the company and support of eight different guide dogs. Though my upbringing made me bold and confident, I have no doubt that my dogs have made me even more so.

I have learned a lot about communicating with and working with these wonderful creatures. Dogs, like humans, feel fear. But with training and preparation, my guide dogs learned how to use fear in a positive way. They've taught me many lessons by their courageous example. Each chapter in this book explores specific strategies for being brave and controlling fear that my various dogs seemed to specialize in.

I look forward to sharing my dog experiences with you. I hope you will gain a better perspective on the value of establishing a close relationship with your dog friends. What? You don't have dogs in your life? I urge you to change that, especially after reading this book.

I hope you will understand from the following chapters that you can learn to use your fear and fear reactions to your advantage. You will learn that you can create a mindset that will empower you to have more control in your life. You may not be able to control some things that happen to you, but you ALWAYS do have control over how you respond to and deal with situations. Of course, a dog in your life can help if you allow it. And having God in your life will help as well. So, let's get to it. I hope you will discover as much about yourself as I have learned about myself.

# Prologue

**"IT'S JUST A COLD," KAREN ASSURED ME.**

My wife's voice sounded horrible, hoarse, and raspy.

"I really think you need to go to urgent care," I told her.

"They'll just tell me it's bronchitis," she said, stifling a cough. "I'll be fine. I just need to rest for a couple of days."

I didn't totally believe Karen. I was concerned, but I didn't feel I could force her to go. Karen and I trusted each other deeply. I knew she had grown up knowing her body, especially since she had spent her entire existence being paralyzed and using a wheelchair. Her parents taught her to always be aware of her physical condition and to not take chances when something made her feel out of sorts. Still, I worried.

Fantasia, Karen's attentive yellow Lab, lay on the floor next to Karen's wheelchair. As we spoke, she stood and nosed Karen, then put her front paws up into her lap. "It's okay, girl," Karen said, stroking her. "Good dog."

*Maybe she's right*, I thought, as I continued to pack my suitcase. I hated to leave her, but I had agreed to attend the 2014 National Washington Seminar for the National Federation of the Blind in Washington, DC, weeks before Karen had come down with . . . whatever this was. In fact, we had both gotten sick the same weekend. I recovered quickly, but she seemed to be getting sicker.

LIVE LIKE A GUIDE DOG

"Are you sure?" I asked again. "You sound like you're getting worse. Maybe I shouldn't go."

"I'll be fine," she said in a tone that might have been more convincing had it not been followed by a wheezy cough. "Did you remember to pack underwear?" Karen teased.

"Yeah, I've got it," I said, grinning.

"You're sure?" she said. Her playful comment made me feel a little less worried.

"If you're sure you're good, I'm going to go get dinner started," she said.

I closed the suitcase and zipped it shut as Karen turned her motorized wheelchair toward the door, with Fantasia beside her. Was it my imagination, or was Fantasia being especially solicitous with Karen this week, even hovering a bit?

*She'll be fine,* I reassured myself. Despite being born a paraplegic, Karen had always been incredibly independent.

I set the suitcase on the floor.

*Karen's friends are not far away. I will ask them to look in on her,* I decided.

*And of course, she has Fantasia by her side.*

And so, on January 24, 2014, my guide dog, Africa (who was Fantasia's daughter), and I were driven to San Francisco International Airport to catch a flight to Baltimore and be taken to the NFB National Center for initial preparations for the seminar. We left not knowing just how soon everything would unexpectedly change.

# 1

# SQUIRE
## Awareness builds confidence

Our volunteer puppy raisers need to
develop awareness of what's going
on in the environment, not just for
themselves, but for the puppy. From
the puppy's perspective.
**JAMES DERN,**
*Senior Manager, Puppy Program,
Canine Companions for Independence*

**WE MUST HAVE LOOKED ODD.**
    Jeff Locke and I walked through the campus of Guide Dogs for
the Blind (GDB)—trainer and student. Jeff held the dog end of the
guide dog harness and leash in one hand as if it were on a real guide
dog, and I held the other ends of both in my left hand just as I would
if I were working a real dog. Jeff stopped and started, occasionally
moving the harness up, down, forward, back. He reminded me of
what commands to give at different times.
    For example, when I said "Sit," Jeff lowered his end of the harness.
Then Jeff told me to command my dog to go forward. "Forward,"
I said. The harness raised, and Jeff began moving forward.
    This peculiar sight was common at GDB headquarters in San
Rafael. A dog trainer, walking beside a blind person, would simulate

for them what it felt like to walk with a dog in a guide harness and leash. In my class, most of the blind students were middle-aged. Except for one: a fourteen-year-old boy with strawberry blond hair and a lot of energy. Me.

Suddenly, Jeff ceased moving forward, and I felt the harness stop. I kept my wits about me, remembering a lecture that emphasized when guide dogs do something you don't expect, there is a reason.

Jeff waited for a moment, giving me time to investigate and figure it out. I moved my foot around. Aha! The edge of a curb.

"Good boy," I said. My "dog" had done exactly what he was trained to do. Now I was being trained in how to reinforce and continue that training.

"Forward," I said confidently, and Jeff moved the handle forward.

"This is where the harness should be, to keep your harness handle grip at your left knee," Jeff explained. He slowly moved the handle forward a little too far, on purpose.

"Juno, steady," I said, pulling gently on the leash.

"Juno" training prepares blind handlers to work with an actual dog. Juno is the name of the imaginary dog, which is not a dog at all, but a simulation.

To the blind student, the training feels pretty much like working with a dog. Meanwhile, the trainer simulates the movements of the dog and watches what the trainee is doing, customizing the training exercises while evaluating the student in order to eventually match the student with the perfect guide dog. It also helps handlers feel less afraid and more confident. The training provides a place for the partners to practice as a team, and for the student to experience the world from a dog's perspective.

"Let's practice some down-sits," Jeff said. He stood in front of me, holding the leash. For now we'd set the harness aside to focus on obedience training, which is done only with the leash.

"Juno, heel," I said firmly.

Jeff walked toward me and did a U-turn around my back to simulate the dog going to my left side and sitting, as commanded.

"Good boy," I said, continuing to praise Juno's proper behavior.

"Juno, down," I said. Jeff moved the leash down as if Juno had laid down on the sidewalk. We waited a few minutes. "Okay," Jeff said. "Ask for a sit, without moving forward."

I grasped the leash firmly and said, "Juno, sit," while at the same time giving a slight upward motion. The dog is supposed to simply rise from lying down to sitting, keeping its haunches on the ground, and Jeff moved the leash to simulate those movements.

Not every blind or low-vision person uses a guide dog. In fact, less than 10 percent do. Not everyone wants a guide dog. The level of commitment required for the responsibility of handling and caring for a guide dog is more than some people want to do. Finally, to use a guide dog effectively, one must not only have good mobility and orientation skills, but they must want to take on the added requirement of building a team, for which they must be the team leader. Guide dogs are simply not for everyone.

Guide dogs do not "lead," they guide. Every handler must know where they want to go and how to get there, and using commands we communicate to the dog where we want to go. The dog's job is to make sure we walk safely. As I like to say, I am the navigator, and the dog is the pilot.

Jeff simulated the dog walking too far ahead of me, lagging, veering off course, and even turning the wrong way, teaching me how to keep the dog moving forward as he should. But most importantly, Juno training allowed Jeff to observe me. How fast did I walk? How confidently did I take corners? Did I know to stop at intersections?

Each trainer team had a group or string of dogs. At the time when I got my first guide dog, Jeff had a string of about a dozen dogs that he and his apprentice trainer, Bruce Benzler, had spent months training. Once our class of students arrived at the school, Jeff and Bruce not only trained us in the basics of using a guide dog but also played matchmaker to select the exact right dog for each student. Each trainer team knew their pups' personalities and temperaments. Jeff and Bruce constantly observed and evaluated me to decide which dog would do best with an energetic teenager getting his first dog. Both Jeff and Bruce taught the class of eight, often switching places so both of them fully got to observe all of us.

What we didn't know is that they constantly conferred with each other on what dog they felt would work best with which student. For example, a dog that is more tentative in its movements and personality wouldn't be a good match for someone who is extremely confident and who likes to get up and go. Or someone who struggles to sit still. They worked with each class member as well as participating together in class lectures for three days. Working with a simulation allows handlers to gain skills without causing their dog undue fear.

Even if you are not blind, you can become more courageous by taking small steps to learn and increase your awareness. We often fear the unknown. So the more you become aware, the less you will experience fear. This is true of both dogs and humans.

Guide dog training teaches dogs to be highly aware of their surroundings and deeply attuned to the commands of their handler. That awareness helps them to guide safely and fearlessly. While we as blind travelers often may go to places not familiar to us, it is our responsibility to learn how to get around. Most importantly, we must not show uncertainty or fear of the unknown to our guide dogs, or the dogs will become more stressed and fearful themselves.

In the training office in our dorm, I squirmed on a hard plastic chair. My body quivered with excitement. Like many teenage boys, sitting quietly was not my strong suit. Especially when I'd been waiting all morning, and in fact, for days, for this moment.

It was "dog day."

After listening to lectures, and doing Juno training for three days, the moment I'd been anticipating had arrived. I took deep breaths, fidgeted, and tapped my sneakers on the tile floor.

"Mike, sit quietly. I'm going to let Squire come in now," said

Bruce. "He's a dark red golden retriever that weighs about sixty-four pounds. I need you to be still, and don't say anything. Don't call him. Just wait, and let's see what he does."

*Don't call him? I want to tackle him and hug him!* I shifted in the chair, making its metal feet scrape loudly on the linoleum floor. I took one more deep breath and held it.

I heard Bruce open the door, and immediately the room echoed with the staccato tapping of Squire's nails on the floor. Squire snuffled loudly as he crossed the room, getting closer to me by the second. I gripped the sides of the chair to keep myself from reaching for him.

Suddenly, his soft doggy breath was on my face. He sniffed me all over—methodically and rapidly taking my scent in. When he sat down next to my chair, everything got quiet.

"Well, it looks like you've got a friend already," Bruce said. "Go ahead and pet him."

We had a dog at home, so I knew better than to launch myself at a dog, even one as meticulously trained as Squire. In my head I was singing his name, giving it three syllables, like "Su-per-man!"

Squi-aiy-yer!

I reached slowly toward the sound of panting, my fingers connecting with silky ears and a strong head. I rubbed Squire's head and powerful shoulders, gently stroked his soft coat, then reached around him to give him a hug. He nuzzled me and licked my hand, and immediately I thought, *I'm Superman—able to do anything!* Still, I admit I was a little nervous too. My world was about to expand dramatically.

Not that it was particularly small before that day.

---

I have been totally blind since birth, but thanks to my parents I viewed it as an inconvenience but not a disability. When my blindness was discovered in infancy, the doctor recommended institutionalizing me because, as he said, "No blind child could ever grow up to be able to contribute to society. All this child will be is a drain on your family."

My parents listened politely but took me home and proceeded to raise me to be a kid like everyone else. I may have navigated the world using some different techniques, but I fully participated in that world. I didn't let blindness scare me or slow me down. As I was growing up, I never really thought about blindness, much less thought of it as a real problem.

God blessed me with two parents who knew that the only way I would learn to live in the world was to let me explore, just like all my sighted relatives and friends. I familiarized myself with my South Side neighborhood in Chicago just like my older brother, Ellery, and my cousins, Robby and Steve, did. The fact that they could see and I couldn't wasn't a big deal, mostly because my parents decided not to make it one.

Sometimes I learned awareness the hard way.

"Wow!" I said, running my hands over the smooth plastic of a toy pedal car, a gift for my third birthday. "Car!"

"Step in here and sit down," Mom explained. "Put your feet on the pedals, and you can make it go."

The pedal car was just my size, and I loved the feeling of scooting along the hallway of our apartment—a great outlet for my boundless energy. I was excited to "drive" myself around.

"Beep, beep!" I shouted, hitting the steering wheel with my hand. I took off down the hallway of our home, pedaling furiously. My first few test-drives included some minor sideswipes of the walls, but I soon became adept at using my hearing to drive my little car around our apartment. Well, mostly I used my hearing well.

A week or two later, I'd become the Mario Andretti of our living room. I raced down the hall and whipped around a turn. *Bam!* My face hit something solid, and I yowled in pain.

"Michael!" My mom came running.

I had driven straight into the coffee table that was just high enough for the hood of my little car to slide underneath. I bashed my face into the side of the table. I'm told there was a lot of blood. Mom gave me a towel to hold on my chin while we drove to the emergency room.

I needed six stitches to close the wound, but I was brave for the doctor and didn't cry. When we got home, my mother just shook her head and said, "Michael, you're just going to have to learn to watch where you're going." So I did.

What I didn't realize as a three-year-old was that my mom was teaching me to learn from my mistakes and to not be afraid when challenges came my way. She didn't take away my toy car or say it was too dangerous. Instead, she guided me toward greater awareness.

This sense of awareness is something psychologist and author Jordan Peterson discussed with podcaster Theo Von in 2022. A portion of their conversation has become the soundtrack for countless memes and TikTok videos. Here's what Peterson said:

> If you are going to make your kids tough, which they
> better be if they are going to survive in the world, you can't
> interfere when they're doing dangerous things carefully.

This advice, offered decades after my parents raised me, sums up their parenting strategy perfectly. Perhaps you weren't raised this way—most kids aren't anymore. But you can implement what Peterson suggests: Do dangerous things carefully. You'll become tougher and braver. When you test your courage—fully aware of the risks—and come through it stronger than when you started, your confidence will naturally grow.

When I was five, we moved to Palmdale, California, where I got to start all over again familiarizing myself with an entirely new neighborhood. My parents were my strongest advocates and encouraged me to do things, make mistakes, and learn from them. I went to school with sighted kids and did just fine.

I became knowledgeable about my surroundings. I can still conjure up a map of my childhood neighborhood in my head—just like most sighted people can. I didn't realize it at the time, but building the skill of awareness also deconstructed or diminished my fears.

As a little kid, it never occurred to me to be fearful—mostly because no one told me I should be. Frankly, I didn't even think of myself as blind. I knew other kids and adults could do this thing called "seeing," something I seemed not to be able to do. However, as I grew up, I discovered that I could do things other people couldn't do, like solving algebra equations in my head, and "hearing" the coffee table. I began to recognize that each of us have individual gifts, and not having others' gifts didn't make me better or worse than anyone else.

My dad, George Hingson, and I often discussed this. He had no problem telling me that I was blind, but he also reminded me that blindness was not a problem if I didn't let it be one.

"How will I be able to do what others do by seeing?" I asked him.

"How do you do things now?"

"I listen and figure things out."

"Right," my dad said. "If you continue to listen and use all the skills you have and will learn—skills given to you by God—you will be successful and able to do whatever you want in life."

My dad loved me and spent a lot of time with me. I had no reason to doubt him. I realize now that his confidence in me gave me confidence in myself. To others, that confidence may look like courage. To me, it was my normal approach to life.

We had several pet dogs while I was growing up. None of them, as I recall, took special interest in me. They loved all of us, and our whole family loved each of them. When I was six, we adopted a mutt named Lady from a shelter, but she lived with us only two years before contracting distemper. I vividly remember January 4, 1958, when my parents told me that Lady had to be put to sleep. I was quite sad and really missed her.

That September we welcomed Rudy, a five-year-old standard size dachshund, into our family. He loved being close to everyone, always finding ways to be underfoot, even with me. He seemed to think of me as just another playmate, not a blind kid who needed special treatment. Rudy lived with us five years before he passed naturally. Later that year we adopted a miniature dachshund named Pee Wee.

Before Squire entered my life, I navigated the world by feel and by listening. I didn't use a white cane because no one ever taught me that. I learned it later in life. My parents just expected me to figure things out, so I learned to pay attention. I didn't realize it at the time but being aware of your situation and surroundings is essential for managing fear and being brave.

A dog's acute sense of hearing and smell makes them tune in to the world around them. Sometimes awareness can cause you (or your dog) to be afraid—you sense danger. Sometimes that awareness protects you from danger—it tells you to be cautious, or to avoid certain places or situations. For example, when my dog and I are halfway through an intersection, and I hear a car coming toward us, I don't just stand there. I hustle to the sidewalk on the other side. Even though crossing the street can be dangerous, I don't avoid it altogether. I'm just careful. The goal is not to never be afraid, but to leverage your fear to bravely face whatever comes your way.

Growing up in a family that expected me to function well right alongside my sighted peers forced me to be hyperaware of my surroundings. I learned to "hear" the coffee table, posts, and doorways. Yes, I became a better driver after hitting the table. Learning to ride a bike was a little more challenging—but again, since my parents seemed confident I could do it, I believed them.

---

"Why are your eyes white like that?" Cindy asked me. Cindy and her family had just moved into a house across the street and a few doors down.

"I'm blind," I explained matter-of-factly, as if I were saying, "I'm left-handed."

"What's that?" Cindy asked. We were both about seven years old.

"It means I don't see the way other people do."

"Oh. Okay. Want to go play on my swing set?" She clearly wasn't worried about my lack of light-dependence.

"Sure," I said, taking off down the street, with Cindy right behind me.

In addition to the cool backyard swing set, Cindy had a full-sized bicycle. She loved riding it up and down the streets of our little desert town.

"You wanna ride it?" Cindy asked one day. "I can teach you."

"Yes, please!"

"Okay," she said, helping me onto the bike. "Put your foot here," she said, guiding my right foot onto a pedal. "Pedal backward to stop; pedal forward to go," she offered helpfully. She ran beside me, holding the back of the seat and shouting instructions, but I still crashed. Still, I wasn't about to give up. After a few falls, I figured out how to keep my balance and the bike upright. But how was I going to avoid obstacles?

*Of course! My pedal car training.* I had learned how to listen for curbs, parked cars, and other obstacles. The same strategy could be implemented here.

Eventually I became quite adept at navigating the neighborhood on two wheels. I remember rolling through the streets of Palmdale on Cindy's bike and eventually on my own bike.

I remember it like it was yesterday. The wind in my face felt amazing. As I pedaled, I listened intently. The rubber tires sang to me, changing their pitch just slightly as I approached a parked car or drifted too close to the curb. The skills of echolocation I honed when I was younger by simply navigating the neighborhood on foot and my pedal car served me well.

Cindy and I were riding our bikes one day when she suddenly asked, "How do you get around?"

"I listen."

"But you can't see!"

"Well," I said, "do you really have to use your eyes to see?"

As Cindy and I rode up and down our street, I described to her things that I heard that clued me in as to how to ride safely. Cindy got it.

Rolling along, I made a gentle clicking sound with my mouth and listened. The slight echo of the noise changed when there was an object near me or in front of me. No one taught me to do this—it was an instinctive way of seeing my surroundings that I had figured out when walking around. My mom had told me to watch where I was going, so I had figured out how to do that. My brother compared me to a bat, but I didn't care. Echolocation was my superpower, a tool I developed to increase my awareness of my surroundings, which helped me navigate the world with less fear.

I also paid attention to small details. The end of our driveway had slightly different cracks from others nearby. After a while, knowing my way around became second nature, just like it does for any kid who explores their neighborhood.

One day as I returned home from riding my bike around the neighborhood and walked in the door, I heard the telephone ring and my dad say "Hello."

"Yes," he said a moment later. As the conversation progressed it became clear that my dad and the caller were talking about me and my bike riding. And the caller was not happy.

"What about it?" my dad said.

"I understand. Uh-huh."

Pause.

"Did he fall off the bike?"

Pause again.

"No? Did he crash into anything? No again? You're sure?" Dad didn't filter the sarcasm from his voice.

I could hear the caller's high-pitched but muffled protest.

"Uh-huh," Dad said. The conversation suddenly stopped. After a moment of quiet, Dad hung up the phone.

"He hung up on me," he said.

It must have really driven some neighbors crazy when I not only rode my bike around the block, but then biked to Yucca Elementary School every day. But it didn't bother me, and after all, it was my parents' idea for me to do so.

My upbringing trained me to be aware, but not allow fear to overwhelm me. It's not that I didn't sometimes feel scared. But I learned early how to control it—and use it. In a moment when we feel fear, which is a natural, physical reaction, we can either panic and be blinded by our fear, or we can leverage the hyperawareness that is a part of fear to help us walk forward. I also realized that the more aware you are, the less you will feel afraid. Because we primarily fear the unknown.

The guide dog looks to its handler for direction—not just where to go, but how to approach any situation. When I feel afraid, I begin not by denying it, but becoming aware of it. I make a conscious decision to keep from panicking (at least on the outside). I notice and pay attention to the involuntary physiological responses that fear can elicit, and I begin to control my breathing, my body movements, and all my external behaviors so that my dog can stay calm and so I can mitigate those physiological reactions. Rather than spiral into panic mode, I focus on self-awareness and self-control.

In turn, my dog reads my steadiness and responds by doing their job of guiding without fear. The dog's calm response to my calmness helps me to manage my fear even more. My dog draws courage from me, and I draw courage from my dog. It's a beautiful experience. Together we reassure one another that we can be brave.

As Bruce Benzler told us during one class, "If we fear or become stressed, then so will our guide dogs." That lesson has always stuck with me, and one day it would save my life.

After dog day in San Rafael, we students spent several weeks learning how to navigate the world with our new guide dog beside us.

"Mike, the leash lets you communicate with your dog. The harness lets him communicate with you," Bruce reminded me. We walked around the campus of Guide Dogs for the Blind with several other students, practicing the delicate dance that is guiding and being guided.

"Forward," I said to Squire, and started to walk. But I ended up ahead of him.

"Mike, wait for Squire to take the first step. Keep your left foot by his right paw." *Easy for him to say*. But if you pay attention, you can sense where the dog is, and how the harness shifts when he begins to move. Then follow his lead even as you simultaneously direct him.

"And say 'Forward' like you mean it," Bruce added. "Remember, you need to learn to trust Squire and let him guide just as Squire needs to learn to trust you to know where you want to go."

"Forward," I said, enthusiastically this time. I waited, and the harness lifted up and forward as Squire began to move. I worked to match my step to his.

"Okay, in about ten steps, signal him to turn right." I felt the sidewalk beneath my feet, then moved my right hand to the right with a slight flick of the wrist.

"Right," I told Squire.

Via the harness, I felt Squire respond to my command and turn, and I walked around the corner perfectly with him.

"Great job!" Bruce said, matching my enthusiasm. "Use the harness to know where he is and keep yourself out of his way, but next to him."

Our training class was four weeks long. So Squire and I got roughly three-and-a-half weeks of working together under Bruce and Jeff's supervision. On our last day, a Saturday, we gathered for a graduation ceremony. Because I was the youngest, I was chosen to be the class valedictorian. I wrote a brief speech in Braille. I don't even remember now what I said, but I am sure I thanked Jeff, Bruce, and

**Guide dogs know that awareness builds confidence, which helps you overcome fear of the unknown by making it known.**

the entire Guide Dogs for the Blind staff. I know I talked about what a difference Squire would make in my life.

Before graduation, we got to meet the people who raised our guide dogs. Nancy, Squire's puppy raiser, was a 4-H member. The high point of the day, as you can imagine, was when our dogs were officially presented to us.

Right after graduation, Squire and I flew home—my first time on an airplane. I was more curious than afraid. My father worked at Edwards Air Force Base and airplanes were a common topic of discussion around our house. Dad was involved with experimental aircraft such as the X-15 rocket plane, so I already had a pretty good notion of what flying was. Of course, there is nothing like actually being in a plane and flying.

My biggest concern was how Squire would handle this new flying experience. I shouldn't have worried. We boarded the Convair A4 and the flight attendant directed us to the "lounge" at the back of the plane. Here, two bench seats faced each other. I sat down and fastened my seat belt, and Squire lay down in front of me. The aircraft taxied to the runway, gained speed, and we were off. Squire took it all in stride. He didn't even get up during the flight to look out the window!

I spent the hour-long flight talking to the others in the lounge and also talking to and petting Squire. My seatmates wanted to know all about Squire and about guide dog training. The time passed all too quickly, and we landed at Burbank Airport. My parents were there to greet me and the hero dog. Of course, Squire immediately made friends with them.

Finally, we returned home and settled into a "normal" life. I'd been around dogs most of my life, but I'd never had one so attentive and well-trained. I was smitten—and eager to see how my life would change with a dark red golden retriever walking beside me everywhere I went.

I rolled over in bed, relishing the lazy last days of summer vacation—or trying to. Pee Wee, our family's dachshund, had other plans. He jumped on the bed, landing square on my chest, and licked my face. "Oof, Pee Wee!" I gave him a morning ear rub.

A moment later, Squire's nose pushed Pee Wee out of the way so he could nuzzle me as well. "Hey, man, we need our breakfast," they seemed to say.

"Okay, okay, I'm getting up." Pee Wee raced down the hallway, and Squire took off after him. This was their favorite game. When they reached the living room, Pee Wee would launch like the Slinky Dog he resembled and soar onto the couch. Then Squire would grab Pee Wee like a toy, flip him off the couch and onto the floor on his back, wrestling and growling playfully. In less than a month, they'd become great friends.

But as soon as I got to the kitchen, they abandoned the game and pranced around me, eager for their food.

"Hey, Mom," I said, both dogs circling me.

"Good morning." Mom was sitting at the kitchen table with her cup of coffee. I walked to the cabinet, pulled out a plastic bin, measured out a cup of kibble, and put it in Squire's bowl. I scooped a smaller portion for Pee Wee, pouring it into his bowl in the opposite corner of the kitchen. As the dogs scarfed down their breakfast, I went to the fridge and pulled out the butter and strawberry jam, then pulled a loaf of bread from the bread box. I put a slice of bread into the toaster and pushed the lever down.

"Is there any bacon left?"

"It's on a plate next to the stove. I convinced your dad to leave you two slices."

"Thanks!"

"Mike, school starts in a couple of weeks. I think we should go over there a few times so you and Squire can learn your way around."

"Sure, Mom." We'd been talking about high school all summer. Up until that year, I had navigated school without assistance, but Yucca Elementary's layout was much simpler. Palmdale High

School's campus consisted of many small buildings and courtyards, typical for California. It was one of the many reasons my parents had applied for me to get a guide dog.

I sat down at the table, munching my toast and bacon as she talked. High school! I did feel a bit apprehensive, as any freshman would. And I wasn't sure how Squire and I would be received. But I hoped we would be very popular, especially since I had a handsome furry guy as my wingman—uh, wingdog.

As we drove to the school midmorning, Mom began describing the campus. "At the front, there are four long rectangular buildings, parallel to each other, perpendicular to the parking lot," she explained. "These buildings make up the series 100 section. You'll get off the bus right in front of the building that has rooms 141, 142, 143, and so on."

Though she had only a high school education, Mom knew that awareness is power, and exploring builds awareness. She knew sheltering me (or my brother, for that matter) wouldn't serve us in the long run.

"Okay," Mom said as Squire and I got out of the car and walked beside her from the parking lot. "This is where the buses stop. Go straight ahead, and your locker is third from the left. Yours is easy to find—it's the only one with a keylock instead of a combination." Knowing I couldn't see the numbers on a combination lock, the school had agreed to my parents' request for an alternate lock.

"From here, go left and then around the corner to the right," Mom continued. "The first room on the right is Mr. Dills's classroom, where you'll have general science, first period."

I wanted to run through the campus, asking a million questions. I took a deep breath, put my hand on Squire's head to steady myself, then gripped his harness and leash. My goal was awareness—the first step to being brave.

Squire walked obediently next to me, watching for obstacles, but listening for my commands. His watchful presence boosted my confidence and courage.

Thanks to Mom's coaching, I already had an idea of what to expect. But Squire did not. He needed me to tell him where to go, and I needed him to help me avoid obstacles and other people. I memorized which way to go from Mr. Dills's classroom to the next class on my schedule, a music elective with Mr. Darrington.

Mom walked beside me, taking me through the next part of my schedule. "Here are the math classrooms. Do you remember which room you're in and how to find it?"

"Room 241—the first door on the left."

"Excellent. And when do you need to be there?"

"Right after lunch." I felt the sidewalk go slightly downhill, and I stored this information away, adding it to the map I was building in my head of the school grounds. Squire's step quickened as he read my growing confidence. I smiled. After only a few weeks, I could tell that this dog felt what I felt. He saw the world for me and was eager to explore it with me.

"This is a snack bar, where you can buy food," Mom explained—immediately piquing my interest. "This courtyard is where you'll eat lunch. There are benches all around the perimeter where you can sit. And there's a restroom just off the other end of the courtyard."

Squire was buzzing with excited energy at my side. Despite the many interesting smells and sights in this strange new environment, he focused on his job of guiding me, listening to my commands to go forward, turn right or left, or stop and sit. After a couple of days of walking me through my schedule, Mom stepped up the challenge.

"Okay, now I'm going to watch you find your way from this classroom, where you have English third period. Which class is next, and how do you get there?"

"I need to go to the locker room, by the gym." The school required me to enroll in a special PE class for kids who couldn't participate in regular PE. We didn't do much physical activity. But I still had to suit up for gym (or rather, suit up for sitting around). I had hoped they would let us jump rope. I was actually pretty good at it.

We walked down the sidewalk, Mom silently trailing us. I walked along, listening for the spaces between buildings, noticing subtle changes in the grade of the sidewalk.

I moved my hand to the right. "Right," I told Squire, who immediately made a sharp right turn. I walked a bit farther and signaled Squire to turn left when I could hear the opening. I walked forward again and listened carefully, hearing the subtle changes that indicated a door on my right. Not the first one, but the second one. I commanded Squire, "Right," and he turned right just like he should. "Good boy!" I said as we entered the gym.

"Great job, Mike," Mom said from behind me. "This may be a bit more challenging when the sidewalk is full of other students, but I know you will do just fine."

Over the next two weeks, Squire and I, with Mom lurking behind, explored and practiced. I learned how to find each of my classrooms, and how to get from one room to the next simply by memorization.

Squire did not have to memorize the campus. Eventually, he would become very familiar with our routine. But I couldn't just let him pull me around from class to class. That is not how a guide dog works. In fact, if possible, you should mix the route up from time to time, just to keep your dog alert. He needs to look to you for direction. He also needs to avoid getting in a rut, so that when you need to change the routine he won't try to "stick to the routine" as dogs (and people) sometimes like to do. Together, dog and handler work as a team to get from one place to another safe and sound.

As I explained earlier, a guide dog doesn't "lead" a blind person. The dog "guides." The dog's job is to keep himself and his person walking safely. The handler must know where they are going and how to get there. Eyesight is not required to master this skill. The dog lets the handler know of unexpected obstacles, such as a construction barrier or a car. Both of us are always aware of our surroundings, and that feels empowering.

Sighted people rely on visual clues to find their way around. But they also remember landmarks when they're driving or memorize the layout of familiar places such as a school. Students aren't stopping to read the signs to the science lab or room 241. They just know where to go. And eventually, I had that same knowledge. In nearly any place I go, I pay attention so I can find my way, with or without my dog. I rely on sound, smell, and physical characteristics like a slight incline in the sidewalk to "see" my surroundings.

Those heightened senses aren't something blind people are just born with—we have to develop them by training ourselves to pay attention and to prepare for anything.

The truth is that even sighted people rely on their other senses. When you ride a bike or cross a street, you often hear cars approaching from behind you. A bicyclist relies on their sense of hearing and acts accordingly. Rather than turning their head to look at the car, and inadvertently steering right into the vehicle's path, they move over. Everyone uses, or should use, all their senses to perceive what's going on. Eyesight can be helpful, but it's not the only game in town.

By the time my high school freshman year began two weeks later, I could go to any room on the campus. Using the simple tools of awareness and preparation eliminated a lot of fear. I knew I could make it from class to class in the six minutes between periods. In my four years of high school, I never arrived late for a class.

Those simple steps of preparation not only made it possible for me to thrive in a public high school alongside my sighted peers, but it taught me a valuable lesson. You can combat fear by increasing your awareness and by preparing. Once I memorized the school's layout, I had an advantage and felt much more confident.

Squire was highly trained, but he had a wicked sense of humor sometimes. About halfway through my freshman year, I was walking down a hallway when I heard a group of girls talking in front of me. I figured Squire would guide me around them. Not Squire. Before I could stop him, he barged right through the middle of the group. Suddenly I heard one of the girls scream, and the whole crowd parted like the Red Sea. I thought, *What just happened?*

This was 1964 when shorter dresses were the latest fashion. In fact, our school required girls to wear dresses measuring between two inches above the knee to two inches below the knee. Later that week, the same thing happened where Squire barreled us through a crowd of girls. Again, there was screaming. Afterward, a friend came up to me.

"What's going on?" I asked.

"Your dog," my friend said, laughing. "Squire was moving his head from side to side as you walked through the group, checking out the girls. His cold, wet nose touched one girl's bare leg. She screamed and almost slapped you. When the girls saw Squire, they scattered."

Actually, Squire did seem to enjoy his game until the girls at school figured out Squire's antics. I would let them pet him after I took off his harness so they wouldn't interfere with his training.

Between my junior and senior high school years I arranged to visit Dr. Ken Ford, chairman of the physics department at the University of California, Irvine, where I contemplated attending college. My parents and I drove to the campus and went to his office.

After we were seated Dr. Ford said, "Tell me about yourself, Mike. Why do you want to major in physics and why do you think UCI is a good fit?" I answered his questions, and we talked about how I would study physics without being able to see. After an hour he said, "I believe you will be a good addition to the school, and I hope you will apply here." I did apply and was accepted for the beginning of UCI's 1968–69 college term.

The summer before college I attended a six-week college preparatory class for blind incoming college freshmen. The course took place at the University of California at Santa Cruz, located about 350 miles north of Palmdale. My parents drove me up there. Squire was not invited, as part of the program was learning how to use and work with white canes. Before attending, I purchased a cane and practiced a bit. I discovered that while it was different from using a guide dog, I did quite well. This was, of course, because I was always quite aware of my surroundings.

When the course began at UCSC I met the mobility instructors who assured me that I could learn to use a cane and that I could get around with it. I smiled internally since I already knew this. It took about ten minutes for the instructors to decide that I was capable of traveling with a cane. As I tell people, "I can teach you to use a cane in five minutes. However, teaching you to have the confidence and faith to use the cane takes months."

———

In September 1968, my parents drove me a hundred miles south from Palmdale to the University of California, Irvine campus. The school had recently opened, and its student population was smaller than most universities, which pleased me. My dorm, Loma, seemed to house all the UCI jocks.

As Mom and I had done in preparation for me attending high school, I spent time walking around the UCI campus, but now with the help of some students and new friends. All went well for the first few weeks. Then one night I was in my room studying, while Squire lay curled at my feet under my desk. After a while I stood up and stretched for a quick break. Squire sighed in his sleep.

"Mike!" one of my classmates, Richard, called to me from his room across the hall. "Could I ask you about the third problem in our homework assignment for Dr. Bork's class?"

"Sure," I said. I pulled my door shut and walked across the hall.

Soon we were deep in a physics geek discussion.

Very quietly—after all, you know I have excellent hearing—three scoundrels slinked into my dorm room.

"Hey, doggy," one said. Squire, friendly and trusting, greeted them with a wag.

"Come on, pup, here we go," one said, grabbing Squire's leash off the hook on the wall and clipping it to his collar.

Stifling laughter, the three boys led Squire down the hall.

"He's going to freak out when he can't find his dog," one said, laughing.

Richard and I figured out the equation we'd been wrestling with. I walked back to my room and sat down at my desk, but my feet didn't feel any canine bulk underneath.

"Squire?" I called. Had he just moved to his bed in the corner of our room? Nope. "Squire!" I called again. My throat got tight and dry. I struggled to remain calm.

"Rich, have you seen Squire?" I said, quickly stepping back into the hallway.

"Your dog?" Richard was brilliant at physics but a little absent-minded.

"He was under my desk, but now he's not in my room!" I said.

Suddenly, we heard a loud bang, like a gunshot. I jumped. Richard ran to his window. "Your dog is running across the parking lot!" Squire was being chased by his three captors, who thought it would be hilarious to set off a firecracker while kidnapping a dog.

"Squire!" I screamed. My heart was racing, my ears ringing. *What if he's injured? Why would these people want to hurt me and my dog?*

Richard and I ran outside. The pranksters had caught Squire and one of them sheepishly handed me his leash. My hand was trembling as I took it from him.

"What were you idiots thinking?" Richard and I demanded.

"It was just a prank, man," said one. "Don't be such a downer."

"A downer?" I said, fuming. "How would you like it if someone suddenly shined a 1,400-watt light in your eyes and at least temporarily blinded you? This is no normal dog. I hope you didn't permanently traumatize him."

I knelt down and petted Squire, who was shaking. He nuzzled me, looking for reassurance. "It's okay, boy, I'm here." Squire pushed his head against my chest, whimpering.

As I stroked his shoulders, he settled a bit and licked my face. But the damage had been done. From that time on, Squire, who'd been mostly fearless, was afraid of loud noises. Thunderstorms made him cower and run to me for comfort.

Squire never totally got over this fear, but with work, his behavior in loud settings did improve. His fear was a normal response to this unfortunate incident. However, he still guided capably. He stayed open and curious—and when he needed to be, he was exceptionally brave.

———

UCI had only around 2,700 students when I was there, with buildings spread over a large campus. So Squire and I typically enjoyed a nice long, quiet walk from one building to another as we went from class to class.

Until the day our walk was not quiet. Or nice.

"Forward, Squire," I commanded as we walked to calculus class. You may wonder how a blind guy could do calculus. Well, why not? I had to solve the proofs in my head as well as writing Braille notes. Actually, I used the same processes as everyone else. The only difference was that I used Braille while my sighted classmates used pencils or pens and paper. My professors gave me oral exams, and I explained the steps of each proof out loud. Higher math wasn't much of a stretch for me—my dad had taught me to solve algebra equations in my head when I was six.

As we walked, I heard barking.

"Squire, hop up," I reminded him. "Hop up" was a command to remind a guide dog to pay attention. I knew that "the pack" was nearby—a group of dogs that belonged to some students. Unfortunately, the owners just let these dogs roam free while they were in class. The pack made me a little nervous—and also a little peeved at the irresponsible behavior of their owners. I tried to ignore them.

A moment later I heard the dogs approaching behind us. Suddenly Squire jumped away from me, spinning to face the pack, growling ferociously. His maneuver caught me off guard, and his quick turn pulled the harness handle out of my hand.

The pack stopped in its tracks, surprised by Squire's defensive move. I managed to keep hold of Squire's leash even as he moved toward the pack. I could feel him crouching down and hear his loud and commanding growl. I had never experienced this behavior from him, but I was awed at my dog's courage. He knew he was supposed to keep us both safe, and he had decided that in order to do that, he needed to confront the pack.

The disorderly dogs stopped in their tracks, obviously surprised. Their barking ceased, and several had their tails between their legs (so a witness to the incident told me later). Slowly, the dogs slunk away.

"Squire, heel," I said. As he stopped beside me, I grabbed the harness again, which wriggled as he wagged his tail furiously, as if to say, "Did I do good or what?"

I knelt down, rubbing his head and shoulders. "Good boy, Squire," I said. "Such a brave boy."

Squire showed no fear. Instead, he showed strength and loyalty. Despite my efforts to stay calm, I'd felt pretty nervous when I heard the dogs approaching.

Squire determined that he had to address the issue of this pack of dogs who threatened us. Essentially Squire told them, "Get out of here and leave us alone!"

Squire may have felt some fear but overcame it to face a specific situation directly. He felt scared but did it anyway. Squire reacted courageously and helped our team stay safe. We never encountered that pack of dogs again.

Squire taught me, by his courageous example, something important that day. When you face the thing that scares you, it need not be so scary after all. Awareness is simply knowing what scares you and facing it head on. One way to be brave is to get as much information as you possibly can.

I am sure both love and a desire to keep both of us safe motivated Squire. He was not trained specifically to guard and protect, but his instincts clearly ran deep. He might have felt afraid, but he overcame his fear at that moment. I never saw that kind of behavior again from him.

What are you afraid of? The more aware you are of your surroundings (with or without people) and what to expect in any situation, the better you'll deal with unexpected or frightening things. Awareness allows you to leverage your fear and deal with what is going on.

An essential part of awareness is understanding fear itself. From a scientific perspective, fear is a biological response to an external stimulus. Our bodies respond to what happens around us, often in ways we don't even think about. If you feel cold (external stimulus), you might get goose bumps, or eventually start shivering (biological response). If you're too hot, you may start sweating or get red in the face. In the same way, your fear is simply a biological response to an external or internal stimulus. Just as you can't stop yourself from sweating or shivering, you can't stop yourself from feeling fear in certain situations. But it doesn't have to run your life.

Many of our fears are internally created. Very rarely will you find yourself in an actual life-or-death situation. Most of the time, you are afraid because of what you *think* will happen rather than what is *actually* happening.

Put another way, many fears simply aren't connected to reality. What you feel is real, but the circumstances you're imagining are not. At times, your fear is a response to a genuine threat. At that moment, your fear keeps you safe. But most fear is a response to an *imagined* reality. This puts you into a "fight or flight" mode when you don't need to be—which can lead to injuring your body and stealing joy from your life.

When you understand the true nature of fear, it becomes easier to overcome. You are able to closely examine your anxiety and determine if there is any substance to it. Some of your worries may have merit, but many don't. Or they might be pointing you toward a past trauma, an unresolved issue, or a hidden wound.

For example, a dog that has been mistreated might cower even when you try to pet it gently. Or it might bark at people who resemble its abuser.

You can view anxiety in a positive light, seeing it as an opportunity to work through and resolve past hurts and fears, so that you can focus on what is happening in the present moment. In other words, anxiety issues an invitation to increase our self-awareness.

One of the most important opportunities afforded to us by our parents is to learn how to live life and, as much as possible, to experience new things they never encountered. Some families do this better than others. My parents worked as hard as they could to help me be well prepared for whatever I encountered. They knew I would not stay sheltered at home as I grew. Whether or not they realized it, they did teach me about being prepared for life's encounters and challenges. Of course, we may well not be prepared for everything that comes our way.

I know many people who, as they age, are losing their eyesight. Nothing has prepared them for this. This is unfortunate as, in reality, while they may not have expected to possibly become blind, they could have learned not to fear life changes, whatever they may be. The specific threat of blindness frightens people—mostly because we tell ourselves that blindness is more debilitating than other things. More importantly, people losing their vision need not experience this alone. While the ophthalmological profession feels that anyone losing eyesight is a failure to their doctors, such people are not failures and should be encouraged.

There are many organizations, such as the National Federation of the Blind, the nation's largest consumer organization of blind persons, who show constantly that blind people can live just as productive lives as others, no matter what their age.

So while not necessarily being directly prepared for blindness, people can learn to be more prepared to deal with unexpected life changes. I faced that with every guide dog I received. I faced changes when I unexpectedly had to change jobs or face other issues. We can fear or we can learn to control our fears and move forward.

<hr />

One night in the late spring of 1972 I called home.

"Hi, Mom."

"Oh, Mike, how are you?"

"Well, I'm doing fine. But I'm a little worried about Squire."

"What do you mean? Is he sick?"

"Not exactly," I said. "He just seems to be slowing down, and he's not as sharp as he used to be. Last night when we were walking to the dorm, he seemed sort of hesitant. I think his eyesight is getting worse at night. I've noticed it a couple of times."

"Well, Mike, he's ten years old. We knew he'd have to retire eventually."

"I know. But is it still okay if he comes to live with you and Dad when I retire him?"

"Of course."

"Okay. I'll call Guide Dogs and apply for my next dog." My voice caught in my throat saying those last two words. "He's such a good dog, Mom." *Would I ever find a partner as amazing as Squire?*

"He's been a terrific partner," Mom said. "Honey, don't worry. Your dad and I will take good care of him. He deserves a comfortable retirement."

The work of guiding takes a heavy toll on a dog, both physically and mentally. The dogs love their work and their people, but the intense concentration and commitment required often mean they retire at about age nine or ten.

Squire guided me through the campus of UC Irvine for the rest of that school year, until I graduated with a bachelor's degree in physics. The school gave Squire an honorary degree in "lethargic guidance." He received a diploma, which I still have more than fifty years later.

In the summer of 1973, after my first year of graduate school at UCI, I went back to San Rafael to meet my second guide dog, Holland.

I had learned so much from Squire. Together, we'd bravely faced all sorts of new situations, expanding our world and making us both grow in awareness and courage. But there was even more that Holland would teach me.

## Guidance from the Word

*For the LORD gives wisdom;*
*from his mouth come knowledge and*
*understanding. . . .*
*Discretion will protect you,*
*and understanding will guard you.*

**PROVERBS 2:6, 11**

## Prayer for Courage

God, when I feel afraid, help me to become
more aware. Help me to be aware of your
presence in each moment and to pay
attention to you.

# 2

# HOLLAND, PART ONE
## Preparation prevents panic

Anytime we bring a dog into a
new and unfamiliar situation, it's
important that we prepare him
for the environment he's going to
be entering. . . . It's up to you to
help make it a more comfortable
experience.

**CESAR MILLAN**

**"SO, IS THIS YOUR FIRST GUIDE DOG?"** I asked my roommate
at Guide Dogs for the Blind. We had completed the requisite three
days of lectures and Juno training. Now we waited patiently to be
introduced to our dogs.

"Nope, this is my second dog," he replied. "My first dog retired
about two months ago. I've been using a white cane but can't wait to
get back to having a dog."

"I kept Squire right up until I came back here to GDB, but I do
know how to use a cane as well. Sometimes it's easier. I went to the
National Convention for NFB in New York this summer, and I used a
cane instead of taking Squire. Just seemed like a good option with the
crowds. He's slowing down a bit—I've had him since I was fourteen."

"Wow, that's really young to get a guide dog, isn't it?"

"Yeah, but sometimes it's easier to learn new things when you're young. And Squire is an amazing dog. We both learned a lot along the way."

A soft knock on the door interrupted our conversation. "Come on in!" I called out, eager to meet my new teammate. I knew the knock was for me because each double dorm room had two doors, one on each side of the room. Each resident went out and in through their own door. Both doors faced a hall that went the length of the dorm. So, it was my turn now. *What will Holland be like? Will he come right over to me as Squire had done nine years before? Will he be as brave and fun as Squire?*

I was eager, and even anxious. Every time I have received a new guide dog since, I have had the same reaction. I wouldn't want it any other way.

Don Frisk, the senior trainer, stepped into our room. "Mike, come with me."

We walked down a hallway to his office.

"Sit down here," Don said, directing me to a chair in the middle of the room. "Mike, as you know, we have matched you with Holland, a male golden retriever. You know the drill. I'll let him in, but don't call him or say anything. Let's see how he reacts."

I remembered Squire's enthusiastic greeting of years before. But this time, Don opened the door and Holland began slowly making his way around the perimeter of the room, sniffing and exploring.

Holland sniffed me in passing but I felt like a piece of chopped liver that wasn't even worth eating. At just eighteen months old—still a bit like a puppy despite his thorough training—he was curious about exploring a new space. Apparently, he found the office furniture more interesting than me. What kind of a deal is that? I listened intently, trying to figure out what he was doing—even what he was thinking. I did realize not every dog was Squire, so I patiently waited.

Finally Don said, "Why don't you call him?"

"Hey, Holland. Holland, come."

Holland calmly walked up and sat down in front of my chair. I patted him a bit, stroking the top of his head. He stayed there, enjoying the attention.

I knew that the trainers had carefully observed me, and I trusted their decision to match me with Holland. The initial aloofness didn't worry me. He was, as I learned, a very affectionate dog. And the bond between us became very strong, once we started working together.

If I had to describe Holland in one word, it would be *unflappable*. Nothing fazed him. Including, apparently, meeting me.

As I sat in Don's office, listening to Holland check out everything in the room, I didn't feel worried or afraid. I had learned enough about dogs by that point to trust the process. I simply wanted to observe and stay very quiet. What impressed me more was that when I called him, Holland came right over, as if to say, "Yes?"

"Ask him to heel, and take him back to your room," Don told me as I clipped a leash to Holland's collar. We headed down the hall, side by side. In our room, I sat on the floor and Holland sat in front of me.

"Good dog, Holland," I said, scratching him in different spots: behind his ears, under his chin, on his chest, learning which he liked best (He liked them all!). "Hey buddy, I'm going to be your person now. I know you're used to these trainers, but you and I are a team now. My name is Mike, I'm twenty-three years old, and I'm a grad student at UC Irvine. You and I will attend my second-year master's degree classes in physics. Now, you're gonna have to tell me all about you. Any hobbies? Favorite foods?" My gentle banter let my new dog know that he was safe with me.

Holland lay down and put his head in my lap, accepting me as his human. "What a good dog you are. We're going to have lots of adventures." But for now, we had just a few short weeks to get to know each other.

Guide dog training is a bonding boot camp, if you will, to prepare you for whatever obstacles or challenges you may encounter as you make your way through the world with a dog at your side. If anything can make you feel brave, it's guide dog training. The whole purpose is to prepare you for the unexpected—a key step to being brave.

Later that afternoon, Holland and I walked around using only the leash, then attended a lecture. Holland lay calmly at my feet. Before I climbed into bed that night, I clipped Holland to a cable attached to a ring on the floor right by my bed so that he wouldn't wander around. My roommate and his newly assigned dog had a similar setup on the opposite side of the room.

Over the next few weeks, Holland and I had training exercises, went to meals, attended lectures, even took walks—first through downtown San Rafael, and eventually through San Francisco with our trainers and other dogs and students. After working with Squire as he aged, it was fun to work with a young dog with a real spring in his step. We began to form a tight bond—a bond that would carry us through the next thirteen years.

Each time I've gotten a new guide dog, I have chosen to have an open attitude, a beginner's mindset, rather than thinking I know everything there is to know. A good guide dog naturally does the same. He's curious and open. He knows his job, but he also knows how to flex.

It's a fine line: You need to be confident and not show your nervousness, but you also need to stay open to learning. Each time, I begin the process of preparation anew. When we are curious, eager to learn and try new things, we're less likely to be afraid, and more likely to prepare effectively. We can envision a better way forward. We won't be upset if things are not "the way they've always been." In reality, even guide dog schools use this mindset to develop, create, and implement new and better training techniques.

After nearly sixty years of walking beside a guide dog, I've seen training techniques evolve. But at the heart of all training is the principle of preparation. You're offering the dog an opportunity to learn how to handle what they will later encounter.

———

Squire attended my first year of graduate school. Even though I began the application process for a new guide late in my senior year of undergrad, it took time to complete everything, and then I needed to agree on a scheduled time to be at GDB to get my new guide. So it was the summer of 1973 before I traveled to San Rafael.

The Fall 1973 quarter had begun for my second year in graduate school. One day Holland and I were in my dorm room, listening to the radio. We had tuned in to KUCI, the university's station where I had recently become the program director. I liked to listen to our announcers in part because it was my job to help them do the best job they could do.

A song ended and the DJ started talking.

"Holland, do you hear this? This guy's been a DJ for months, and I really think he hasn't improved one bit. He might have even gotten worse. He says *um* about every other word."

Holland's tail thumped the floor. One of my favorite things about Holland (and Squire before him) was that they usually agreed with me, or at least they listened to my comments. Holland nuzzled my hand as I reached down to pet him to emphasize his obvious support. I stroked his head in appreciation.

A few days later, I met with that particular DJ and a few others who seemed to be struggling with their on-air delivery. "Before you go on the radio, what do you do to prepare?" I asked. "Do any of you ever record yourself to listen to your speech patterns and how you sound? That might help you learn more about what works and what doesn't work on the radio."

"Oh, man, Mike," said the worst offender. "No way. I couldn't stand to do that."

I couldn't convince him or some of our other DJs to take this simple step to improve their performance. So without them knowing, I took it for them.

"Listen, can you just set up the microphone so that it records automatically?" I asked Dave, our station engineer. "We don't need to record the music, just when they are talking."

"Sure, that's easy," he said.

The next day we began recording the DJs every time they took to the airwaves. After a week or so, we gave the recordings to our team, saying if they wanted to keep their radio gig, they needed to listen to themselves.

*I'm taking a risk,* I thought. *What if my DJs get mad at me? What if they all quit? I can't manage a radio station without them. Still, I know this will improve what we're doing. I have to help them see that I'm on their side.* And yet, as program director, it was my job to make sure the broadcasts were the best they could be.

"Notice what you do right, and what you should change," I said. "This would be easy if someone else asked you to listen to them and evaluate their work. Pretend you're listening to someone else and give constructive feedback—to yourself. Then, use what you learn to prepare for your next time on the air. Before you go on, think about what you want to say. Be prepared!"

Most of my DJs reluctantly listened to themselves, and within a few weeks I began to see a marked improvement in their on-air performances, and a remarkable uptick in their confidence. Their deliveries became smoother. They no longer mispronounced words as often. Their timing no longer felt awkward. They'd eliminated the *ummms* and *uhhhs* from their banter. By the end of the year, those who had taken the time to listen to themselves and give themselves feedback had vastly improved.

This simple step of self-awareness had an almost immediate impact. Because they heard themselves as other people heard them, and had to think about what they could change, they got better at speaking on the radio. It was amazing. We got them to think a lot about what they could do differently and then actually make those changes. They became braver public speakers and ultimately thanked me. Some of them went on to do radio professionally while others had careers that involved public speaking.

Actually, when it comes to fears, public speaking ranks right up there with fear of heights, fear of blindness, and even fear of death! But taking simple steps of preparation and self-awareness can help you manage that fear. My amateur DJs hemmed and hawed because they were afraid of making a mistake. They went in cold, trying to "wing it" when they ought to have prepared a little more. They were nervous about speaking in public—even over the radio. Self-awareness and preparation helped them manage and control their fear, so they could thrive.

At first, I was nervous and somewhat reluctant to make too strong a suggestion to my DJs. I wasn't sure how they'd react. However, after thinking about it, I talked myself into being confident about my plan. Frankly, I think my confidence did as much as anything to convince people to listen to themselves. I also told my DJs that I wasn't asking them to do anything I didn't do myself. I explained to them that I recorded my shows from a radio in my apartment and listened to them, trying to learn how to improve. I think some people thought, *If he is brave enough to hear himself, then I guess I can try it too.* Later on, when my career path led to public speaking, I again followed my own advice—which helped tremendously. Today, I listen to every speech I give. I record them and spend time listening to what I say and how I say it.

Wow, I had a lot to learn! These days, I'm getting pretty satisfied with my talks, but I will always listen to myself and figure out how I can improve. Each speech prepares me for the next one. I've learned that I am not my own worst critic, but rather I am my own best teacher. If I can't teach myself, no one else can break through my mindset. It really is first up to me.

During college and grad school, I became active in the National Federation of the Blind (NFB). After joining in 1972, I served as the president of the Orange County chapter and began attending national conventions the following year. In 1974, I was at the national convention in Chicago at the Palmer House.

Federation president Dr. Kenneth Jernigan approached me in the presidential suite at the convention. Jernigan had led the Iowa

Commission for the Blind for more than a decade, turning it into the most effective training organization for the blind in the country. In 1968, after the founder and first president of the NFB, Dr. Jacobus tenBroek, died from cancer, Jernigan also became the National Federation of the Blind president, a position he would hold for eighteen years.

"Mike, we have an opportunity for you," he said, explaining a joint project with an inventor named Ray Kurzweil.

"The guy's got a machine that can read printed pages out loud. It's going to change everything," Dr. Jernigan said. "I didn't believe it at first either. But Kurzweil talked me into letting the head of our Washington office, Jim Gashel, visit him in Cambridge, Massachusetts. Jim brought printed material—I figured it would really test Dr. Kurzweil's machine. Well, it read the pages. The machine scanned them, then read them out loud. It was pretty amazing."

"Well, that's pretty interesting technology, but what does that have to do with me?" I asked. After all, I was in grad school in California, thinking of possibly going into teaching. And Ray Kurzweil and his fancy new machine were in Cambridge, Massachusetts.

"So, we've agreed to help Kurzweil develop and distribute this machine," Dr. Jernigan said. "He wants to get it out where people can use it. Places like universities and even the New York Public Library. We're applying for grants so we can roll out machines in beta test sites to refine the function and design with each one and make recommendations for a final production model for Dr. Kurzweil."

"Okay," I said. "That's a great idea. But I still don't get what you want me to do."

Dr. Jernigan explained that the NFB would seek funding, through grants to the federation, to purchase five of Kurzweil's prototype machines at $50,000 each. Then the federation and the Kurzweil company would work together to place the machines in public spaces where blind people could access them.

Today, people are used to carrying technology in their pockets, without giving it a second thought. The Kurzweil prototype machine weighed 400 pounds and was about the size of a washing machine. It scanned one printed line at a time, taking nearly a minute to scan a full page and then to begin to read the text aloud.

"So, the project budget includes an eighteen-month position for someone who can travel to each installation, teach people how to use the machines, fix them when they break, and work out the bugs," Dr. Jernigan continued. "Someone who can document issues and work with us to correct them, develop training materials, troubleshoot and make suggestions for improvements, and write a training curriculum for the machine. Each subsequent machine will be a new version, based on what we learn. And we think that person should be you."

"Me? Dr. Jernigan, I'm flattered. That sounds like a really interesting opportunity."

"It will take us a while to get everything in place, but once we do, you'd start by moving to Massachusetts where Kurzweil is located."

*Move to Massachusetts? With only Holland to help me navigate?* I smiled to cover my apprehension. "Sure, that sounds great," I said, though inside I wasn't at all so confident. It sounded exciting but intimidating. Still, was my acceptance of the position arrogance on my part or the chance to do something pretty unique and be part of a real adventure? Probably a bit of both. Hey, I was twenty-four and ready to take on the world. Even so, I must admit that inside I was afraid to take on this seemingly daunting job. Literally living out of suitcases and in hotels for a month or two at a time in one location, then moving to the next? No real place to call home for eighteen months?

The Bible tells us repeatedly, "Do not be afraid." When I was in my twenties, I didn't know this, but I do now. Most of those verses tell us why we don't need to be afraid—because God is with us. It's hard to just say, "Don't be afraid," because fear is a normal, human experience. But we can be brave because God is with us. And I somehow knew God would be with me wherever I went.

What scared me more than the idea of moving to a strange city was the alternative—not being employed at all. More than 70 percent of employable blind people are unemployed. Not because we're incapable of doing the work, but because companies are not willing to hire us. I knew any new graduate—sighted or not—would struggle to find job experience. It's the classic conundrum: You need experience to get a job, but you need a job to get experience. But it's even more challenging for blind people because of the discrimination we face.

I wanted to use my education, to make a contribution to the world, to have a purpose—and I sometimes felt afraid I wouldn't have that opportunity. So I couldn't pass this one up. What I didn't know then was how saying yes would set in motion a series of events that would change my life. Harnessing my fear, using it to move me forward, did indeed change my destiny. I prepared for a move to the East Coast. To "do it scared" and move ahead despite my uncertainties. To use preparation to turn my fear into courage.

While the NFB secured funding and laid the groundwork for getting the machines to various locations, I finished my master's degree, then took some business classes that I hoped would prepare me for this new role.

Two years passed before the project began. In October 1976, I put my furniture in storage and packed up some suitcases. I'd never really spent time away from home, other than going to UCI and traveling to San Rafael for my guide dogs. But Holland and I got on an airplane one Sunday and off we flew to Boston.

The federation had arranged for me to stay in a short-term apartment. But I had to familiarize myself with a whole new city, learn how to get to the Kurzweil headquarters via public transportation, and start my first real job. I have always felt that life is an adventure. Now, I had to adopt my adventurous attitude and move forward.

---

Holland and I walked through the American Airlines terminal of Logan International Airport. Before my trip, I'd gathered information on the airport's layout and learned about the city's subways and

Boston as a whole. The Kurzweil folks promised to help me get acclimatized to the area.

"Can you tell me where I can catch a cab?" I asked an airline ticket agent.

"Sure, right out those doors," he said. I guessed that he was pointing, so I listened. After a second, I pointed toward where I thought I heard traffic noise and said, "Over there?"

"Yep," he said. I don't think he realized I was blind until he saw me walk away with Holland beside me.

Out on the sidewalk, a man came up to me. "Need a cab, sir?"

"Yes, please."

He opened a car door in front of me, and Holland and I walked toward it.

"No dawgs in the cab," the cabbie said with a thick Boston accent.

"He's a guide dog," I told the driver. "I'm blind."

"Really?" the cabdriver said. I could tell he was thinking it over. This was nearly fifteen years before the federal Americans with Disabilities Act was passed, but many states already had laws requiring that guide dogs be allowed anywhere their people went.

"Massachusetts law . . ." I began.

"All right, fine," he said. He got out and took my suitcases, tossing them in the trunk and slamming it shut. "I hope he don't shed all over my caah."

"Not at all," I said, trying not to laugh as Holland and I climbed into the voluminous back seat of a Checker cab. Golden retrievers are shedding machines, but I always kept Holland clean and brushed, so hopefully he wouldn't leave too much fur in the cab. There was plenty of room for him to sit on the floor of that boat of a car. Also, I had trained Holland to never climb on car seats. Dogs are safer on the floor.

"Home Away Apartments at 322 Beacon Street," I said. "It's in the Back Bay area."

"You got it," the cabbie said, and drove quickly, weaving in and out, using his horn much more often than his brakes, a driving style I'd soon learn was typical of Boston drivers.

"Here you go, pal," he said. "That's $9.25." I handed him a ten-dollar bill and said, "Keep the change."

When the cabbie got out of the car to get my suitcase, he asked if he could meet Holland. It was all about good human relations. Holland knew how to be an ambassador for guide dogs. So I removed Holland's harness and let the two of them interact with each other for a few minutes. As usual, both Holland and his new friend had fun. It was hard to finally say, "Come on, Holland, time to go back to work." As the Checker cab pulled away, I thought, *That cabbie won't hesitate to pick up other guide dog teams after meeting Holland.*

Then I heard, "Michael? Welcome to Boston. I'm Don."

Don, the apartment building owner, grabbed my suitcase and led me inside. Our apartment was on the first floor to make it easy to let Holland out. Which he definitely needed now.

"Get settled, and I'll give you a tour of the neighborhood," Don said. He unlocked our apartment door, then handed me the key. I stepped into the apartment and began exploring, with Don behind me.

"This is a studio apartment. The kitchen is right here as you first walk in, and here's the fridge, and the stove is on your left," he said. "The bed is straight ahead as you come through the front door and the bathroom is to your right, down past the foot of the bed.

"You'll like the neighborhood. Back Bay Boston is a great place to live. The T (the subway system) station is close, and you are within walking distance of the Star Market. I'll walk you around when you're ready."

I took a deep breath. *Three thousand miles from home for the first time, in a city I'd never visited before.* "Wow," I said out loud. "Holland, we're doing this. We're in Boston!" Apprehension, fear, and excitement swirled inside me.

Don showed me around the apartment building, including the locations of the mailboxes, the laundry room, the back door and other emergency exits. Then he gave us a walking tour of the nearby streets. He explained to me the locations of local restaurants and shops. I breathed in the cool fall air, tinged with a hint of the smell of the sea.

Don was super at explaining the area to me and helping me to become oriented to the Back Bay world. "Beacon here is one of your main thoroughfares. The Charles River is just a few blocks north of here. The whole area's laid out on a grid, so that should make it easier."

"Can you please show me where the subway station is?" I asked. "I'll be taking it to work eventually. But I'm planning to take a cab tomorrow." Don's help was invaluable and within a short time I learned the neighborhood around my new temporary home.

Holland and I did a lot of research on our own, asking pedestrians lots of questions, finding shops and restaurants, both the ones Don mentioned and others, memorizing how to get to the subway stop several blocks away. Before long, we knew the neighborhood by heart—without any digital assistance. To this day, I travel best when I familiarize myself with areas before I arrive.

The very best way to learn and prepare, and to be brave, is to just do things. The next few weekends, when we were not at the office, Holland and I would walk into shops and simply say hello and ask, "What is this place? What do you do or sell here?" I let my curiosity be stronger than my fear of making mistakes or getting lost. I found some great pizza places and what became my favorite shop: Steve's Ice Cream. Yes, even in the height of winter. Nothing like a good double-scoop of mint chocolate chip in a cone with sprinkles to make the world better. Unfortunately, there were no ice cream options for Holland.

Think about when a dog meets someone. They don't wonder if the person will like them or reject them. They usually just wag their tail and approach, using body language to say, "Wanna be friends?" I knew if I simply chose to be friendly, I would feel less afraid.

Dogs are open to trust much more than us humans. We should try to be more like a dog. You might be surprised at how much farther

**Guide dogs teach us that when we prepare diligently, the unknown and uncertain becomes known and familiar, and we feel braver.**

you will get in developing relationships if you are more open to the idea of trust.

Most people happily told me about their business and welcomed me. Of course, it didn't hurt that I had a handsome and outgoing golden retriever with me.

I asked Don which shops delivered groceries (this was the 70s, way before Uber Eats, DoorDash, or Amazon food delivery) and set up a weekly delivery with Star Market.

---

After I spent a few weeks at Kurzweil Computer Products' offices, learning everything about the reading machine, including how to do basic repairs, Kurzweil delivered one of the machines to my apartment, so that I could learn how to use it. Holland and I worked remotely a few days a week, tinkering with the machine and getting to know its functions, and writing a training curriculum. I went to the local library and checked out some books I always wanted to read but hadn't been able to because they were not in Braille or recorded.

I was particularly eager to listen to *The Mysterious Island* by Jules Verne. Like many others, I loved *Twenty Thousand Leagues Under the Sea*. Thanks to my new reading machine, I finally got to read the sequel. What a tremendous feeling as Verne's words came to life even if the reading machine was speaking with a clearly synthetic voice. No matter. Reading a printed book and learning about this new technology were what really counted.

One of my new Kurzweil coworkers, Al Becker, the vice president of engineering, became a great ally and friend.

"Mike, have you been to Durgin-Park yet?" he asked one day.

"No, but Holland likes parks."

Al laughed. "It's not actually a park. It's a famous restaurant in Quincy Market that's been here forever. They've got great seafood and the best prime rib in Boston. How about we go this weekend?"

"Well, thanks. Yes, that would be great," I said.

Al told me to order the prime rib, which I did. Dinner was great!

Al and I often spent time together on weekends, and he gave me a guided tour each time we went out. Later Al's sister, Susie, and her huge sheepdog, Lewis, joined the expeditions.

———

Holland and I became quite adept at navigating our way around Boston. But a few months after we arrived, we encountered something that we weren't prepared for. When we stepped outside to go to work one morning, we were hit by a blast of really cold, damp air.

On the morning news, the weatherman had mentioned that we'd gotten six inches of snow the night before, and now the temperatures had dipped. Although I spent my early childhood in Chicago, I had no recollection of snow. And growing up in the California desert, I'd rarely experienced it before, at least to any significant degree. I was not prepared.

The sidewalk under my feet felt slippery and wet, but manageable. "Forward," I said to Holland, who stepped confidently beside me. But within a few minutes, he was acting strangely, jumping around, almost dancing in the harness. I didn't know what was wrong. "Forward, Holland," I said, shuffling a bit because the sidewalk felt like it had a layer of moisture on it, but also some grit. I could hear an odd scraping sound.

"Good morning, Michael," Don said. "I've got the walk all shoveled for you. But watch your step." I had never shoveled snow in my life, so I was thankful that Don was on top of that responsibility!

We made our way down the sidewalk to the subway station. We'd gone less than a block when suddenly my feet had no traction whatsoever. As I stepped forward, my feet slid out from under me. *Wham!* I was suddenly sprawled on the sidewalk. My arms flew up instinctively, and I lost my grip on Holland's harness and leash. *What on earth? Oh no, where's Holland? My elbow hurts.* My panicked thoughts were jumping around as much as Holland had been doing a few minutes before.

But Holland stayed by my side, nosing me to see if I was alright—though he seemed to be slipping around as well. I sat up and took off one glove to feel the ground. It was hard, smooth, and cold—a sheet of ice. *Now what?*

I crawled on my hands and knees until I found a safer, grittier part of the sidewalk. Then I heard a woman's voice. "Are you alright?"

"I think so," I said, slowly standing. I felt shaky and flushed, despite the cold. *What just happened?*

"Well, look at those shoes," she said, obviously sizing up my slick-soled leather dress shoes. "You won't get far in those. You need a pair of rubbers!"

"Rubbers?" I couldn't even imagine what she was talking about.

"Sure. They're flexible boots you can pull on over those dress shoes. They'll give you better traction and keep your feet dry. We get a lot of slush around here and it'll ruin your leather shoes. Rubbers protect them. There's a shoe store down the next block that sells them."

"Thank you so much," I said. "Which side of the street is the shoe store?"

"It's right there," she said. "See the sign? That's a cute dog you got."

"This is my guide dog, Holland. He's a working dog, so please don't pet him."

"Wait—you're blind?"

"Well, yes. That's why I have a guide dog."

"Well, I'll be," she said. "Come on, the shoe store's right up here. I'm walking that way. I'll show you. Just tell the man you need some rubbers. Also—you should see if he has a rag to wipe off your dog's paws. The salt irritates them."

"Salt?"

"They put rock salt on the sidewalks to melt the ice. Though as you experienced firsthand, it doesn't always do such a great job." Being a physics kind of guy, I should have thought of that, but, oh well, one doesn't think of everything. That explained Holland's odd movements—he'd been squirmy because his feet hurt!

*What exactly have I gotten myself—and my dog—into?* Doubt began to creep into my mind, threatening to overwhelm me. *What if I had hit my head on the sidewalk?* I took a deep breath. *Use your fear,* I told myself. *Go forward.*

At the shoe store, I purchased a pair of rubbers and immediately put them on, hoping they'd keep me from slipping again—I was already running late for work. I'd have to leave earlier on snowy days. Later that week, I bought winter boots and a heavier overcoat. "Looks like we're not in California anymore, Holland," I said in my best Judy Garland imitation.

Over the weekend, we got even more snow. When I lived in California, I never really paid much attention to the weather reports. But in Boston, I needed to prepare for each day's commute by paying close attention to how much snow had fallen, what the temperature was, and any other weather-related information. At my apartment I even learned the value of storm windows and why several layers of glass kept things warmer than just a plain single-pane window.

The next Monday morning, Holland and I walked to the corner.

"Good thing I've got the right footwear," I told Holland as we walked. "It's been snowing all weekend."

We approached the corner, and Holland stopped—telling me there was an obstacle in our way. I could hear the traffic in the street about ten feet in front of us. I started to walk closer to the curb, but Holland held back. I reached tentatively with my foot to feel the space in front of us. My toe connected with a solid block of cold snow. I reached over and felt it with my hand. A two-foot-high wall of snow blocked our way.

Again, a helpful passerby saw my dilemma.

"Are you trying to cross?" he asked.

"Yes, I want to go across and to the left," I told him.

"The plows pile the snow on the curbs. But they've got a path over here," he said. I came to realize that a mound of snow framed each sidewalk and street.

At each corner, a narrow passageway, only about a foot wide, had been cut through the bank of piled-up snow creating a path from the sidewalk to the street. It was wide enough for one person to walk through but too narrow for Holland to walk beside me. I had to walk ahead of him, and he followed. Mostly, guide dogs are trained to walk beside their handler, not in front of them or behind them. But the unflappable Holland took it all in stride. Walking single file on a path flanked on both sides by snowbanks that were taller than he was, was strange and different for Holland. But he trusted me, and we figured it out together.

We learned how to navigate those snowbanks and to find the narrow passageways through them. I kept a rag in my coat pocket and extras in my desk drawer at work to wipe Holland's paws off. I wanted my teammate to be comfortable and safe. I was amazed at Holland's resilience and willingness to adapt to strange situations. His calm acceptance of these new situations inspired me to do the same. Once again I remembered Bruce Benzler's words from guide dog training: "If we fear or become stressed, then so will our guide dogs."

*Holland is being brave for me. I need to be brave for him.* To be honest, I think Holland was having a lot of fun, especially at my expense. Seriously, he never showed fear and did take everything in stride. His demeanor helped me a lot.

I even tried ice-skating with Al and Susie. As we made our way around the rink, Holland sat on the edge, watching and wondering what on earth I was doing! Hadn't I learned that ice was dangerous and should be avoided at all costs? Holland had a point. I did great until the end when I fell and sprained my ankle. I'm grateful for the experience, but I decided to hang up my silver skates after that.

Even with snow boots, I would occasionally slip on the ice. I fell more than once. But we didn't let those mishaps scare us. We got up, brushed the snow and slush off, and kept moving forward. There was always something to learn. For example, since neither of us could read signs, I had to ask people a lot of questions. Where's the Star Market? How do I get to the restaurants in the area? Which side of the tracks does the Cambridge-bound subway train stop on? My job was to learn all that information so I could properly communicate to Holland what I wanted him to do.

I was so proud of Holland who courageously did everything I asked, without complaint. It was a lot for both of us, but I knew I needed to support and help him by staying calm and not acting afraid or upset. I sometimes wondered what I had gotten myself into, but I never thought of giving up.

---

Just when we had Boston figured out, Holland and I relocated again, this time to Des Moines, Iowa. Kurzweil's newest version of the machine was ready to be installed at the Iowa Commission for the Blind where Dr. Jernigan was the director. No pressure—just because Dr. Jernigan directed the agency, was the president of the NFB, and had hired me? I needed to do the job well.

At least the commute was easy. Holland and I were staying at the Kirkwood Hotel, two blocks from the commission's headquarters.

"Come on, Holland," I said one evening. "I need to work on the training manual, and my notes are over at the Commission." I slipped his harness on and we headed out the door.

There was still snow on the ground. *Good grief. Winter lasts into April here!* Still, I decided to let Holland have a little playtime. I took his harness off and made a snowball.

"Holland, get it!" I said, throwing the snowball in the air. I could hear him grab the snowball before it hit the ground. "Come," I said, and he bounded up to me. "That's my snowball," I said, taking it from his mouth, then tossing it up again. "Is that your snowball? Nope, it's my snowball!"

Holland loved this game, bringing me the snowball each time so I could toss it for him again. Because we were on a street corner, I simply tossed the snowball straight up in the air so he wouldn't go too far away.

"Alright, buddy, let's get over to the Commission so we don't have to work too late," I told him. "It's already almost seven. Was that fun? For a California dog, you certainly like the snow, don't you?" I could feel him wriggling, wagging his tail as he walked beside me. "Good dog, Holland."

When we got to the building, I reached down to pet him and realized he had something in his mouth.

"Holland, what do you have?" Holland sat calmly on the sidewalk—with a snowball in his mouth! He'd carried it carefully for two blocks from the hotel. "Holland, you are kidding me! Your mouth must be frozen."

Holland simply wagged his tail but held the snowball tenderly in his jaws, in that soft retriever mouth style.

"Holland, give me that snowball," I said, reaching down. Holland stayed sitting beside me, but deftly swiveled his head, evading my efforts. Apparently, he wanted to have the last word: *"My* snowball!"

Finally, I got him to give it up. I unlocked the entrance to the Commission with the key I had been given and we went inside and up to my office on the third floor, right next to the conference room where the Kurzweil reading machine was housed. Holland napped by my desk while I worked for an hour before we headed back to the hotel.

Snowballs aside, Holland seemed to simply accept our new assignment as it came. After attending the NFB national convention in New Orleans, Holland and I moved to the next installation site in July 1977 which was Blind Industries and Services of Maryland (BISM) in Baltimore. For two months, we trained users and continually refined the machine.

And so it went. The New York Public Library received their machine sometime around November 1977, so Holland and I lived in New York at the Hotel Seville for a few months where the two of us— now snow-navigation experts—experienced the Northeast Blizzard of

1978. Nearly a foot and a half of snow fell on the Big Apple during the first week of February. You haven't lived until you can walk down the middle of Madison Avenue in complete silence because there weren't any cars in the city that could navigate the deep snow that fell in only a few hours. Soon after, we went to Boulder, Colorado; then in April, we installed the final machine at the Orientation Center for the Blind in Albany, California, a city in the Bay Area. The Center was a residential facility, so Holland and I were able to make it our temporary home.

———

Walking through airports, riding in cabs, dealing with winter weather, staying in different places for a month or two at a time—nothing fazed Holland. As I said earlier, this was before the Americans with Disabilities Act became law, so I always called ahead to wherever I'd be staying to make sure they understood that I traveled with a guide dog. I did the same when I made airline reservations. This simple step of preparation made things a lot easier and less scary. I do not do that anymore since the law is clear. Guide dogs and other service dogs are allowed in any place or on any transportation conveyance wherever the public can go, including rideshare vehicles.

Did I feel fearful? Sure! I was facing the unknown. My parents had prepared me to be able to function in the world. However, no one prepared me for navigating icy city sidewalks or told me about how sidewalk salt can irritate a dog's paws. And suddenly falling was scary. But because I'd handled many different situations in my life, I could handle this one. I'd prepared by putting myself in challenging situations over and over, so that this felt in many ways like just the next step on my journey.

When guide dogs go through training, that's exactly what happens: They experience challenging situations which prepare them to handle just about anything.

That has been true for me too. When an opportunity came my

way, even though it involved some challenging steps I never anticipated taking, I envisioned myself taking those steps. I did teach—just not in the classroom. That made it less scary and more exciting. And it gave me more specific ways to prepare.

Sometimes, you prepare by intentionally engaging in experiences that will help you be brave and thrive. But sometimes, the things that happen unexpectedly prepare you for whatever is next, if you have the mindset to see things that you didn't choose as opportunities. You remain flexible. If you see each moment as preparation, whether intentional or not, you'll be able to live courageously.

At each installation, I'd demonstrate how to set up the machine and use it. No one ever said this out loud, but I could just tell people thought, *Well, if a blind guy can work this thing, it must be pretty easy to use!* (This same dynamic occurred later in my career when I sold computer hardware and software.) Of course, most people continued to underestimate me then, and sighted people today continue to underestimate me and other blind people. The pervasive view remains that people need eyesight to lead and live "normal" lives. Not true at all. Even though I didn't realize it, I was learning to talk, communicate, and relate to others with everything I did, which would serve me well in the future.

At the end of the Federation's reading machine project, Ray Kurzweil hired me to continue to carry out studies to help improve the technology. In October 1978 I moved to Winthrop, Massachusetts, and rented an apartment. Every day, Holland and I commuted an hour each way to the Kurzweil facility in Cambridge.

While preparation helps us feel less afraid, sometimes life throws you a curveball. How can you be brave when you face something you had no way to prepare for? You have to adapt and seize new opportunities when they come your way. Holland and I would learn the importance of being both bold and flexible, and trusting God, soon after our career at Kurzweil began.

## Guidance from the Word

*Have I not commanded you? Be strong and courageous. Do not be afraid; do not be discouraged, for the LORD your God will be with you wherever you go.*

**JOSHUA 1:9**

## Prayer for Courage

Dear God, thank you that I can know you're with me wherever I go. Help me to be open and curious so I can prepare to be brave.

# 3

# HOLLAND, PART TWO
## Flexibility and faith move you forward

A dog doesn't care if you are rich or poor, educated or illiterate, clever or dull. Give him your heart and he will give you his.

**JOSH GROGAN**

**HOLLAND AND I ENJOYED LIVING IN WINTHROP,** commuting into Cambridge and continuing to visit Boston on the weekends.

In late May 1979, Andrew Parsons, vice president of marketing, called me into his office. "Mike, have a seat. We need to talk."

*Uh-oh*, I thought. I took a deep breath. *Don't worry, just listen,* I chided myself. *Be brave.* I sat down, Holland beside me. I rested my hand on his shoulder and took a deep breath.

"You're doing a great job," Mr. Parsons began. "Your work here is important, and it adds a lot of value to the company." *Okay. So far, so good. But I don't think he called me into his office just to give me an "attaboy" talk.* And I was right.

"However . . ." he continued. "Unfortunately, your work doesn't produce revenue for the company, so your position is not sustainable. You've done great work, but . . ."

I listened silently, but inside, fear began rising up. My face felt hot; my throat tightened. Like many other engineering start-ups, Kurzweil hired lots of people, but not enough revenue producers. So I was being fired from a job I excelled at. I could feel my heart pounding in my ears, and my palms began to sweat.

After a brief pause, Mr. Parsons said, "We have to let you go. Unless . . . (he drew out the word), you would be willing to go into sales."

"Sales?" I asked, swallowing hard. *I've never done sales.*

"Sure. You're a people person. You'd probably be good at it. And we'll train you. You wouldn't be selling the reading machine. We'd want you on the team selling our new flagship product, the Kurzweil Data Entry Machine or KDEM. Mike, this machine is a game changer. It can digitize thousands of pages of print a day. It can convert printed pages into computer readable forms. Think of it! Legal briefs, newspaper clippings—so many uses!"

In that moment, my life turned upside down.

I had traipsed all over the country and thought I could finally settle in Boston. And now I was getting fired unless I was willing to go into sales? I was a scientist and I wanted to be a teacher, not a salesman! But . . .

In the next breath I felt a nudge, pushing my fears to the side. A sort of calming presence gently told me: *Accept the offer.* I knew, of course, that finding another job would be challenging. If someone offered a path through the obstacles, it made more sense to walk through them on that path. Like the paths that were cut through the snowbanks, there was a way forward provided here too. Just not the kind I expected.

A split second later, a deeper reality began to sink in. A more encouraging truth.

*Don't be afraid. I'll be with you*, I felt God reassuring me. *Be strong and courageous. Step out and say yes. Don't hesitate. Go forward!*

"I'd be willing to do sales."

"Great," he said. "We were hoping you'd say yes. The first step will be a Dale Carnegie sales course. We can get you signed up for that today."

"Wow, that's, um, great," I said. My head was spinning slightly—this was happening quickly.

In that pivotal moment, I had a choice: fear or faith. I could have listened to the objections in my mind—*You don't have experience in sales. You're a scientist, not a salesman. There's so much you don't know.* My fear spoke loudly in my mind. I could have refused to be flexible—and ended up unemployed. But instead, I listened to that nudge that gradually grew louder and overcame the voice of fear—that inner knowing, which I knew was the voice of God: *Say yes. Begin an adventure. I'll be with you wherever you go. Don't be afraid, for I am with you always.*

From there, God guided my steps and used the team at Kurzweil to take me on a new career path. I faced many challenges along the way, but whenever I felt scared, I used that energy to motivate me. I knew I had to work hard—just getting by would not cut it. I had to be flexible and have faith. I realized I needed to be the best I could possibly be. I jumped in right away to amass skills to succeed. I completed a ten-week Dale Carnegie sales course, which boosted my confidence and provided excellent preparation to begin selling.

As it turned out, I had a knack for sales. During my sales training I realized that selling isn't just about "pushing a product." The best salespeople really are teachers too! They explain the ways their products can help customers and prospects, and if they're great salespeople, they also honestly divulge when and why the products won't do the job. (That's a really hard one to swallow, but it is necessary to know that to be the best.)

Holland and I traveled to cities and even countries where I had never been before. If Holland could adapt to all the things I threw at him, I could learn to cultivate the same faith and flexibility.

I know absolutely that God urged me to take the position, in an area of business where I had no experience. In fact, God and I talked often about that choice and how it led to other things in my life. Yes,

I mean it when I say that God and I converse about such things. It is all about being open and taking the time to listen, and then to move forward in faith.

Growing up, I remember my dad and I often had discussions about God and prayer. I remember one conversation in particular when he told me, "Too many people constantly tell God what they want. Then they sit back and wait for what they want to appear. Mike, do you really think you have to tell our omnipotent, omnipresent, and omniscient God what you want, much less what you need?"

"No, I guess not," I replied. "If God knows everything, and knows what's best, I don't need to tell him what to do."

"Right. He knows. What you need to do is to talk with God, acknowledging that all things are possible with him, and that you believe he can make it possible to do whatever you want or need done. Then your job is to listen—I mean really listen—for the answer. The answer may well not be exactly what you expect. That's okay. The point is, listen for God's answer. The more you listen and hear, the more you will connect with God and see in one way or another the results you need."

That conversation, and many others like it, helped me to understand that prayer ought to be more about listening than talking. More about paying attention than demanding things from God.

Years later, my dad's words and example of faith guided me in that meeting with Andrew Parsons. The fear of the unknown tried to take over, but by 1979 I knew enough to overcome any perceived fears and move forward.

Holland also had to adapt and have faith in me. From our home base in Boston, we traveled as a team all over New England and Canada.

In 1980 Kurzweil began developing a talking computer terminal which was very cutting edge. I became the product manager for that item while continuing to sell the KDEM. The talking computer terminal got Xerox's attention. They wanted the technology Kurzweil had, and so they bought the company. As a result, I worked with the Xerox team at their Palo Alto Area Research Center (PAARC) quite often.

One day in the spring of 1981, Roy Cundiff, Kurzweil's vice president of sales, called me into his office.

"Mike, we'd like you to move back to California and sell to the West Coast for us, but also help integrate Kurzweil into Xerox PAARC."

Since I was from California, I was happy to get back home. I called my cousin Rob, a real estate agent in Orange County, and he helped me find a condo where Holland and I could live and work. In October 1981, exactly five years after we'd left, Holland and I moved home.

———

While working for Kurzweil, Holland and I traveled extensively. While my dog and I made a great team, I knew I eventually wanted to have a non-canine partner as well!

In January 1982, Harold Snider, a friend from the NFB, called me to say that he was going to be in Orange County for a project. Harold consulted for the Society for the Advancement of Travel and the Handicapped and was coming from DC to California to scope out a convention site and possible tour activities for the convention goers. Harold invited me to go with him and his driver to Knott's Berry Farm and then to dinner.

When Harold arrived, he said, "Mike, meet Karen Ashurst who is acting as my driver today." Harold and Karen picked us up and off we went. As we neared Knott's Berry Farm, Harold explained to me that Karen drove her car with hand controls because she was paralyzed from the lower chest down, due possibly to a birth injury, and used a wheelchair. When we arrived, he asked me to help get her chair out of the trunk, and we were off to explore.

That night we all went to dinner. The party included Harold; Karen; my date, Marci; and me. As always when at a restaurant, Holland was tucked under the table at my feet.

"Sir, can you please remove this chair, so I have room for my wheelchair?" Karen asked the waiter.

"Of course, ma'am," the waiter replied. Karen was seated right across from me, and to my right was Marci, whom I had been seeing for a couple of months.

"Mike, what line of work are you in?" Karen asked after we'd ordered our meals.

"I'm in sales with Kurzweil Computer Products," I replied. "We manufacture and sell computers that can read and digitize printed pages. How about you?"

"I run a travel agency focusing on making travel accessible to people with disabilities."

*Wow. What an intriguing person*, I thought. But because I was dating someone else, and traveling constantly for work, I didn't think about Karen romantically—at first. Although I did figure out how to get her phone number.

"Well, I travel a lot," I said. "I wonder if you can help with arrangements for me?"

"Of course."

Two months later Marci decided she wanted to move back to her home in Washington state—without me, of course.

Initially, I contacted Karen for work-related business, having her book my hotels and flights. Travel agents did all the work in those days.

Occasionally I'd call Karen for a casual conversation. I enjoyed talking with this lively and intelligent woman. We started going to movies together and having longer conversations about everything. I found myself calling her more and more frequently. As Karen would later say, "We just fit."

---

In early May I began arrangements to go to Hawaii to visit some KDEM prospects. Of course, who should I call for tickets?

"Anyone Can Travel, this is Karen."

"Hey, Karen," I said.

"Hi, Mike. What's up?"

"Kurzweil wants to send me to Maui to visit some customers."

"Rough life," she laughed. *I love her laugh.*

"Yeah, it's tough, but someone's got to do it," I replied. "But I was thinking—my parents have never been to Hawaii. I'd like to take them with me. Can you book three round-trip tickets for us to Maui, departing May 10 and returning May 24?"

"Of course," she said. "That's really nice of you to take your folks. I'm sure they'll enjoy it. I can get you two rooms at the new Hyatt Regency hotel on Maui. Tell you what. I can get the tickets by tomorrow, and I'll stop by your condo and deliver them to you."

"Oh, that's thoughtful, but you don't have to do that."

"It's no problem. See you tomorrow around eleven," she said breezily.

The next day, Saturday, Karen drove to my condo. Holland and I greeted her in the parking lot.

"I was just taking him out," I said. "Do you want to take a walk with us?"

"If you push, I'll navigate," she said. I handed her Holland's leash and stood behind the chair. "Forward!" she said, laughing. We strolled to the corner and then back to the parking lot.

Back at my condo, we sat and talked for far longer than was necessary, but I didn't want the time to end. I took off Holland's harness, letting him know he could relax. Karen knew Holland was doing his job when the harness was on, but he loved getting attention when he was "off the clock."

"Good boy, Holland," Karen said. "Who's a good boy? Oh, you like having your ears scratched, don't you?" It made me happy to hear Karen interacting so comfortably with Holland.

We were in our early thirties and knew what we wanted in a life partner. That day, I realized that this woman was who I wanted as my life partner.

"Well, I should get going," Karen said.

"I'll walk you out," I said. "Holland, you stay here."

Once Karen was in the driver's seat and her chair stowed behind her, she sat with the window open.

"Good to see you, Mike," she said.

"Good to see you too." I leaned in the window and gave her a big kiss, before I could let my fear talk me out of it. Talk about a step of faith!

Karen later told me she had hoped I'd ask her to lunch that day. I wasn't thinking about food! Sometimes we guys are simply clueless.

Things progressed rapidly. Karen met my parents when she drove us to a hotel near the airport the day before we left for Hawaii. We all went out to dinner the night before.

I called her from Hawaii—twice a day, every day. When I got home, Karen was traveling for work, but again, I called her twice a day.

———

A few weeks later, I came back from the 1982 NFB national convention in Minneapolis feeling very sick. It didn't escape Karen's notice when she picked me up at the airport.

"Are you alright?" she asked.

"Um, I'm not feeling great, actually," I said. Holland whined from the back seat.

She put the back of her hand gently against my forehead. Her hand felt like ice.

"Mike, you're burning up!"

"I don't feel hot," I said. "I've got the chills." I shivered and felt like I might pass out.

"I'm taking you to the house right now. You can't stay by yourself."

"Holland will watch out for me," I said deliriously. "Won't you, boy?"

"Rowwww!" he replied, as if trying to tell Karen, "No! Don't listen to him! He needs help!"

She drove quickly to her parents' home. She helped me from the car and into the house, where I promptly fell onto the couch in exhaustion. Holland had stuck close beside me as I walked in, then lay down on the floor against the couch, as if on guard.

"What on earth?" Karen's mother asked.

But Karen was already on the phone, setting up a doctor's appointment for the next morning. "Mom, can you give Mike some aspirin? And find the thermometer? I think he's got a fever."

Karen's mom took my temperature. "It's 105!" Karen kept her cool, talking with the doctor who told her to sponge my head and wrists with cool cloths, to continue with the aspirin, and get me to his office first thing in the morning.

Eventually, the doctor told Karen that he suspected I had Legionnaires' disease, but he couldn't be certain. Karen insisted that I stay with her and her parents to recuperate. They cared for me while she worked.

While I was sick, Holland mostly stayed beside me, watching over me. He knew something was wrong, and he'd sometimes sit by the couch and put a paw gently on my arm. Holland also took the opportunity to play with the Ashursts' dog, Tramp. They definitely hit it off and entertained all of us. I drew strength from Holland's presence, even though I was out of it. Whenever I began to rouse from my fevered sleep, he was there, nosing me or putting his paws on the couch.

I also drew strength from the love of Karen's family, and my unfortunate situation did bring me closer to them. It also gave Karen and her parents a chance to get to know me and Holland even better. They fed and cared for him while I was recovering.

This may not seem like a big deal. But one way you build teamwork and trust with a guide dog is by being his source of food and care. Until then, I had been Holland's sole caregiver. So as I lay on the couch at Karen's parents' home, and as Karen fed and cared for Holland, he accepted her as part of our team. He was quite food-motivated, which helped. He also enjoyed going for walks beside her wheelchair, but he never wanted to go too far from me.

But I think Holland also realized that certain situations call for flexibility. If you insist on things being done the way they've always been done, you will feel afraid of change. That fear may show up as anger or stubbornness, but it will still have the same impact: It will keep you stuck. In order to move forward, you have to be willing to change. And you have to be willing to accept help—from God as well as the people and possibly even the dogs he puts in your life. That's sometimes hard for me, but in that moment I realized it was the right thing to do.

Eventually I recovered. After those difficult weeks, I knew I had found someone very special. And I was definitely ready to change my life in order to keep this woman in it!

Here's how Karen described our courtship:

> Mike never really proposed. One day we were driving near my apartment in Santa Ana, and the subject of marriage came up at a stoplight. By the time the light turned green, we had decided to get married. A few days later Mike showed up at the travel agency. I was busy on the phone with a customer, and Mike didn't care. He grabbed my hand and slid a diamond ring on my finger. "I think I have to stop talking to you now," I told my client.

For the record, I recall asking her to marry me while we sat at that stoplight!

---

We got married November 27, 1982, at Irvine United Methodist Church—less than a year after we'd met and after only about six months of dating.

As the music began, Holland and I took our place at the front of the sanctuary where the two ministers (we couldn't decide which one to ask, so we had both) were standing. The music blended with the

Guide dogs know that in order to move past your fear, you have to be willing to change and be flexible. And you have to be willing to accept help.

quiet buzz of conversation as people found their seats. But it seemed a little too quiet.

"There aren't many people here," I observed. "Aren't we starting at 4:00?" I flipped open my Braille watch: 3:55 p.m.

"Yes, but the church is only about half full," one minister said.

"We're expecting 225 people," I whispered. I adjusted the tie on my white tux, and Holland sat quietly beside me.

"Well, a lot of them seem to be running late," he whispered back. "Maybe they all got lost?"

The music kept playing. Karen and her dad were still in the vestibule, obviously wondering where our guests were. I could hear people whispering a bit more as 4:00 p.m. came and went.

At 4:12, the doors of the church burst open, and a crowd of people rushed in to take their seats. We later learned that these guests had been in their cars in the parking lot, listening to the final moments of the USC–Notre Dame game on the radio. Both Karen and her dad were USC alumni, so they of course understood. And we were delighted that USC won on our wedding day! So we knew the marriage was going to last. How could anyone argue with that kind of positive success?

The wedding march music began, and Karen's dad pushed her wheelchair down the aisle. She wore a high-necked white gown and a white hat. My canine best man wagged his tail as he watched them make their way toward us.

We said traditional vows, with our families and friends proudly watching. I stood there holding Karen's hands and just feeling a joy and connection unlike any I'd experienced before. It just felt right.

The minister finally pronounced us husband and wife, and then said to me, "You may kiss the bride." I was more than happy to follow his direction. As the recessional began, I pushed Karen's chair back down the aisle, Holland walking proudly beside us.

The reception was held at El Adobe, our favorite Mexican restaurant in beautiful San Juan Capistrano. As the sun set, we danced on the patio overlooking the ocean, to Anne Murray's "Could I Have

This Dance (for the Rest of My Life)?"—one of our favorite songs. "Isn't she beautiful?" I said over and over as I twirled Karen's chair around the dance floor.

I never felt fear about marrying Karen. We took a step of faith, sure, but we didn't worry. We decided that we would have a lifetime of adventure together. I know—she's in a wheelchair, and I'm blind. So, who cares? I think every person has gifts and challenges. Ours are perhaps a bit more obvious at first glance. Karen and I needed each other. You can overthink stuff (doesn't a lot of fear come from overthinking?), but we didn't. I had no idea how everything would go, other than the fact that I felt absolutely certain that we could and would make it work.

Teamwork is about having our individual strengths and feeding off each other. Everyone needs a support system, a partner. There are things that Karen did well and things that I did well, and those things complemented each other. As my team expanded from two (Holland and I) to three, I felt blessed.

As I used to say, "She reads; I push." Of course, when she got a power chair in 2003 because her shoulders were giving out, she didn't need me to push. But we still needed each other. We recognized that each of us had skills that we brought to the relationship, and over the decades we incorporated those strengths into our lives together. We learned to flex and adjust to each other.

Karen and I began our lives together in Mission Viejo, which was near her travel agency office in San Juan Capistrano. I continued the work I'd been doing, traveling often. Until . . .

On a sunny Saturday morning in late June 1984, our FedEx delivery man rang the doorbell. I opened the door, and he handed me a thin envelope. "Have a good one," he said as he hustled back to his truck. I somehow knew that this day might not be so good.

Inside the envelope was a letter—not written in Braille. My employer, who knew I was blind, sent me a letter I could not read. Of course, I did not have my own $50,000 Kurzweil reading machine either.

In college and grad school, I'd hired readers to read textbooks and correspondence that were not in Braille to me. Now that job fell to my lovely wife.

I handed the letter to Karen. "This makes me a little nervous," I told her. "But read it."

"It's from Xerox," Karen said. She read out loud, but I could barely listen once I heard, "Your services are no longer needed." No thank you, or sorry, just "You're gone."

"Well, I can't say I'm really surprised. I guess there's some consolation in that I'm the last non-Xerox salesperson to get laid off." But my words covered my fear—I was suddenly unemployed.

Since the merger, management was slowly replacing Kurzweil salespeople with Xerox people. I'd been anxiously anticipating that letter for more than a month. Corporate takeovers typically don't help the existing team. Despite the international sales experience now on my resume, and the fact that I'd done my job well, I knew I faced obstacles that sighted people didn't.

"Well, good thing you've been working on your resume," Karen said. "We kind of knew this was coming. You'll find something."

"Right," I said, even though it felt anything but right.

*Be brave*, I told myself. *Walk by faith.* But inside, I battled doubt. Karen and I were still newlyweds, married less than two years.

*Forward. No pity parties allowed. It's now your full-time job to find a new job. Part of being brave is to be flexible and try new things.*

One month turned into two, then four, then six. I was getting scared. Six months of sending resumes, calling associates from my years at Kurzweil, putting the word out that I wanted a sales job in the tech sector. In the mid-1980s, tech was a rapidly changing but growing industry. The Apple Macintosh debuted in 1984, but people still struggled to wrap their minds around the concept of a "personal computer." The idea of each worker having their own computer seemed completely revolutionary.

Businesses that came on board realized that computers were astonishing innovations in the workplace, making this an exciting and intriguing field. I thought it might be a ripe opportunity for me to pursue.

Finding a job wasn't working out well. In fact, it wasn't working at all. I had several possible employers tell me that they couldn't hire a blind person no matter what my resume showed. I even had one executive recruiter set up an in-person interview for me in San Jose, California, nearly 400 miles north of where we lived. I would have to fly. The tickets arrived, but the night before I was to travel, the recruiter called and said, "Mike, I notice on your resume that you have a number of activities relating to blind people. Is someone in your family blind?"

"Yes. I am."

"You? Well, I am going to have to let the company know. Probably they won't want to interview you."

"Why? All of you liked my qualifications and my resume. Nothing has changed."

"Yes, it has. You are blind." The next morning the interview was called off and the airline reservation was canceled, all due strictly to prejudice, not reality.

The incident made me furious. But anger is often a secondary emotion. It typically has other feelings that lead up to it. And I hated to admit it, but that primary feeling, the one under the anger, is often fear. *What if other companies discriminate against me in the same way? What if no one wants to hire a blind man? What if I can't find a job?*

As if these setbacks weren't enough, my dad was in and out of the hospital. The doctors believed a spore had entered his body when he'd served in Africa in World War II. Whatever the cause, he now battled numerous health issues.

I loved my dad and talked to him often. He had always been my biggest advocate. He'd fought for the opportunity for me to attend school, ride a bike, get an education alongside sighted people. We'd been ham radio operators together. And now I was losing him. Early in 1984, he was in the hospital, in a coma. He came out of it but was never quite the same. He had numerous blood transfusions, but they didn't seem to help.

He passed away on November 1, 1984. The doctors blamed congestive heart failure. The idea of facing the future without my dad scared me. Every rejection letter I got seemed to mock me—all the work he'd done to make the world a more inclusive place for me had obviously not been enough, and now he was gone. Even so, deep down I knew he would want me to be creative and move forward.

---

"So, I've been thinking," I said to Karen one night at dinner. "What if I were to create a job for myself?"

"What do you mean?"

"I mean start a company that sells computers with this new technology—computer-aided design (CAD). What architects and engineers have been doing with a pencil and ruler at a drafting table can now be done on a computer with CAD. It's fascinating—and I think it's a great business opportunity."

"Well, do you think it's financially viable? Are companies going to be willing to invest in something that feels like it might replace their expertise?"

"I think there's great potential," I said. Actually, I wasn't sure, and maybe a little terrified. But I kept that thought to myself. *What do I know about starting a company from scratch? Not much. I've never done it.* I'd watched my dad run a business. He and his brother-in-law, Uncle Abe, had a television repair shop. *If I can convince Karen, I can convince myself. Maybe it's time to take a leap of faith.*

"I've been selling cutting-edge computer technology," I told

Karen, trying to sound confident. "I've been involved in the research at PAARC. I think it's a good fit. I know people in the industry. Plus, we need something to pay the bills."

So a friend and I started The System Connection to sell computer-based CAD systems—both software and hardware. I applied for a low-interest loan from the Small Business Administration. It took time, but we finally got the loan, which helped a great deal. Even so, until financing came through, we lived off credit cards and the few early sales we made.

CAD is a commonly used technology now (some high schools even offer classes in CAD), but in the mid-1980s, it was brand new. Prior to its introduction, architects still worked at drafting tables, meticulously drawing plans with pencils and rulers.

Our software could create a floor plan in a fraction of the time it took to draw it by hand. That floor plan could easily be revised if a client wanted to add a window or move a wall, without having to completely start over. We even had a three-dimensional CAD system so that we could build a model of a house and do a virtual walk-through on the computer screen. It was advanced technology.

Some old-school architects were skeptical at first, and the computers didn't exactly sell themselves as readily as I'd hoped. The early-adopting customers realized that they could still make as much money, but now they would charge for their expertise rather than for time. But some resisted, listening to their fears about technological changes.

Another unforeseen challenge: The market continued to change quite rapidly. Our business model included selling a system—both the PC and the software. But by the middle of 1988, a growing number of companies priced PCs so inexpensively, we couldn't compete. Hardware and software evolved into two very different businesses.

But I pushed forward, dizzied by the rapid changes of an industry I thought I really understood. I knew I had to be flexible, but I wasn't sure how. In the midst of that fear and uncertainty, I experienced yet another loss.

In late 1985, Holland, who had walked faithfully beside me for thirteen years, seemed to be slowing down. I could tell he needed to retire—he was nearly fifteen years old—so I began the process of applying to get a new guide dog. We could just keep Holland as a pet. Like Squire, he deserved a comfortable retirement.

"Come on, buddy, let's go out," I said to Holland one morning in early 1986. His nails clicked on the kitchen floor, his steps hesitant and uneven as he moved toward the back door I was holding open.

I walked out with him, enjoying the warmth of the sun on my face. I waited as Holland snuffled around the yard. But suddenly I heard a grunt and a thud.

I rushed toward him and nearly tripped over him. I knelt beside him and stroked him.

"Holland? Holland!" He lay still.

"Karen!" I yelled, gently shaking my dog, trying to rouse him, fighting the sick feeling in my stomach. *No, please.*

I put my hand in front of his nose, felt his puffs of rapid, labored breath. He lay perfectly still, except for the rise and fall of his ribs.

Karen wheeled out onto the patio. "What happened? Why is he on the ground like that?"

"I don't know! He just collapsed."

"Can you pick him up? I'll call the vet."

We somehow got Holland into our car and rushed to the vet's office. An assistant carried him, still unconscious, into an examination room and laid him gently on a table. I stroked his head gently. Tears ran down my cheeks and I didn't bother to wipe them away.

"Mike, Karen, I'm so sorry," the vet began. "We're not sure what happened, but we think Holland may have suffered a stroke or heart attack. I can resuscitate him, but I don't recommend that. He's just not going to have a good quality of life."

I reached for Karen, putting my arms around her shaking shoulders as she sobbed quietly. Holland was fifteen-and-a-half years old—a good long life for a retriever. He had walked beside me and witnessed so many important milestones in my life.

*God, this is hard*, I prayed silently, one arm around Karen, my other hand on Holland. *My business is failing, and now my dog too?*

*It's time to say goodbye*, I realized. *It doesn't make sense to prolong Holland's suffering.*

In a time when the future looked so uncertain, it broke my heart to have to let go of someone who'd been a constant and reliable companion for so long.

But a few weeks later, Klondike, another golden retriever, came bounding into our lives. Even as I mourned the loss of Holland, I knew he had taught me by his brave example. I had to move forward and walk by faith.

## Guidance from the Word

*Therefore do not worry about tomorrow, for tomorrow will worry about itself. Each day has enough trouble of its own.*

**MATTHEW 6:34**

## Prayer for Courage

God, I sometimes feel worried about the future: my job, my relationships, my health, my legacy. Today, I place all those in your hands, trusting you to replace my fear with confidence.

# 4

# KLONDIKE

## Perseverance strengthens your spirit

I love seeing what dogs do when
they see a problem for the first time.
What do they understand about the
problem? What kind of intelligence
will they display? What skills will they
use to solve it?

**BRIAN HARE**

**IT WAS FORTUITOUS** that my arrangements to get a new guide dog
had progressed so far that when Holland died I was only three weeks
away from heading back to San Rafael. On my third dog day, I was
matched with Klondike, a sweet and mellow golden retriever.

By now I had been partnered with a guide dog for more than two
decades, so most of what we learned was review—although there were
always new developments and training protocols. But a few days into
training, we hit a roadblock.

"Okay, everyone on the bus," Terry Barrett, the supervisor, called
out. We were taking a field trip into San Francisco to practice navigating city streets with our dogs.

When it was my turn, I took hold of Klondike's leash. He couldn't walk beside me in the narrow bus aisle, so I didn't hold his harness. Instead, I mounted the bus steps with my dog right behind me, then let him follow me down the narrow aisle. "Heel," I said confidently. Klondike calmly walked onto the bus, we found a seat, and he tucked under the seat in front of me. With the rest of the class, we headed to San Francisco.

"When we arrive, you'll get off the bus one by one," Terry reminded us as the bus made its way through the narrow streets. The bus finally pulled to a stop, and the other students and their dogs began filing off.

"Mike, your turn," Terry called from outside the bus, where the other students were gathered.

"Klondike, sit," I said, and he rose dutifully from the floor where he'd been lying down at my feet. As I had before, using the leash only, I walked with Klondike down the narrow bus aisle to the front of the bus. But as we approached the front of the bus, Klondike's pace slowed.

The closer to the exit we got, the more hesitant he became. I pulled on the leash, but instead of following me, he stopped cold. I reached to pet him and could feel him trembling. He planted his feet and panted hard. I almost had to drag him the last few steps to the exit.

"What's the matter, boy?" I asked. *What on earth? I've never had a dog do this.*

I kept tugging the leash, finally convincing him to step hesitantly down the metal steps and off the bus. I got him clear of the bus door, then knelt down in front of him, stroking him gently as he continued to pant and shake. "It's okay, fella," I said. I hugged him gently, and his shaking subsided a bit.

"What's going on, Mike?" Terry walked toward us.

"I'm not sure. Yesterday when we came into San Francisco, Klondike was fine the whole trip. Today he was afraid to leave the bus. I practically had to drag him off. He seems almost afraid to walk."

"Just be patient with him," Terry said. "Any of these dogs can develop some fears and we may never know why. All you can do is be supportive. Encourage him and gently urge him forward."

"Are you sure?"

"Yes. He'll come around. Don't worry about it just yet."

What I didn't know then but have since learned is that many dogs go through what is called a "fear period," where things that didn't bother them before abruptly begin to frighten them. Most of them get over it if their handler responds with love and support. You must not push too hard to make things worse. Instead, invite your dog to take small steps of courage and praise them when they do so.

I felt some doubt, but I decided to try to help my dog persevere and overcome his fear.

"Forward, Klondike," I said as I took the harness handle and began trying to walk, trying to sound cheerful. He held back at first, pulling against the harness. "That's a good dog. You've got this. Forward!"

After a little nudging and encouragement, Klondike began—tentatively at first—to walk. Within a block he was walking fine, and the rest of that trip went well. But doubts clouded my mind.

The next day, Klondike again displayed fear—trembling, balking, whining—as we were getting off the bus in San Francisco. This fear reaction had never happened in San Rafael or anywhere else. On that trip I tried to stay patient and help my dog. I knew Terry and the other trainers were watching carefully. Some dogs simply can't handle the stress of guiding. Would Klondike make it, or would he have to be "career changed"? About half the dogs who enter guide dog training don't make it as guide dogs and find a different career, often as a pet. These dogs are NOT rejects. They simply, for whatever reason, are not cut out for the job of being a guide dog.

On our next trip into the city, Klondike, or Klonny as I'd begun to call him, got off the bus with only a brief pause. "Good boy! Look at how brave you are," I told him. His fear seemed to be ebbing away. By the fourth day he was back to his old confident self and never exhibited that kind of fear again.

LIVE LIKE A GUIDE DOG

It is always good to have a friend and companion with whom to commiserate about fear. We may communicate in a slightly different way with a dog, but the basics are the same: love, encouragement, support, and being there. The bus incident showed me an important principle—you can't give up when you run into roadblocks. You just have to patiently work your way through them. Perseverance is really about problem-solving—not giving up in the face of those problems, but finding a solution. The very act of solving the problem can help us become more confident and courageous.

Guide dogs show us that if they persevere in the face of challenges, the simple strategy of not giving up will grow their courage. Perseverance strengthens your spirit. With my encouragement, Klondike kept going, even when he felt afraid, and as a result, he became braver.

Still, after years with the bold and friendly Holland, this dog was going to require a different approach. Perhaps God had brought Klondike into my life at that time to teach me how to be patient and persevere because of the challenges I was facing at work.

———

A week later, we were home.

"Another golden retriever? He looks sweet," said Karen. She set a bowl of water on the floor for Klondike, who sniffed it cautiously before lapping it up.

"Yes, but he's nothing like Holland, that's for sure," I told her. "He acted a bit fearful at times during the training. He was afraid to get off the bus when we went to the city."

Karen petted Klonny who, for all his timidity, didn't seem to be bothered by her wheelchair. As we got into a routine, he seemed to be less nervous. Maybe I just had to carry on and get used to a quieter dog.

In many ways I was thankful for a relaxed, mellow dog. I had other things to worry about. I desperately continued trying to keep my business afloat. Continuing to pursue that venture was way more challenging than getting my dog off the bus. And way more scary.

At the same time, my mother, who had been a heavy smoker for most of her life, started having health issues. On the way to a doctor's appointment, she slipped and fell, breaking her hip. They also discovered that she had colon cancer. She had two surgeries within a week—one for her hip, the other for her colon. It was too much, and she had a heart attack and stroke in the hospital. She was still living in Palmdale, and Karen and I lived in Mission Viejo, about three hours apart. When I learned of her stroke and heart attack, Karen and I went up to see her in the hospital. My brother also was there. A day after I arrived, she died in the hospital. Just three years after my father had passed, I lost my mother as well.

Amid that season of loss and grief, I felt afraid. My parents had taught me to be brave. They'd given me tools to thrive and live courageously in a world built for sighted people. But in that season, I wasn't thriving at all, or so it seemed. And now, they weren't around. What was going to happen to me, to my business? The financial stress was hard on our marriage as debt continued to mount. It seemed like every conversation felt strained and was somehow about our finances.

As if these losses weren't enough, my business partner had asked to be bought out in 1987, saying he didn't think our business would work. I limped along for another two years, but we really couldn't make ends meet. I put company expenses and all of our living expenses on credit cards. That's not a strategy I recommend, by the way. But at the time I couldn't figure out a different solution. Ironically, I became blinded by fear in that season of my life.

---

One day the phone rang. As usual, I considered not answering. But this was in the days before caller ID and who knows—maybe it was a customer for The System Connection? I decided to risk it and answer.

"Hello?"

"Mr. Hingson, this is Oscar, calling on behalf of Citibank. Are you aware that your credit card payment is overdue?"

"Hello, Oscar," I said wearily. It's a sad day when you are on a first-name basis with the collectors. "Yes, I'm aware. I will try to send in a payment this week."

"That's what you told me last week!" he said.

"I know," I said, sighing.

"You know, you should really make your payments," he told me. "You shouldn't be trying to rip off the credit card company. Think of all these handicapped people who are, you know, actually struggling."

*Handicapped people?* I didn't know whether to laugh or cry. My weariness gave way to anger. "You know, why don't you come down here and sit with me and my guide dog and my wife who is a paraplegic, and tell me about handicapped people? Shut up! We're doing our best."

———

In late 1988, Klondike and I were at my office toward the end of the day. He lay on the floor as I made phone calls.

"Well, if you change your mind, I'd love to bring over a demo and show you what our systems can do," I said, forcing cheerfulness. "The CAD system is easy to use and we'll train your employees in how to use it. . . . Excuse me? What's that? Okay, thanks for your time."

I hung up the phone and sighed. Tension and worry knotted up the muscles in my neck.

"Klonny, come," I said. I needed a little canine encouragement after another unsuccessful cold call.

Klondike walked over, and I stroked his silky ears. "It's been a long day, buddy. Just a couple more calls and then we can head home."

Klondike licked my hand. Then suddenly, he dropped to the floor. I reached down and could feel his body convulsing.

"Klondike!" I knelt beside him as he jerked and quivered for more than a minute. Panic surged through my body. Eventually, my dog lay still. A foul stench filled the air—Klondike had apparently lost *all* control. I stroked his back and could feel his labored breathing. I remembered what had happened with Holland. *No, not again.*

I grabbed the phone and called Karen. I was scared I'd lose my dog, and I didn't even know what to do to help him.

"I think Klondike just had a seizure," I said.

"I'll call Dad," Karen said. Karen's dad, Don, was a former army medic.

He arrived about twenty minutes later and confirmed what I already thought. "Judging from the mess, Klondike's clearly had some kind of seizure."

We quickly cleaned up Klondike (and my office floor) and called the vet to let him know we were on our way.

Don's diagnosis was supported by Klondike's veterinarian. "Let's see if Klondike has another seizure or if this is a onetime thing," he suggested. We went home, and over the next few days I kept close tabs on Klondike.

Two days later he had another grand mal seizure. Karen and I took him back to the vet, who told me, "I think your dog has some form of epilepsy. Here are some medications that might help."

But the meds didn't seem to work, and Klondike continued to have grand mal seizures. Our vet couldn't figure out what was wrong, and after one particularly bad episode, he suggested we take Klonny to a canine neurologist. A burning question raced through my mind: *Would I need to retire Klonny so soon?*

"Maybe we should try the neurologist, like the vet recommended?" Karen said.

In my mind, I imagined money pouring out of my hands and into the coffers of a canine neurologist. I was already fearful about our finances. The idea of having to spend money we didn't have on a specialist for our dog seemed crazy. But other than this occasional (admittedly serious) problem, Klondike served as an excellent guide dog.

I knew he sometimes struggled, but he was brave and did his best to do his job. He was still young but had come far in his ability to guide. He had overcome his fear of buses, had persevered, and now he typically guided with confidence and assurance. He had committed himself to me, and this was a time I certainly needed to be committed to him.

The neurologist tested Klondike thoroughly. His blood work showed a thyroid deficiency—which could explain his mellow demeanor. Dogs, like children, are more prone to seizures if they have low thyroid levels.

"I recommend Synthroid, and also phenobarbital," the doctor said.

"I think we should try it," said Karen.

After we got him on those drugs, Klondike never had another seizure. He comfortably and confidently guided for another seven years. In fact, because the medicine boosted his thyroid function, he became more active, alert, and engaged, with a wonderful, outgoing and confident personality.

Sometimes for people, fear and anxiety are made worse by chemical and hormonal imbalances, as they were for Klonny. You can try to simply persevere but sometimes you have to get the medical help you need, rather than just trying harder to overcome it on your own. This is true for people as well as dogs. Ironically, some people are afraid to take medication that would help them overcome their fear. Klonny showed me that, sometimes, you have to address both physical and emotional roots of fear.

Meanwhile, we continued to try to keep The System Connection afloat, but unlike Klondike's situation, we couldn't find the right prescription.

When we go through seasons of loss, we get scared. We mourn what we've lost, and battle fear that we'll lose even more. It can be hard to go forward. To persevere.

Klondike, for all his struggles, didn't give up. And we didn't give up on him either. As a team, we found the right solution to help him, and he bravely moved forward. His steadfast efforts inspired me.

As happy as I was that I'd found the right solution for my dog, I still wrestled with fear about my ongoing business struggles. As the company owner, I got paid last—if at all. I tried to do right by my employees, but it was killing us. I finally sold the company for a fraction of what I'd invested in it. But what would come next? I didn't know. We felt overwhelmed, and the situation put a lot of stress on our relationship. That's how we ended up in an attorney's office.

———

Karen and I sat across a desk from a sympathetic attorney. "Your situation is, unfortunately, not that unusual," he said.

"But really, you are exactly the type of people that bankruptcy was created for. If you can avoid it, that's great, but you should not feel bad or guilty. I can help you file for Chapter 13 bankruptcy right away if you want."

I held Karen's hand and swallowed hard. I'd really thought that we could make a go of the business. But I had failed—or rather, had not foreseen how much the industry would change, how the prices of PCs would plummet. I could blame circumstances beyond my control, but the fact was, we now had a decision to make.

My mind swirled. Was this the "solution" to our problems, the right prescription that would allow us to move forward?

"We need to think it over," I said.

Karen had been quiet in the attorney's office, but in the car, she unloaded.

"Mike, we've been living off our credit cards for far too long," she said as she drove down the freeway. "We've burned through our savings. What if we lose our house? Maybe bankruptcy is the best option."

"I know, I know," I said wearily. "I don't want to declare bankruptcy. I don't want to be 'the type of people that bankruptcy was created for.'"

"Well, I get that, and I don't want it either. But the truth is, maybe that is what type of people we are. Maybe it's the only way."

**Guide dogs show that if they persevere in the face of challenges, the simple strategy of not giving up will grow their courage.**

We drove in silence for a while. My mind churned. "I don't know," I said. *I'm scared*, I thought, but I didn't admit it out loud.

After dinner that night, Karen was calmer. "Want to listen to the next chapter in that Catherine Marshall book?" she asked. "Maybe it will take our minds off things for a while."

Karen and I often listened to audiobooks together. In that season, we enjoyed Catherine Marshall's books, including her memoir, *Meeting God at Every Turn*. The author wrote honestly about her own struggles in life, and how God had met her in those challenges.

Now we were reading her book *Beyond Our Selves* and were at a chapter that included the story of a man drowning in debt. Like us, he had to decide if he would declare bankruptcy or not. Rather than take our minds off our troubles, the story seemed to echo them. The man in the story consulted with George Müller, the famous founder of orphanages in England known for his experiences of God's miraculous provision. Inspired by Müller's faith, the man decided not to file for bankruptcy. Did I have that much faith? I was afraid I might not.

Jesus, in one lesson he taught about prayer, told his followers, "Go into your closet" to pray. In other words, don't make a big show of public piety. But I took that direction literally. I didn't want to be overcome and overwhelmed by fear. Instead, I needed to leverage my fear into action. And the first action I needed was stillness.

The next morning, I scooted my shoes out of the way and sat on the floor of our small walk-in closet. Alone, with no noise to distract me, I sat still. I took a few moments to just breathe, to settle. And then I prayed.

*God, I don't know what to do. But I'm not here to demand answers or quick fixes. God, I just need your presence and your wisdom. I'm exhausted. I wish I could call my dad. But I'm calling on you, my heavenly Father.*

Slowly, in the quiet, God's peaceful presence swept in, slowly pushing my fears away. I thought of Jesus' invitation recorded in Matthew's Gospel: "Come to me, all you who are weary and burdened, and I will give you rest."

*I'm here, God. I'm coming to you with a lot of burdens. I need your rest, your peace.*

There is power in simply being still, in letting God surround you with the light of his love. Sometimes being brave begins with surrender. I wanted to experience the promise of Scripture: "Perfect love casts out fear."

In the solitude, I could meditate and not think or worry about anything. I could hear God. *You're not a failure. Keep going forward. I'm with you. Don't be afraid.*

In my physical prayer closet, I clung to those reassurances. I could set aside my fears of creditors calling and bankruptcy and all the rest, and just let God love me. I continued to do this every morning, focusing on God's love and light before I had to face the day. It gave me the strength to continue.

It's a beautiful paradox: When we disengage, we can then engage more fully. The quiet presence of God, who loved me like my earthly father, prepared my mind and heart to deal with whatever stresses came my way. I began to personally experience the truth of the verse that says, "Fear not, for I am with you." Because I knew he was with me, I felt braver.

Sometimes God soothes our fears with words or impressions, as God did in that time of prayer. But God also speaks through other means—like the book we just happened to be reading that week, or something that Karen found during breakfast a few days later.

---

Karen turned to the want ads in the morning paper, as she did every day. I'd become rather weary of looking for a job and chasing leads that didn't pan out. I was afraid I'd never find a job.

"This one looks good," she said. "The company is called Artecon.

They're looking for a salesperson. I think you're qualified for it—it's selling computer systems. It sounds like a good fit. Let's send them a resume."

"Well, I'm not sure what kind of systems they sell," I said. "But I guess I can learn. It's worth a try."

Artecon sold a very innovative and efficient technology: hot-pluggable removable disks. You had a hard drive on your computer, and the drive would be in a special canister. Users could store their data on their own pluggable disk and could pull it out of the hard drive without completely shutting down the entire computer system and needing to reboot it for the next person. That may sound slightly crazy now, in an era of smartphones, laptops, and cloud storage, but at the time it was cutting edge.

I got to work on a cover letter. And got a little stuck.

"Karen, what do you think? Should I mention that I'm blind in my cover letter? I mean, if I don't say I'm blind, with my experience, I'd probably get an interview. But then when I show up, they'll go, 'Wait, you're blind? How are you going to get to work? How can you do this job? We can't hire you.' They'll ignore everything on my resume because of that. But if I say in the letter I'm blind, they won't even give me the courtesy of an answer. Remember that company that canceled the night before the interview because they found out I was blind? Well, what do you think? Should I say I'm blind in the cover letter?"

Karen was quiet for maybe half a second. "You're an idiot."

I started to object, then stopped and decided to play along. "Um, okay—why am I an idiot?"

"What is the most important thing you learned when you took that Dale Carnegie sales course? The thing you always told all your salespeople?"

She was obviously way ahead of me and clearly wasn't one to mince words.

I stalled for time. "Well, I'm not quite sure which thing you're thinking of. I learned a lot of things in the sales course."

She exhaled impatiently. "You have always said that the most important thing that salespeople need to keep in mind, especially when people are objecting to something regarding your product, is this: *Turn perceived liabilities into assets.*"

*Ah, yes.* I felt like a cartoon character when a little light bulb suddenly clicks on above his head. *Turn perceived liabilities into assets.* Emphasis on *perceived.* When a customer says a product is too expensive, you explain how your product is going to be able to save them so much money that it will pay for itself. When they say the system is too complicated, you talk about the level of support and training that comes with it, and how it will put them ahead of their competition.

Perseverance is essential to living courageously. And one way to persevere is to see things differently. Perceived liabilities can be assets, and seeing them that way allows you to move forward. For example, when an architect told me that a CAD system would only cause him to lose money, as it was so much faster than drawing by hand, I recommended that they shouldn't charge for their time, but rather for their expertise. They didn't need to lower their prices because they could provide their clients the benefit of quick modifications when needed by using this new CAD system. I realized I had to do a similar selling job to sell myself for this job.

I got to work on the letter. The last two paragraphs of the letter went something like this:

> The most important thing that you need to know about me when you're considering my application is that I happen to be blind. As a blind person, I have had to sell all my life, in order to survive and accomplish things. I've had to sell to convince people to let me, as a blind person, buy a house or rent an apartment. I've had to sell to convince people to let me take my guide dog into places. I've had to sell to convince people to let me take my guide dog on an airplane and into restaurants.

So I've had to sell to do anything that I wanted to do. When you're hiring somebody for this job, do you want to hire somebody who comes into the office, works for eight or ten hours a day, and then goes home because the job is over? Or do you want to hire somebody who truly understands sales for the science and art that it is, and who sells twenty-four hours a day because that's his way of life?

We sent the letter off. We waited for two weeks. I spent a lot of those two weeks on the floor of my closet, asking God for strength and praying for a miracle. And we continued to peruse the want ads, sending off more resumes, refusing to give up.

Then one day the phone rang.

---

"Michael Hingson?"

"Speaking," I said, then held my breath.

"This is Doug Cooper. I head up sales and marketing at Artecon. We got your resume and letter. I'm incredibly impressed with what you said. We want you to come down for an interview."

"That would be great," I said. And on July 2, 1989, I joined the sales team at Artecon with the responsibility of handling sales for the Mid-Atlantic region of the United States.

Now, you may be wondering how I got to work. No one, especially salespeople, worked remotely in 1989. We lived in Mission Viejo, California, at the time, an hour's drive from Artecon's office in Carlsbad. Have I mentioned I don't have a driver's license? (Although I did have a car for a while in college, which I sometimes drove—that's another story.)

But a job offer was a job offer. So Karen drove me from Mission Viejo to Carlsbad five mornings a week. Karen, Klondike, and I would leave the house at five to beat the traffic. Which meant I'd be in the office by six, and got a lot done before everyone else arrived.

And usually, I'd take a bus back home, to a bus depot near our house where Karen would pick us up.

We continued to read Catherine Marshall books on those morning commutes. Her teachings about faith and trusting God provided just what we needed at that season of our lives. She really helped us keep perspective—or I should say, God helped us through her words. We still had a lot of bills to pay, but at least now I had an income. Little by little, we persevered. We slowly paid off our debt, avoiding bankruptcy.

We commuted for six months, then eventually moved to Vista, about five miles away from Artecon's offices. Not surprisingly, Klondike was the hit of the place. And Karen was hired as the manager of document control.

Life was comfortable for the first time in years. We'd found the remedy for Klondike's seizures and for my career.

At the Artecon office, my desk was just across from the men's restroom. The company office was a sea of cubicles. I didn't take Klondike with me when I simply walked around my cubicle to go to the men's room.

One day I returned to my desk and Klondike wasn't there. My first thought was of Squire and his kidnapping, but I rejected that notion. A minute later, Karen called.

"Are you looking for your dog?"

"Maybe," I said, smiling.

"Well, he's downstairs here with me. He arrived at my desk a few minutes ago, carrying his leash in his mouth." Klondike had carefully walked himself down from my office on the second floor to Karen's desk on the first floor.

"So what is he doing now?" I asked.

"He's asleep under my desk," she laughed.

"I'll come and get him later. I've got some calls I need to make."

After that, I either tied Klondike's leash to my desk or simply let him go visit Karen if I wasn't paying attention. Our coworkers got used to seeing my dog walking himself through the building to Karen's cubicle.

———

We joined San Marcos United Methodist Church just after moving to Vista and quickly got involved. When I was growing up, my parents and I had many conversations about God and faith. And I certainly made prayer and meditation a regular part of my routine. I was grateful to God for guiding me to this new job and blessing my efforts at Artecon. I felt like he was inviting me into a deeper faith, reminding me that the reason we don't need to fear is because he is always with us.

But I hadn't been to church in years. Karen had lots of church experience, so she guided us through it. About two years after we joined, the church engaged an itinerant minister, Reverend Kimball Coburn, to spend a weekend preaching the gospel and conducting classes.

On the second evening of this revival weekend, Reverend Coburn delivered an inspiring sermon, and at the end, he stepped to the side of the lectern. "Let us turn now to the Communion table," he said. "If anyone would like to come up for Communion, and to affirm their commitment to Jesus, please come forward."

"Let's go up," I said to Karen.

"I was just thinking the same thing," she whispered back.

I stood up and so did Klondike, assuming his services were needed. "No, Klonny, stay here," I said. He stood for a few seconds, seemingly puzzled.

"It's okay, boy," I said. "Stay."

He lay down and put his head on his paws in disappointment. To him, Karen was taking over his job of guiding me.

"Good dog. You *stay*," I said firmly. Klondike sighed.

Karen and I went to the front and joined the communion line. About thirty seconds later Karen said, "Oh my goodness!"

"What?"

"Klondike has come up, and he's right in front of us, waiting his turn for the bread and wine."

Reverend Coburn moved along the line, giving each person a wafer dipped in grape juice, sometimes stopping to pray with people, until he reached Klondike.

"Well, hello," he said to Klondike, who gazed at him and wagged his tail. "Umm, whose dog is this?"

"He's my guide dog," I admitted, a little embarrassed. "I guess he doesn't want to be left out."

"Well, if he's answered the altar call, who am I to turn him away?" Reverend Coburn said. Without missing a beat, he administered the sacraments to Klondike, who took it politely.

For years afterward, Reverend Coburn loved to tell the story about giving Communion to his first dog who had ever answered his altar call.

We lived in Vista for four more years. And things went really well. Until . . .

———

As Artecon grew, the company saw opportunities to get government contracts. My boss talked about opening an office in the Washington, DC, area. Although our family and friends lived in California, Karen was open to the idea of moving to Virginia. Especially if it might lead to other career opportunities for me.

In late 1995, Artecon's president came into my office.

"I've changed my mind," he said. "It would serve the company better if you open an office for us in New York."

"New York?" I echoed. "What happened to DC?"

He ignored my question. "Well, you can either move to New York, or you can sell to New Mexico, because that's the only other open sales territory. I've already reassigned your territory here. We really need you in New York."

"New Mexico?" I tried to keep the panic out of my voice, even though I was incredulous. As a sales territory, New Mexico sat at the bottom of the barrel, and wouldn't provide enough income. So really, my only option was to move to New York or look for a new job. We'd just paid off our bills, so the idea of losing my job scared me. *There's no way I'm going to New Mexico. Karen is not going to like this news.*

That evening, I waited until dinner to tell Karen about this plot twist. I felt a little nervous about bringing it up.

"New York? And what, we'd live in New Jersey? *New Jersey!*" she said. "No way. I do not want to move to New Jersey. What happened to Virginia? Virginia is beautiful. New York City is noisy and dirty and unsafe. Can't you take another territory? Why New York?"

She was so strongly opposed to the idea I wondered if this would break up our marriage, which—admittedly—scared me. I didn't want to end up in another attorney's office—a divorce attorney! I tried hard to listen, and to stay calm.

"I know it's not ideal," I said.

"Not ideal? That's an understatement! How will Klondike handle commuting into New York City?" she asked. "He was afraid of the bus during training. You're going to expect him to get on a train and guide you through Manhattan five days a week?"

"He's come so far though," I said. "He's much less fearful than before. I think he can manage it. And Karen, here's the thing. This position could be a bridge to an even better opportunity. Have you forgotten what it felt like to have bankruptcy nipping at our heels? What if I take this job but keep looking for another position at the same time? I feel like there will be more plentiful opportunities on the East Coast, and this job will help me expand my network."

"I don't want to move to New Jersey," she said. She was quiet for a moment, and I knew she was fuming. "But it seems like we don't have a better option."

"Exactly. It will work out." *At least, I hope it will. I'm actually not sure what will happen. But the only way out is forward. So I need to be brave.*

I was uncertain about what lay ahead. But I couldn't go backward. God was opening doors and I needed to walk through them, despite my uncertainty—and my wife's reluctance.

As the time grew closer for us to move, we decided that Klondike might not really do well in New York. He was now twelve years old; he had been guiding for ten years. We worried his health might deteriorate with the harsher weather conditions. My commute would include taking two trains—a challenge for any dog, especially an older one.

Because we were getting ready to move, I called Guide Dogs for the Blind to get on the list for a new dog. I asked if they could find Klondike a family he could retire with. Within a couple of weeks, the head trainer said they'd found a family who wanted him—and they were flying to San Rafael in their private airplane to pick him up!

In February 1996 I went to San Rafael and was introduced to Linnie, my first yellow Labrador retriever guide.

Karen and I had visited Westfield, New Jersey, and worked with a real estate agent to secure a property and begin the construction of an accessible two-story house. In mid-April, Linnie and I went to New York while Karen stayed behind to get our house in California ready to be put on the market. I rented an apartment in Elizabeth, New Jersey, where Linnie and I could live in the meantime.

It was hardly ideal to be living apart on opposite coasts, but if I'd learned anything from Klondike, it was to persevere even when times were hard.

## Guidance from the Word

*I sought the LORD, and he answered me;*
*he delivered me from all my fears.*

**PSALM 34:4**

## Prayer for Courage

God, when life throws challenges at me, help
me to persevere and keep moving forward in
faith.

# 5

# LINNIE

## Empathy builds
## courageous connections

My service dog has definitely
helped me manage fear and anxiety,
because I'm never alone. Having my
battle buddy right there with me at
all times, he's going to take care of
me in any situation.

**JASON MORGAN**

**LINNIE WAS THE MOST PEOPLE-ORIENTED** guide dog I have ever
encountered. My other dogs were more focused on me, and sometimes Karen. But Linnie never met a person she didn't like. Actually,
she never met a person she didn't ask for a belly rub. Oh, make no
mistake, if we were walking and she was guiding, she was as focused as
any guide dog. However, when we were just standing around, well . . .

I first discovered this when we were still going through training.
We had walked from the training facility to the nearby Northgate
Mall. Along with a trainer, our group walked with our dogs around
Macy's department store, interacting with the staff and other custom-
ers, navigating the aisles of displays.

I stood at a counter. "Your dog is so cute," the salesclerk said.
"What's her name?"

"This is Linnie." Suddenly, Linnie dropped to the floor, pulling the harness from my hand, and lying on her back. *What on earth?*

Our trainer who was standing nearby laughed. "Is that dog silly or what? Linnie always wants to get her belly rubbed. Say her name and she'll invite you to be her best friend!"

If Linnie knew she wasn't working and figured out that somebody was looking at her, she'd flip over and be cute. She won people over easily because she was so friendly. She operated on the assumption that others wanted to connect—and as a result, she wasn't afraid.

It's quite normal to fear rejection or fear that other people might hurt us. People sometimes are afraid of me, just because I'm blind. But Linnie showed me that when we focus on connecting with others, we're less likely to fear them. Guide dogs know we can be brave when we try first to simply be friendly and kind.

Linnie wasn't just a taker, though. Our pastor Cherie Jones called her an "old soul" and "the most empathetic dog she'd ever met." I think Linnie simply lived in the moment—whether she was comforting someone who seemed down or asking someone to rub her belly. Sometimes it seemed she knew that giving a sweet yellow Lab a belly rub was exactly what the person needed.

I think sometimes we are afraid to connect with others because we wonder if they will reject us. Or we assume people cannot be trusted. While we should be wise, we will walk through the world feeling much less fearful if we assume, as Linnie did, that other people want to connect and are not out to hurt us.

Linnie settled right in at the Chilton Towers apartment building, in Elizabeth, New Jersey. Each weekday, we took two trains to Manhattan.

It had been years since I'd been to New York, so I had to learn my way around—just as anyone would. I decided to take a cue from Linnie and assume that most people were willing to be helpful or at least cordial. She wasn't afraid to make friends with strangers, and I knew I needed to do the same.

To get to the office from Elizabeth, I had to walk a couple of blocks from our apartment to the train station and catch a train bound for Penn Station Newark (different from the Penn Station in New York City), which was several stops away. I listened carefully as the stations were announced over the train's public address system.

"Next stop, Penn Station Newark," the voice intoned.

"Hi," I said to the person next to me on my first trip into the city. "Would you happen to know how to get to the PATH train that goes to the World Trade Center?"

"It's down one level. You go straight off the train and down the stairs, and you'll be right on the inbound platform. I'm actually heading into the city myself, so I can show you."

"Thanks so much."

"Cute dog," he added. On cue, Linnie immediately flipped on her back for a belly rub.

Together, we walked out of the train, across a platform, then down a set of stairs. I paid close attention as we walked, noticing distances and landmarks between the staircase and the train. By the second or third day, I was able to find my way to the PATH train without having to ask anyone.

On the way home, I simply reversed the process. If I wasn't sure where to go, I simply asked for directions—which is exactly what anyone would do—sighted or not. On each train, they usually announced the upcoming stop, so I knew when to get off. Until one day . . .

*What a long day. I'm exhausted.* Linnie seemed tired, too, and dozed at my feet. We'd taken the PATH train to Penn Station and just managed to catch the Northeast Corridor line train. The train made several stops before I noticed something wasn't right. *That's funny. I haven't heard any of these stops announced.*

*Something's off. I've been on the train longer than usual.* Elizabeth was the third stop, but I was so tired, I hadn't been counting stops— I just listened for the announcement. But I hadn't really been paying attention. Panic started to rise in me. I took a deep breath. *Okay, connect with people around you,* I told myself.

"Excuse me," I said to the woman sitting next to me. "What stop is coming up?"

"Well, the last stop was Elizabeth, so the next one will be Linden," she said.

*Uh oh.*

"Well, Linnie, looks like we might have a longer commute tonight," I said. At Linden, we disembarked. Since neither Linnie nor I can read signs, we asked a couple of other commuters how to get to the opposite side of the tracks so we could catch a train back to Elizabeth.

I stood on the platform waiting, feeling a bit foolish—and a bit nervous. *I know my way out of the station when I'm on the other platform, but now I'll be coming out a different way. I can't believe they didn't announce the stations! And I can't believe I wasn't counting the stops!*

Linnie nosed my hand, sensing my concern. Connections can allay our fears. That day, and many other days, people had been quite willing to direct me or offer help if I asked. Occasionally I encountered rude people. But when I was polite, people typically responded in kind. Linnie's nosing me reminded me that I shouldn't show her stress or fear. I petted her and said, "Don't worry, Linnie. Everything is fine." And it was.

Finally, the right train pulled into the station. We got on, rode back to Elizabeth, and got out. Thankfully, other commuters streamed toward the exit, and we went along with the crowd. When I got outside the station, I asked directions once, then found myself on a familiar street and was soon at our apartment.

Linnie took our commute (and the occasional detour) in stride. I knew I'd made the right decision to let Klonny retire. What would have overwhelmed many other dogs didn't faze Linnie in the least.

<hr />

We nicknamed the apartment "Camp Elizabeth" because family members were always coming and going. Karen would come out to meet with the builder as construction on the house continued. I'd sometimes fly back to California for the weekend. Sometimes Karen's parents would also visit.

Karen's brother, Gary, his wife, Julie, and their little daughter, Alagna, sometimes visited too. Gary was a certified mountain ski guide in France. In the winter, he'd often lead an *off-piste* (meaning "off the marked or groomed trails") ski tour in France, then come back to the United States to lead ski tours here. When ski season ended, Gary was a cabinetmaker and a general contractor. However, come winter, skiing was the only game for him.

One weekend when I was in California, I left Gary a key to our apartment since he was coming through town. At the end of the weekend, Karen, her parents, Linnie, and I returned together.

"Okay, Linnie, here we are," I said as we got off the elevator in the hall outside our apartment. I unhooked her leash and removed her harness, and she danced around me. *She seems more enthused than usual to be home.* I was glad to be home, too, after flying across the country and back in one weekend.

I unlocked the door and opened it, and Linnie rushed past me. With a giant leap, she launched herself onto our "guest bed"—which was an extra bed in the living room—right in between Gary and his wife, Julie! They were certainly surprised to be awakened by a sixty-pound yellow Lab landing on their bed!

The next day, Gary offered to take Linnie with him on his morning run. I showed him how to use the flexi retractable leash.

"This button stops the leash from extending," I began. "You've got to be careful . . ."

"I know. I got it. Come on, Linnie!"

I had warned Gary of Linnie's other weakness besides belly rubs: bunnies. She couldn't help it—she loved chasing rabbits. When she was in harness, Linnie *noticed* bunnies—and she'd let me know by whining or pulling a bit, but she mostly stayed focused on her work. But on a run, on a flexi leash, she felt free. She knew she was off the clock and that meant all bets were off if she saw a rabbit. I doubt

Linnie would ever catch a rabbit or know what to do with one if she did, but she was fascinated by them. And determined to chase them if she wasn't in harness. Maybe she thought she could befriend them.

A while later, Gary came home, Linnie in tow. "Look what your dog did to my hand!" he said. I resisted the urge to be a smart aleck and say something like "Let me have a look at it!" Linnie had spied a rabbit and taken off after it. Gary instinctively grabbed the flexi leash instead of pushing the stop button on the handle and ended up with a nasty rope burn on his palm. Gary never made that mistake again—and he didn't let it deter him from keeping Linnie as his running buddy. When he'd grab the leash and say, "Come on, Linnie," she would immediately be up and ready to go. I appreciated Gary giving Linnie some exercise.

---

For all the coming and going at Camp Elizabeth, there were many weekends when Linnie and I were there alone. I didn't really know anyone in the area, and since my living arrangements in Elizabeth were temporary, I didn't have a lot of opportunities to make friends.

One Saturday afternoon, I lay on the couch, channel surfing and feeling a little sorry for myself.

*I hate not having Karen here.* I turned off the television. *I'm just going to take a nap.* I rolled over onto my stomach.

I had just fallen asleep when I felt a weight land on my back. *Linnie?* I felt her doggy breath in my ear, as she gently settled herself on top of me. She put her muzzle on my neck and stretched out her legs on top of mine—like a snuggly Labrador blanket.

It was as if my empathetic dog was saying, "I know you're feeling lonely. But don't worry, I'm here with you. Don't be afraid. Besides, I miss Karen too."

I smiled, my loneliness slowly ebbing away, replaced by gratitude for my dog. "Good girl, Linnie." As we both drifted off to sleep, I just thought, *Thank you. Thank you.* I will never forget that afternoon with Linnie. She knew what I needed, and I let myself simply receive the comfort she offered. Once again, she reminded me that connection can ease our fears.

———

In July 1996, I made yet another trip to California to help Karen with the sale of our house and to help pack up our belongings. Linnie and I flew out of Newark to LAX, where we could connect to a flight for San Diego. Since I had at least an hour and a half before my connecting flight, we made our way to the Admirals Club, the American Airlines lounge.

As we walked in, I heard a gravelly voice with a thick New York accent. "I'm trying to get this paperwork done. I gotta go. I gotta go catch my flight, so can we move this along?"

*I know that voice. . . . Columbo!* Karen and I loved to watch the popular detective show by the same name, which starred Peter Falk, who was now standing at the counter in the Admirals Club next to me. I'd also seen him in movies like *Robin and the 7 Hoods*, one of my favorites, in which he plays a gangster.

"Mr. Falk, I'll get this processed as quickly as I can," the airline agent said. "Give me a minute and I'll have you on your way."

*I'm going to stay cool and not ask him for an autograph.* But I did decide to chat with him.

"Don't you hate paperwork?" I said.

"Yeah, no kidding," he said. "But you gotta do what you gotta do." He paused. "So, what's your dog's name?"

"This is Linnie." Upon hearing her name, Linnie did what she always did when someone gave her even a little bit of attention. She lay down and flipped on her back, inviting the famous actor to rub her belly.

He knelt down and kindly obliged her as we chatted for the next five minutes. Finally he said, in that unmistakable voice, "Linnie, I can't stay here and scratch your belly all night!"

**Guide dogs show that we can be brave when we try first to simply be friendly and kind.**

"Sure you can," I said. "Just ask her! She'd be happy to have you do it."

He laughed.

"Mr. Falk, here's your boarding pass," the agent said. "You're all set."

"Great, thanks. Goodbye, Linnie. I gotta catch my flight!"

When I finally got to Karen's parents' home later that night (Karen was staying with them), I said, "You won't believe who Linnie and I met at LAX."

"Who?"

"Columbo! In the flesh! Peter Falk! He sounded just like he does on TV!"

"Wow!" Karen said. "So, who did he spend more time with, you or Linnie?"

"Linnie, of course." I gave the family all the details of Linnie's celebrity encounter.

———

I thought about Linnie and her assumption that strangers were simply friends she hadn't met yet. For her, it took very little effort to be brave, because she was tuned in to people around her, instead of being anxious about herself. Why can't we all be more open like Linnie? I think if we believed the best about others, and focused on connecting with them, it would help us to be brave. When we turn our focus off ourselves, we often find our courage grows.

Dogs can experience anxiety, as Klondike did that day on the bus at guide dog training. But most dogs do not regret past actions or worry about future events. They live in the moment and don't do what-ifs.

It's harder for humans. We have to train ourselves to be present. Cultivating mindfulness can help us overcome fear and is essential to being brave. And being empathetic toward others, as Linnie was, can help us to focus less on ourselves and our fear.

Dogs don't have to do mindfulness training. But they absolutely must be continually trained to overcome distractions. But some dogs seem to have an uncanny ability to be fully present. Linnie was such a dog, as long as there were no bunnies in sight.

In August 1996, we found a renter for our home in California, and Karen and I moved into our newly-built home in Westfield, New Jersey. The house was on a pie-shaped lot—very narrow by the street but fanning out into a wide, lush backyard, framed by a wooded area. The landscape was very different from what we were used to in California.

That Christmas, we spent the holidays with Karen's family in San Clemente. For years, we'd had a tradition of throwing a "tree upping" party. Neither of us were especially good at putting up a Christmas tree and decorating. So we would provide the food and invite friends over to help make our house festive for the holidays. That's what we did at her parents' home.

We invited Pastor Cherie, who was now leading a Methodist ministry called The International Walk to Emmaus and happened to be in town at the same time.

Cherie sat down beside me and Karen on the couch.

"Linnie is an amazing dog," she said.

"I agree," I said. "But what makes you think so?"

"She just goes to the person who needs her, the one who's in the most pain. It's pretty incredible how she can read a room."

"What do you mean?" Karen asked.

"When she walked in and you let her off the leash, Linnie went straight over to my friend. I happen to know that she's going through a difficult season in her life. Linnie always zones in on the person who's emotionally in the most need. And only after she goes to that person does she start working the room to greet everyone else."

---

After Karen's first New Jersey winter, we were thankful when spring finally arrived.

I stood in the backyard, holding Linnie's leash. We didn't have a fence between our property and a busy road, so I always clipped a leash to her collar.

I stood in the shade of the tall trees that ringed our lawn, breathing in the green scent of spring.

We walked back inside, and I took off her leash. I bent down to pet her, and she assumed the position. I obliged, but as I ran my hands over her belly, my fingers felt a small bump.

"Linnie, what's that? Let's go upstairs and get that looked at." She bounded up the stairs ahead of me.

"Karen, can you come here for a minute?" I knelt down, and Linnie licked my face.

"Linnie, down," I said. She lay down and I gently rolled her onto her side.

Karen wheeled into the room. "I feel something odd here," I said, showing her the spot on Linnie's belly where I could still feel the small, hard lump.

"It's a tick!" Karen said. "Let me get a plastic bag to put it in, and we can try to pull it out."

Linnie lay patiently on the ground while I probed carefully, then pinched with my fingernails and successfully removed the tick.

"Do we need to get her tested for Lyme disease?" I asked.

Karen called the vet, who explained there really wasn't a way to test the tick or Linnie for Lyme disease, so if we'd gotten the entire tick completely off, we shouldn't worry about it.

After that I was always careful to check Linnie for ticks when I brought her in. But she seemed just fine.

———

While I wanted to believe the best about people and trust them, there are some situations where you have to confront people or speak up about things that should change. You can be empathetic but also have good boundaries. And I began to realize that I needed to set some strong boundaries in my job—even if it made me afraid.

The longer I worked at Artecon the more I could see some critical flaws in the company, and I had strong opinions about our business model. It may not surprise you by this point, but I sometimes find it difficult *not* to share my opinions, especially when I feel I'm right!

"It's so frustrating," I told Karen one night at dinner. "When customers' products need to be repaired, our team has to order parts from our headquarters in California. The company won't let us keep an inventory here in New York. Obviously, that slows down our service times. It makes no sense!" Our customers on Wall Street had begun to notice the delays, and they were not happy that we, in their eyes, took too long to address product warranty repairs.

Karen listened thoughtfully. "Well, have you talked to your boss about it?"

"I'm not sure how that would pan out. He might not appreciate me criticizing the way things are done. But we're working with big companies on Wall Street—they expect immediate action to fix equipment."

"Well, I don't know if you remember this—but you convinced me to move to New Jersey by telling me that you'd find other career opportunities. Maybe it's time to start looking for those opportunities!"

"Yeah, maybe," I said. "I know I'm not the only employee who's frustrated, though. Maybe I should get some of my coworkers to complain with me."

"You could get fired for doing that," Karen said. "I think maybe you should just start looking for another job."

"I'm praying about what to do," I said. The situation with the engineers was just one of many systems within the company that I considered were mismanaged.

*Even if I ask for change, it might not happen. And Karen's right. I might get fired for even stirring the pot. And if I get fired, I'm going to have a harder time finding a job than my sighted peers because of discrimination against blind people. I just got out of financial trouble— I don't want to go back into it! What is the best way to go forward? Do I have the courage to speak up?*

Armed with the confidence that God was with me and was prompting me to be brave and speak up, I decided to step out in faith and courage.

I made an appointment with my boss, Raleigh Wilson, for a face-to-face meeting in California. A few days later, I was sitting on the edge of my chair in his office, with Linnie's head resting on top of my shoe. Her presence strengthened me.

Raleigh cleared his throat. "So, Mike, what's on your mind?"

"Well, I'm concerned about our ability to respond to requests from our customers for repairs," I said.

I had always found Raleigh to be reasonable and supportive. But we both knew Jim and Dana, the owners, might have other opinions about how to run their company.

"That's the way we've always done it and I don't think Jim and Dana will change," he said. "We need to have a centralized inventory system, not have different inventories at each office."

I took a deep breath, reaching down to stroke Linnie's ears. Then I folded my hands in my lap and lifted my chin. "Look, this needs to change. All of you wanted me to relocate to open the New York office because our financial customers there wanted the actual manufacturer's presence. That needs to include providing proper support. If not, I resign."

"What? Are you kidding me?"

"No, I feel quite strongly that we're hamstringing our engineers and our sales force by running inventory this way. I hear complaints from our New York service people every day as they try to cover for our lack of service inventory. When our maintenance people kept some items in New York, they were able to fix things quickly. Then Jim discovered we had inventory and he demanded that everything be sent back to Carlsbad, which slowed our response time again."

"Mike, I don't know. Let me talk to Jim and Dana."

Later that day, I got a call from a competitor. They told me they were looking for a sales manager to open a New York office for them—would I be interested? Getting the call that day seemed like a confirmation I was doing the right thing. *God, what perfect timing. Thank you for reminding me that you really are with me, so I don't have to be afraid.*

Raleigh spoke to the owners that day, but it was clear they wouldn't budge. I resigned the same day. I took the other job offer and worked with that company for two years. Then one of their customers, Quantum Corporation, a Fortune 500 company, hired me. And they asked me to open a New York office for them, which I did in 1999. Was this becoming a trend or what? I arranged to rent an office on the 78th floor of Tower One of the World Trade Center.

In a way, I think those feelings of frustration, and that hard conversation, were part of God's way of directing me to the next good thing in my life. God's guidance comes when we pay attention. When you have the assurance that God is guiding you, it helps you be brave.

---

In late April 1999, I flew to San Diego for business meetings. I planned to take a red-eye back a couple of days later, after my meetings were done.

After dinner, Linnie vomited in the hotel room.

"Linnie, are you okay?"

I did a quick cleanup, then sat and petted Linnie. As usual, she rolled over for a belly rub, which reassured me that she was alright.

After a while, Linnie and I went to sleep.

We arrived back in New Jersey in the wee hours of the morning, and Linnie seemed her usual self. I chalked it up to being in a strange place—dogs sometimes throw up; it wasn't a big deal.

The next evening, I poured kibble into Linnie's bowl at her usual dinnertime. The sound usually made her come running—if she wasn't already at my feet anticipating her meal.

"Linnie," Karen called. "Come get your dinner."

She paused. It was quiet.

"Mike, where's Linnie?" she asked.

"I'm not sure," I said. "She might be upstairs?"

Karen rolled into the elevator and went up to our room.

"Mike!"

I hurried upstairs.

"Something's wrong! Linnie!" Karen said, panic rising in her voice.

I walked over to the bed, where Linnie lay. "Come on, girl, it's dinnertime!" I said. Linnie didn't move. I stroked her back. She was breathing, but unresponsive.

"I'm going to look in the phone book and find an emergency vet," Karen said. Since it was Saturday night, she knew our vet wouldn't be in the office.

While Karen made the phone call, I carried Linnie to the elevator and took her downstairs. We put her on a blanket on the back seat of our car and drove to the vet Karen found.

"We really don't know what's wrong with her," the vet said, after examining her. "But we want to refer you to Tracey Gillespie, a specialist."

Tracey kept Linnie for a few days to test and observe her. She seemed kind and gentle—an empathetic vet for our empathetic dog.

A few days later, we sat in her office.

"Mr. and Mrs. Hingson, I'm so sorry to have to tell you this," she began. "I'm quite certain that Linnie has glomerulonephritis."

"Glom-u-what?" Karen said.

"Glomerulonephritis," she repeated. "Basically, her kidneys are not working properly. Instead of filtering the waste in her body, they're just letting everything through, including the nutrients her body needs. Your dog is basically starving to death from the inside."

"How did this happen?" I asked. "What causes it?"

"Well, it could be any number of things," Tracey said. "It's often the result of compromised immunity."

"She's been so healthy otherwise," I said.

"Could it come from Lyme disease?" Karen asked. "About two years ago, Linnie was bit by a tick. She's seemed to be fine up until now."

"It very well could be that she contracted Lyme from a tick, but never showed symptoms until now," Tracey said. "It's hard to know for sure. Working dogs are focused on pleasing you and doing their job. They can be extremely stoic, working even when they are in pain."

"So she's in a lot of pain?" I asked. Brave Linnie had never complained but had probably been more than uncomfortable for quite a while.

"Not necessarily," Tracey said. "But enough discomfort that she really can't do her job."

"I don't want her to suffer," Karen said through her tears. "But let's see if we can try to keep her around."

"Yes," I said. My feelings stuck in my throat, unable to make their way out as words. I stroked Linnie, who had come around but was quite lethargic. As she licked my hand, I let the tears fall. Even though she was my fourth guide dog, this didn't get easier.

I called Guide Dogs to tell them what had happened to Linnie. They said they could get me a dog, but it might take a few months. I'd be flying solo for a while until then.

Linnie stayed in the hospital for several weeks, but thankfully she did get stronger. When she finally came home, it was imperative for us to keep her hydrated so her kidneys would be exercised. Every other day Karen gave Linnie a liter of saline solution subcutaneously. Even so, we knew her life span would not be what we expected.

There's some debate in the blind community about the relative merits of using a guide dog versus navigating with a white cane. When I was young, as I mentioned, I simply walked or rode my bike without a cane or a dog. But when I got involved with the National Federation of the Blind back in college, I learned to use a white cane, because it is a helpful tool in certain situations.

Because of the unfortunate (but persistent) misunderstanding that the guide dog is leading the blind person who is "helpless" without his canine companion, some blind people prefer to use a cane, which they believe others perceive as being more independent. Canes are also a little more readily accepted at restaurants and other businesses. The truth is, both a cane and a dog provide similar amounts of assistance to a blind person, albeit in different ways. Both require that the blind person knows where they are going and how to get there.

For the next six months, I navigated my commute into Manhattan with a white cane.

I walked along the mid-Manhattan sidewalk, tapping the cane in an arc in front of me. The sidewalks were crowded with morning commuters. Yes, this was a different feeling for me, but I knew the process, and I also knew I would be just as mobile as when using a guide dog.

*Snap!* Suddenly my cane was no longer tapping the ground but waving in the air.

"Oh, sorry!" a man said, but then he was gone. I stood on the sidewalk holding my broken cane.

*Not again! That's the third cane this month!*

Thankfully, I was only about a block from the World Trade Center, and I simply made my way along, a bit slower than usual. I listened closely to hear the people and buildings around me, and occasionally moved the broken cane in front of me to avoid running into people. Without the information that I get from tapping the cane on the ground, travel was challenging, even on a familiar route. But when I first began working at the World Trade Center, I'd explored it thoroughly (with a cane) and memorized the layout of the entire place. As a result, I could easily make my way across the sprawling complex and up the elevator to my office.

Although people are generally helpful when you ask them, they can also be thoughtless, especially when they are in a hurry. People would jostle and cut in front of me, stepping directly on my cane and breaking it. After a quick "Pardon me, so sorry!" they were off and running. I spent more money replacing canes in those few months than I ever spent on dog food! And I have to say the experience made me a little cynical about some people's manners.

Normally when I travel with a cane, I typically hold it at an angle so I can tap about five feet in front of me. While traveling in New York City that year, I learned to hold the cane at a steeper angle so that it would tap the ground about two or three feet in front of me. It slowed me down somewhat, but fewer people stepped on it when it was closer to me.

Finally, in October, I got a call from Guide Dogs for the Blind, inviting me to fly to San Rafael and be matched with another dog. Little did I know that this dog would take courage to a whole other level.

## Guidance from the Word

*There is no fear in love. But perfect love drives out fear.*

**1 JOHN 4:18**

## Prayer for Courage

God, when I feel afraid, remind me to practice empathy and compassion for both myself and others. May your perfect love drive out my fear.

# 6
# ROSELLE, PART ONE

## Trust and teamwork build bravery

Training a dog is not about teaching them obedience. It's about building a relationship based on trust, respect, and understanding.

**IAN DUNBAR**

**"ROSELLE, THIS IS LINNIE.** Linnie, meet Roselle."

It was the night I came home with my fifth guide dog, Roselle. While it wasn't the first time I introduced a new guide dog to a retired one, this time was different—at least at first. The two yellow Labs circled each other, sniffing suspiciously. Even though Linnie had retired several months ago, she still considered herself the queen of the house. What on earth did I think I was doing bringing another dog into her territory?

At the recommendation of Roselle's trainers, Karen and I had decided to introduce them on the neutral ground of our garage, so that Linnie wouldn't be too territorial.

"They both seem very hesitant," Karen observed. "I swear Linnie looks a little insulted."

While I was glad Linnie didn't try to defend her turf, and neither dog seemed afraid or aggressive, I didn't like the idea of them not being friends. It was odd. Linnie wanted nothing to do with this strange dog who'd apparently followed me home. Roselle remained aloof as well.

We walked inside, but the dogs continued to ignore each other. Roselle immediately introduced herself to Cali and Sherlock, the cats. Cali leaped to the top of the refrigerator, and Sherlock hid under the bed. But Roselle and Linnie treated one another as if the other were invisible.

I decided to just give them some time to warm up to one another. That night, I tethered each to a separate space in our bedroom.

The next day, the silence and avoidance continued.

This had to stop. "I know how to break the ice," I said. I went to Linnie's toy box and came back with the Booda Bone, Linnie's favorite toy. It's a thick knotted rope, about two feet long. She loved to play tug-of-war with it.

"Linnie, what have I got here?" I dangled the rope in front of her, holding tight to the knot on the other end. She sniffed the rope, then grabbed it in her teeth and began to tug, slowly at first, then more insistently.

"Ooh, I think Roselle's getting jealous," Karen said, wheeling into the room.

I heard Roselle panting from a few feet away. She'd come out from behind the couch to find out what was going on.

"Oh, so you want to play now, hmm?" I said. I offered Roselle the other end of the rope, and I held on to the middle.

The three of us tussled with the rope, both dogs play-growling, backing up, circling. Our playful dance apparently made them forget they weren't speaking to one another.

After a few moments, I said, "I can't keep up with two powerful beasts! I give up!" I let go of the rope, and Linnie and Roselle found themselves eye to eye, pulling on the rope, play-growling and circling one another. In that moment, something happened. Their fear and suspicion seemed to melt away. From that moment on, they were best friends.

They also loved to include me in their games. My home office was in the basement, so I'd sit in my rolling desk chair and hold the Booda Bone rope in the middle. I'd have a dog at each end of the rope, dragging me across the cement floor. Their favorite game involved trying to wrap me around a support pole in the middle of our basement as I clung to the rope and rode my office chair. It was like a life-size pinball game, and I was the ball!

I brought Roselle home on a Saturday night late in November 1999, and by Monday she was accompanying me into New York City to work. Quantum Corporation, a Fortune 500 company that provided data protection and network storage systems, had hired me earlier that year as regional sales manager and head of operations in New York. They'd asked me to open an office in New York, hire staff, and begin developing relationships with Quantum's sales partners. For nearly two years, things remained blessedly quiet and routine.

———

Just after midnight in the early morning of September 11, 2001, I awoke to the sound of panting in my ear. Roselle stood by my bed, quivering. She nosed me and whined. Her fear of thunder had woken her, even before the storm hit. The wind rattled the windows, but otherwise it was quiet. Roselle knew what was coming, with that sixth sense that dogs have.

Roselle was afraid of thunder. She would shake, pant, and become agitated when a thunderstorm approached. In fact, we discovered that she could sense a storm nearly a half hour before we could. She was our early-thunderstorm-warning system that never failed.

"Hey, Roselle, it's okay," I whispered, rolling over to stroke her back. She panted hard, as her trembling turned into shaking.

I yawned, trying to pull myself out of sleep without waking Karen, who slept peacefully beside me. Roselle's fear of thunderstorms meant she'd do whatever she could to enlist my help in riding them out.

Roselle whined quietly, nosing my hand again, and I pulled myself out of bed, sliding my feet into slippers and shrugging into my robe. "Okay, girl, come on. Let's go downstairs." Roselle walked to the door with me, rubbing against my legs, reassured to have a trusted companion to help her through the storm that she could feel coming.

When I first brought Roselle home from guide dog training, she wasn't afraid of thunder, or really of anything. The trainers at Guide Dogs for the Blind knew I needed a bold dog that could handle a two-train commute and walk quickly through the crowded streets of New York City. She was mostly fearless and fun loving, but thunderstorms just made her nervous.

Many dogs are sensitive to thunderstorms. Some people theorize that changes in barometric pressure or buildup of static electricity may be what sets them off. Some dogs wear vests or capes meant to diffuse the static. But back then, what worked for Roselle was a comforting human presence while hunkering down in the basement. Roselle always felt less fear if she knew I was by her side, reminding her that we were a team. And she could trust me to take care of her. Like people, dogs like Roselle love to have a good support system.

As we left the room, Karen woke up. "What's going on?"

"I think Roselle knows a thunderstorm is coming."

"Linnie and I will just stay here," she said sleepily. "See you later."

We made our way down the stairs, Roselle's nails clicking on the oak floor, the banister cool beneath my hand. Even though I would have to get up for work at 5:00 a.m., I also knew my dog wouldn't let me sleep through a storm if she couldn't.

In my basement office, Roselle dove under my desk, still panting. By the time we got downstairs, I could hear the storm in the distance. Our canine storm detector had been right again. Soon the thunder boomed overhead, and I sat at my desk, stroking her gently.

"It's alright, girl." She leaned on my feet, whining quietly, as the first rumbles of thunder began. I turned on a news radio program, hoping the quiet talking would calm my pup.

I fired up my computer, catching up on last-minute preparations for the sales meeting that I would be leading later that morning.

Eventually, Roselle's quivering subsided, and the booms of thunder grew further and further apart. After about an hour and a half, the storm had passed. We walked back upstairs to catch a couple of hours of sleep before the alarm would wake us again.

By 8:00 a.m. we would be at the World Trade Center, hard at work.

In the office that morning, a colleague from our corporate office, David Frank, and some representatives from our sales distribution partner, Ingram Micro, met me to prepare to conduct seminars for fifty people from various small reseller organizations around the New York City area. We prepared for a full day of meetings in our office on the 78th floor of Tower One of the World Trade Center. The last thing David and I needed to do before the seminars was to prepare a list of attendees, as required, to fax to the Port Authority security people.

I was reaching for the letterhead on which to print our final list when at 8:46 a.m., we heard a muffled noise, like distant thunder.

*BOOM!*

"What on earth?" Suddenly, the building began leaning hard, about twenty feet. I slid slightly along the floor, grabbing a door frame to keep myself from falling. The building stayed tilted for what felt like an eternity.

While things in our offices remained pretty much in place, we later learned that elsewhere in the Tower, ceiling tiles crashed to the floor and file cabinet drawers were jostled open and spilled their contents onto the floor.

"Mike, what is going on?"

"I have no idea! But it feels like the building is going to fall over!"

*God, please don't let this building tip over*, I prayed silently, gripping the door frame so tightly my hand began to cramp. *What on earth is going on?*

Just as I thought I was going to die, the tower slowly moved back and righted itself. We had no idea what was going on. An earthquake? A bomb? We were both terrified.

I scrambled to my desk, where Roselle had just woken from her nap. I grabbed her leash. I didn't know what was happening, but I didn't want to be separated from her. Oddly, she seemed unperturbed by what had just happened.

"Oh, my God!" David yelled. "Michael, I can see debris, fire, and smoke, and what looks like burning paper floating past the windows!"

I could hear something that David told me was debris brushing the windows. "I don't smell smoke," I said. "But obviously there's a fire. We need to evacuate."

Our guests in the conference room were screaming.

"We have to get out of here—now!" David said urgently.

I'd been through countless World Trade Center emergency training sessions and fire drills. I knew the procedure. I'd prepared, which helped me to control my fear and appear brave for David and our guests. I was terrified, too, but I knew I needed to leverage my fear to make good decisions.

"David, let's do this right," I said, forcing calmness into my voice. My heart raced, but I tried to breathe to steady myself. *Stay calm for your dog, and for the people around you.*

"We all need to get out of here right now!" he said.

"David," I said, "slow down."

"Mike, you don't understand! You can't see it!"

It took work on my part to get David calm and focused. In reality, it wasn't what I didn't or couldn't see that mattered. It was David who wasn't seeing. Remember how I described Roselle's fear of thunder? Roselle was not exhibiting any fear reaction at all. What that told me was that whatever was happening was not such an immediate threat that we had to leave in a panic. Dogs' senses are more acute than ours.

Roselle's tranquil demeanor told me that we could, at least for the moment, remain calm.

"Get our guests to the staircase. Don't panic," I told David. "Don't let them use the elevators, since you saw fire."

David took our guests to the stairs and they started down. While he did that, I quickly called Karen. "There's been an explosion of some sort. We're okay."

"What do you mean an explosion?" she asked, panic rising in her voice.

"We're leaving the building now," I told her, struggling to keep calm in the face of her anxiety. "I'll call as soon as I can."

It may seem ironic now, but we began to shut down our computer systems before David and I evacuated. We thought we might eventually be able to get back into the building. After a few minutes, we gave up because it was taking too long—a crucial decision that turned out to save us precious moments that we needed later on.

I grabbed Roselle's harness. "Forward," I said, again containing my fear, while forcing my voice to remain calm. She immediately went to work, guiding me through the office. David walked beside us as we made our way down the hall, through a large lobby, and into the central stairwell. Roselle dialed in, guiding me around the debris on the floor. Even when dust and debris fell on her, she stayed focused on her job.

We made our way to Stairwell B, in the center of Tower One, and started down the stairs, trying to stay focused in the confusion as more and more people entered the stairwell. I was thankful for Roselle in that moment, in part because she gave me something to focus on in the midst of the chaos.

As David, Roselle, and I began our journey down the stairs, I noticed a peculiar smell. It conjured up memories of Boy Scout camp and kerosene lanterns. With a growing group of people, we walked down the stairs: ten steps down, turn 180 degrees, nine steps down. Repeat.

The smell gradually strengthened, at times coating my throat.

Suddenly, I recognized the smell. It was familiar to me as a frequent business traveler. *Jet fuel.* I mentioned this to the others around me. Someone near me said, "You're right! We were all trying to figure out the smell. An airplane must have crashed into the Tower."

We, of course, had no details. None of us knew what happened, but we did assume from then on that somehow this situation involved an airplane crashing into our building.

As we descended, the smell of jet fuel grew sometimes stronger and sometimes it lessened. I worried about Roselle—dogs' noses are far more sensitive than people's. *She must be overwhelmed by it.* In fact, she never panicked, showed fear, or displayed weakness as we descended the stairs. But the people around her sometimes did.

"I can't breathe," said a woman in the slow-moving line of people. She had stopped on the stairwell just as we reached, I think, the 68th floor. "I don't think we're going to make it out of here."

Several of us gathered around the woman, offering encouragement and reassurance. "It's going to be okay," I said. "You can do it," someone else said.

In a way, all the lessons I'd learned from my dogs, and all the things I'd learned about being brave, came together on that day. I imagined Linnie, with her empathy and connection, and how she would have reacted to someone who was panicking. I was prepared for an emergency because I had memorized the way out of the Tower.

Roselle and I were right below the woman, and I turned to talk with her. "One step at a time," I said. Roselle, glad for the chance to rest, nudged the woman's hand. *Pet me, please.* Roselle's greetings are not exactly subtle. The woman stroked Roselle's velvety ears and Roselle wagged her tail in appreciation.

"This is Roselle, and she's going to guide us down the stairs," I said. Roselle panted happily. The woman took a deep breath and laughed shakily.

"Okay," she said. "Thank you." Roselle touched her nose to the woman's hand, as if to offer reassurance, and we resumed our steady march down the staircase.

Before September 11, I had spent much time learning as much as I could about the center, its layout, the locations of offices, and even the shops on the first floor. I learned all I could about evacuation procedures. I felt I needed to know all I could because if we ever experienced an emergency, I might be in the office alone or I might need to help others get out. Awareness and preparation could help me be brave, and it also meant that I did not have to rely on people reading signs I could not read (and if the power was out, they couldn't read them either). Besides, as the leader of our New York office, I was responsible for anyone in our office. I needed to be the best expert with real knowledge, the only way I know to operate. The other thing that helped me to not panic was Roselle. *Roselle is focused on her work. We're a team, and I have to stay calm so she will too.*

Later, I learned that many others felt reassured by Roselle's presence as we walked down the steps, one floor at a time.

People often ask, "Weren't you afraid?" Of course I was. But it's not about not being afraid. Rather, it's about not letting fear blind you. Roselle, even though she sometimes cowered during thunderstorms, stayed focused on her work. Dogs live in the moment, and she didn't waste time thinking about what could have happened—which is a key part of being brave. Instead, she just guided me down the stairs.

Guide dogs know that when you work with a team you trust, you'll be braver than you ever could be on your own. We often feel afraid when we're alone, but trust and teamwork build our bravery.

Roselle trusted me and obeyed when I said "Forward." I trusted her to guide me down the stairs—all 1,463 of them.

I listened all the way down the stairs, trying to determine what might be happening next. I focused my fear on helping me to be attentive. Was it hot? Was it cold? What were people saying? Were they shouting in panic or getting out in an orderly way? I focused on sensing other people on the stairs, reading their actions, even their moods, their fears. I tried to help people calm down and stay on task by simply staying calm myself. Roselle provided both distraction and comfort to many around us. I helped Roselle by constantly praising her. "Good girl. Let's keep going. Good job."

At one point as we walked down the stairs, David began to panic. "We're not going to make it. Mike, we're going to die."

With as much authority as I could muster, I said, "Stop it, David. If Roselle and I can go down these stairs, then so can you." Later David told me that my snapping at him brought him out of his funk.

After a moment David decided he would walk ahead of us and be one floor below us so he could shout out to me whatever he saw on the stairs and around him.

At each landing, he'd loudly announce his location and what he could see. His voice reassured others on the staircase (which grew more crowded the farther we descended) that we were making progress. I didn't need him to tell me those things, but doing so helped him and the people around him to feel some measure of control, and with it, hope.

David began shouting up to me things like "Mike, I'm on the 48th floor. All is good here. Going on down." David's courage, something I think none of us appreciated at the time, was absolutely critical. He would even joke around, saying things like "I'm at the 44th floor, by the Port Authority cafeteria. But I don't think we're going to stop for a snack."

This commentary didn't really change our strategy—we knew we just had to keep going down those stairs. We weren't even sure what we'd find at the bottom. Staying in the moment—another key part of being brave—helped all of us. David's positive attitude had a profound effect on everyone on the stairs within the sound of his voice. Each of his reports reminded every single person above and below him that we were one step closer to our goal of getting out of that building. Probably thousands of people heard David and knew that somewhere on the stairs, someone was okay and making progress. David gave everyone who heard him renewed confidence to continue.

**Guide dogs know that when you work with a team you trust, you'll be braver than you ever could be on your own.**

He deserves much more recognition for his efforts on the stairs than he ever has received.

"Good girl, Roselle. You are doing such a great job." *She must be so tired and thirsty.*

The stairwell, despite the smell, was still a comfortable temperature, though as more people joined us, the heat increased. *But what if the lights go out?* I wondered. A second later I realized that conversations on the stairs were lessening. Would more people panic, or end up too fearful to go on? The tension seemed to build. I needed to try to do something to get people to relax. What could I say? *That's the answer. If the lights go out, I'll be the one at an advantage, so I'll be the guide.*

"Hey everyone," I called out. "If the lights happen to go out and we lose power, don't worry a bit. I am blind and using a guide dog. Roselle and I are offering a two-for-one special today and will get you out of here. No problem."

"Well, that's a relief," a man said, with a chuckle. For a moment, the mood lightened. Then it was back to business until we finally reached the first floor.

"We're going to have to run through a waterfall," David said. The sprinkler systems were saturating the entire first floor. I could hear water gushing, and my feet were suddenly in several inches of water.

I felt Roselle start to lower her head in an effort to lap up some water from the floor. *If the air smells like this, what's in that water?*

"I know it's tough, girl, but hop up," I told her as we waded through the lobby, pulling up on the harness. My sweet, obedient Roselle complied, even though I knew she was parched.

"Here we go!" David yelled. I could hear the water cascading down in front of us, and I took a deep breath.

"Forward!"

The force of the cold water nearly knocked me down, but at the same time it refreshed me, washing away the sweat and fumes.

We stood in the lobby of Tower One, and I rubbed Roselle's head and back. "Good girl, Roselle, we did it!"

I felt her head start to shake back and forth, and I knew what was coming next. I let go of the harness, held tight to her leash, and let her do what she always does after a dousing: a full body shake. Water flew everywhere. I wiped my face with my jacket and petted her again.

"Good girl. Shake it off!"

People ran everywhere around us, through ankle-deep water full of debris. A man approached us.

"FBI," he said. "Come this way." He directed us to the revolving doors that I knew led to the underground shopping arcade.

"Thank you!" I called as we hurried away. Actually, he followed us most of the way through the first floor just to make sure we exited safely. Talk about brave—that man stayed in the building, helping people find their way to the underground shopping center.

Once we were there, we began to run. Although we'd made it down the stairs, we were not out of the Tower yet. Other people ran or jogged beside us, and within minutes we rode an escalator up one floor and exited into the street, flowing with the huge crowd outside the building.

I gulped fresh air, then checked my watch. Nearly an hour had passed since we left the office. Just then David said, "There's a fire in Tower Two, up high."

*Tower Two? But we just escaped a fire in Tower One. What is happening?*

---

We had no idea what was going on. All we knew was that our friend from the FBI and others told us to leave the area. Out on the street, we began to walk, traveling uptown on Broadway. We found ourselves at the corner of Broadway and Vesey Street with Tower Two in flames near us. I pulled out my phone to try to call Karen, while David snapped photos of the burning Tower.

"All circuits are busy," a recording informed me. *Of course they are. There are people trapped in the floors above the fire, calling loved ones.*

As I went to put away my phone, a police officer shouted, "Get out of here now! It's coming down!" We heard a rumble that quickly became a deafening roar. It sounded like a combination of a freight train and waterfall colliding with a wall of glass. Metal clattered and crashed. Then all we heard was the white noise of Tower Two pancaking down. Everyone turned and ran, including David. I still remember hearing him yelling, "Oh, my God, it's coming down!" as he ran off. A jolt of adrenaline coursed through my limbs. I had never felt so scared in all my life.

You may be thinking, *How could David just run off and leave a blind man stranded?* Don't think that! If my life's experiences mean anything, then you need to understand that I was by no means stranded. I knew the streets of Manhattan like I'd known my neighborhood in Palmdale growing up. And my teammate, Roselle, was right there by my side. I fully understand David's actions and have absolutely no problem with them. I was afraid, but that wasn't David's fault.

Quickly, I picked up Roselle by her harness, turned her around 180 degrees, put her back on the ground and . . . "Forward!" I told her and began running back the way we had come only a minute before. We were heading south with Broadway on our left and a building on our right.

As I ran, I had a conversation with God. It wasn't pretty. *Are you kidding me, God? Why did you rescue me from Tower One, only to have a building fall on us?*

In that moment of panic and chaos, it was as if time suddenly stopped—like a freeze-frame in a movie. The confusion and screaming people around me momentarily faded into the background, and I heard quite clearly a voice that said in my mind: *Don't worry about what you cannot control. Focus on running with Roselle, and the rest will take care of itself.*

An extraordinary calm and peace enveloped me, even as I ran for my life, debris raining down and the dust so thick I struggled to breathe. I knew God was with me and protecting me; he had heard me, and I could trust him. That answer has been guiding me ever since that day. As it says in Psalm 6:9, "The LORD has heard my cry for mercy; the LORD accepts my prayer." In that moment, I felt fear, but I simultaneously felt reassurance. I heard God's voice and trusted it.

*Don't worry about what you can't control* has become a watch phrase for me. To me, learning not to be blinded by fear begins with that simple reassurance because it forces you to focus on what you *can* control. What you *do* know. And with that reassurance, I ran even faster.

Rather than tell myself, *Don't be scared* (I absolutely did feel fear—a huge skyscraper was collapsing near me, and I would be a fool not to feel afraid), I used that fear to inspire me to run as best I could away from the danger, and to hang on very tightly to Roselle's harness. My fear inspired me to take action that saved my life.

If we had not been afraid, we might have walked blindly into danger. Instead, we sprinted from the collapsing towers, debris raining down on us, dust enveloping us. Small bits of rock and shards of glass cut my face.

I kept running with Roselle, encouraging her as we ran. (We don't normally jog unless we're late for a flight, so it was a challenge for both of us!) When we got to the next street, Fulton Street, I turned right to head west.

"Mike!" Roselle and I had nearly plowed into David. "I'm so sorry! I panicked! I thought you were right behind me. I was just going back to look for you."

"David, it's fine. Roselle and I are fine. Now let's go."

As we ran up Fulton, I thought, *What a kind friend.* David was ready to run back to where we had parted—back *toward* the collapsing building—in an attempt to find me. That's an act of courage if ever there was one.

Why did I happen to turn on Fulton? First, logic: I thought the buildings there would shield me from the falling debris. But also, I believe now that God guided me to meet up with David again.

Choices made. Voices heard. If I had not listened to what God told me along the way, it's possible that Roselle and I would not have survived, or perhaps been severely injured. All of my life would have been different. There is no reason to speculate about what might have been. What matters is that I had the faith to listen and act according to my guidance from God. What I did is no different than what anyone can do—what you can do. It starts with full, open faith.

Trusting God doesn't mean we can control the outcome. I sometimes wonder why, on that fateful day, God chose to answer my prayer and protect and guide me. I could say that I don't know, but I believe it was because I chose to listen. Nearly three thousand people died that day. Did God talk with them? Who knows? If nothing else, I hope they experienced his presence.

Faith is about listening and trusting. For example, Roselle guided me away from Tower One. She did what I'd asked her to do, without any hesitation. But when I got more information from the policeman, I needed to share it with Roselle, so we could change direction.

Because we had built a relationship of mutual trust before that day, Roselle handled my unusual motion of turning her around in stride, and obeyed when I moved much faster than usual. Trust and teamwork were essential to our survival on 9/11. In fact, that same trust and teamwork allows my current guide dog and I to survive as I go through my daily routine and as I travel, work, play, and live in my community.

Sometimes, a guide dog stops even though they've been told "Forward" because there's a hazard, an approaching car, a pothole, or some other potential danger that they must warn their handler about. In guide dog training, this is known as "intelligent disobedience." As Holland did when we encountered snowbanks on the curbs of Boston, the dog overrides the handler's command in order to keep them both safe.

A successful handler won't insist on the dog moving, but rather will recognize that the guide dog is doing its job and trust that the unexpected reactions of the guide dog are things to accept and possibly explore, in order to give the proper next command to the guide dog. The dog and handler must learn to trust each other.

As David, Roselle, and I ran up Fulton Street, a cloud of choking dust poured off the collapsing tower and flooded the street like a wave.

"Mike, the dust is too thick," David said. "I can't even see my hand in front of my face."

"Maybe we can find a building to shelter in. I'm signaling Roselle to look for an opening," I choked out as we hurried up the street. "Right, Roselle, right!"

The air was so thick with dust that I could barely breathe. I didn't even know if Roselle could see my hand signal.

But suddenly, I heard an opening to our right, and Roselle began to turn that way as well—then stopped short.

"What is it, Roselle? Come on, girl. Keep going." Roselle wouldn't move. Suddenly, I realized that she might very well have stopped for a reason. I recalled God's words, *Focus on running with Roselle and the rest will take care of itself.* Even in that panicked moment, I trusted that Roselle might be trying to protect me. I reached my hand along the wall, and I probed out with my foot. We were at the top of a flight of stairs that we soon learned would lead us to a subway station. Roselle had done her job perfectly.

We slowly descended, along with several other people who'd been running beside us.

I had to direct Roselle, but she also had to do her job, which included the intelligent disobedience of stopping at the top of the stairs. Our partnership was the key to survival that day—and the key to keeping me from tumbling down a flight of stairs and being injured.

---

At the bottom of the stairs, I heard a woman crying hysterically.

"Someone, please help. I can't see!"

I stopped, wiping the dirt from my face.

"My eyes are so full of dirt, I can't see!" the woman continued. "I don't want to fall onto the subway track!"

"Forward," I told Roselle quietly, walking toward the sound of the woman's sobs. I reached out and touched her arm, and her cries quieted.

"It's going to be okay. My name is Mike. I'm blind and I have my guide dog, Roselle, with me. We'll make sure you don't fall. Go ahead and try to get the dirt out of your eyes."

We had come down to the arcade entrance of the Fulton Street subway station. The tracks were down another level.

"You are ten feet away from the stairs going down to the train platform. What's your name?"

"Carol."

A minute later, someone came up the stairs from the station down below us. "I'm Lou," he said. "I'm an employee of the subway system and I can take you to an employee's locker room where you can sit and get a drink of water."

I offered Carol my arm. "Thanks," she said. "I can see again."

Along with eight others who'd fled the dust-choked streets, we trusted Lou to guide us.

I heard an oscillating fan that kept the air circulating and made the locker room cool. "Mike, there's a drinking fountain!" David sounded like he would weep with relief. The group took turns washing their faces and taking long drinks of water. Roselle flopped to the floor to rest.

I sat on a bench, trying to process what had just happened.

About ten minutes later, a police officer burst in.

"I have orders to evacuate the station," he said. "You'll need to leave. The air outside is beginning to clear. Please leave the area."

Roselle stood up, ready to work again. We made our way through the station and up the stairs. The officer was right. The dust had indeed settled on Fulton.

"Tower One is still burning," David said. "But Tower Two is gone completely. It's completely gone!"

"Are you sure?" I asked. "What do you see? Are you sure Tower Two is gone?"

"All I see are pillars of smoke several hundred feet high. There is no Tower Two anymore."

We stood there in shock for a moment, and then we walked west on Fulton for about ten minutes when the ground began to shake. A distant roar got louder, and the vibration beneath my feet became more intense. *This has to be our Tower.* "Tower One is collapsing!" David told me, despair and disbelief in his voice. Again, I heard the freight train sound, then a waterfall of glass and metal, several blocks away.

At the time we were in a small plaza. "A dust cloud is coming toward us," David said. We ducked behind a low retaining wall and waited for things to calm. Clearly the tower we were working in just a couple of hours ago was collapsing.

After the cloud passed us by and the noise died away, we stood up. "Mike, there is no World Trade Center anymore," David said, his voice flat from disbelief. I felt numb. I survived but was nearly undone. Suddenly, I thought of Karen. I pulled out my cell phone, and she picked up on the third ring.

"Hello?" her voice was tight, higher pitched than usual.

"Karen, it's me," I choked out, then began to cry. "I'm okay. Roselle and I made it out of the Tower. We're with David."

She was crying too hard to speak at first. "It's so good to hear your voice," she finally said.

Through her tears, Karen briefed me on what had happened: It was a terrorist attack, using at least four planes. The first hit our Tower, the second hit Tower Two fifteen minutes later. A third plane attacked the Pentagon. "And there's at least one more plane missing over Pennsylvania," she said. "The president is in hiding."

I found it nearly impossible to wrap my mind around what was going on. *A terrorist attack? An attack on the United States? Hijacking airplanes and crashing them into the World Trade Center and the Pentagon? Who would even conceive of doing such a thing, much less actually committing such an act?*

"Karen, David and I are going to try to get out of the city," I said. "I love you. I'll call when I know more."

David called his friend Nina who had an apartment in Manhattan and asked if we could rest there for a while. It took us a while to get there, and we arrived before Nina, who had gone out to buy groceries. When we were finally together and had something to eat, our strength started to return. After a few hours, Karen called to tell me a friend made it back to New Jersey by train.

"David, it looks like public transit is moving again. I want to go home."

"Are you sure? I don't know if it's safe," Nina said. "You're more than welcome to stay."

"If I can get to Penn Station, I can catch a train to New Jersey," I said. "Roselle and I can do it. It certainly can't be any more challenging than what we've already managed today. Thank you for your hospitality and for giving us a safe place to rest." David decided to head to Penn Station to drop me off and then walk to his sister's house on the city's Upper East Side.

The streets were still full of people trying to get out of Manhattan. After walking a few blocks, we heard a bus. We hopped on, pleasantly surprised that no fare was required, and took it to Thirty-Third and Sixth, a block from the station.

David and I said goodbye—a brief but emotional hug and parting at the train station. It was 5:30 p.m. *I'm exhausted. But since the trains are running, it is off to New Jersey. Roselle and I just want to go home.*

"Forward," I said, and Roselle guided me through the crowd that surged into the station, down the stairs, and onto a very full train for Newark. People immediately noticed the dust and grime on my clothes and Roselle's fur.

"Were you in the Towers?" a woman asked.

"Did you hear the plane hit?" a man asked. It was difficult, suddenly, to answer. I didn't want to talk. I just wanted to go home, but I told people what I could.

Roselle and I got off at Newark and headed to Track 5, where I was relieved to find that the Westfield train was waiting. I called Karen with an update.

At 7:00 p.m., the train pulled into Westfield. As Roselle and I climbed down the steps of the train, I heard the distinctive sound of our van, pulling up to the curb. The side sliding door opened.

"Michael!" My wife's voice had never sounded so sweet. Roselle jumped into the van, and I climbed in after her. Karen was in the back, and I wrapped my arms around her. We both cried and laughed. *Thank you, God. Thank you. I can't believe I'm home.*

"Tom came to help," she said. Our dear friend Tom Painter was driving the van. "It's good to see you, Mike," he said, his voice choked with emotion.

When we arrived home and walked in the door, Linnie greeted us, wriggling and wagging. But then, she sniffed us carefully. We smelled strange.

I planned to take Roselle outside so she could relieve herself. She would have none of that. After I removed her harness, she escaped my hold, ran off, and came back a minute later with her Booda Bone, prancing with it in her mouth. Linnie followed, hoping to play.

"Are you kidding me, Roselle? Have you already forgotten about our day?" I know dogs live in the moment, but I was shocked at how unperturbed Roselle seemed. Or maybe, she was celebrating the miraculous truth that kept running through my mind:

*We're home.*

## Guidance from the Word

*Do not fear, for I have redeemed you;*
*I have summoned you by name;*
*you are mine.*
*When you pass through the waters,*
*I will be with you . . .*
*When you walk through the fire,*
*you will not be burned.*

**ISAIAH 43:1-2**

## Prayer for Courage

God, thank you for the promise of your presence. Thank you for the gift of others who can walk through life with me. You're always with me, and I can trust you no matter what I go through.

# 7

# ROSELLE, PART TWO

## Listening to God
## banishes isolation

Dogs do not worry about the
future or dwell on the past. They
exist in the moment, which can be
something very difficult for humans
to understand, especially with the
stresses of modern life.

**CESAR MILLAN**

**LIVING IN NEW YORK RIGHT AFTER 9/11** tested the courage and
resolve of every New Yorker, including me. I didn't know how to put
my unease into words. More than fear, I felt shock and amazement
that someone would intentionally fly a plane at such a high speed
into a building, killing themselves and thousands of others. I couldn't
wrap my mind around it.

President George W. Bush vowed revenge, but we didn't know
what that would look like. Would our country go to war? If so, with
what country? The nineteen al-Qaeda terrorist attackers came from
four different countries, some of which were our allies at the time. It
was a time of great uncertainty and fear for everyone.

The center of commerce for the city and even the world had
been reduced to a pile of smoking rubble, and yet my employer (and

probably hundreds of other companies) wanted to return to business as usual as quickly as possible. They didn't seem to understand that many of my best clients were attending funerals, and our team had just survived a very traumatic event.

But I knew that Karen and I were forever changed by that day. After hearing so clearly from God, my faith became more important. I was determined to listen to God and trust him to guide me.

Roselle, for her part, seemed unfazed—though later, she would develop health issues that I am certain were related to the dust and toxic fumes she inhaled on that fateful day.

The next morning, after a night of tossing and turning, Karen and I sat at the kitchen table. I drank the same tea I always had to start my day. It felt somehow normal, but absolutely not normal. For one thing, every muscle in my body ached. In fact, I was stiff and in a lot of pain for the next week, and I couldn't walk up and down stairs for several days. I used our elevator even more than Karen, especially to get to my home office in the basement of the house. I don't know about others, but for me, the exercise I normally got on a day-to-day basis did not prepare me and my body for what we experienced on September 11.

"Mike, I have a suggestion," Karen said that morning.

"Please tell me."

"Since some of the people from Guide Dogs for the Blind visited you in the World Trade Center over the past year, you should let them know that you and Roselle survived."

"That's a good idea. People there might not yet have recalled that Roselle and I worked in the WTC, but someone is bound to remember soon."

I got up from the table and slowly headed to the kitchen counter to toast an English muffin.

"You're moving like an old man," Karen said, laughing.

"Everything hurts," I said. "I think the adrenaline is wearing off. I certainly don't typically walk down that many stairs in one day!"

Roselle, on the other hand, was fine. She and Linnie played and even tried to entice me into joining their tug games, but there was no way I could do that.

Around noon, I called GDB and heard receptionist Barbara Browning's voice.

"Guide Dogs for the Blind, how can I help you?"

"Barbara, it's Mike Hingson."

"Hi! How are you doing?"

"Well, under the circumstances I guess pretty well."

"What do you mean?"

"You may or may not know that I worked in the World Trade Center and was in my office yesterday with Roselle when the building was attacked."

"Are both of you okay?"

"Yes, but I am quite stiff and sore from going down 1,463 stairs and walking around New York City for a few hours."

"Hang on," Barbara said. "I need to let people know you are on the phone. Someone is going to want to talk to you, I'm sure."

I spent the next hour or more talking to various people at Guide Dogs, repeating my story. Finally, I was passed to Joanne Ritter, GDB's public information director.

After I recounted what Roselle and I had experienced, Joanne asked, "Do you mind if I write and release a little story about this?"

"Sure, go ahead."

"You know, once our story goes out lots of people are going to want to interview you. What TV show do you want to go on first?" Clearly Joanne was thinking like the PR person she was and is. I wasn't thinking, so I said with a touch of sarcasm, "How about *Larry King Live*?"

The next day, reporters indeed began calling. And by early afternoon, Joanne called to say that I had been invited to appear on Larry King's show on Friday, September 14. Who would have thought that this would happen?

CNN sent a car to transport me, Karen, and Roselle to the

studios in New York. When we arrived I learned that Mr. King was in California and would be doing his part of the broadcast from there. Larry interviewed me for around six minutes, and it wasn't the only time we interacted. I returned to the show four additional times. It provided me an opportunity to help people (including Larry) better understand guide dogs, what they do, and how they are trained. I feel like our conversations helped break down stereotypes about blind people and guide dogs, a primary reason I agreed to do media interviews in the first place.

My last time with Larry King took place on the fifth anniversary of the terrorist attacks. He was in New York, and we met down near Ground Zero. At the end of that interview, I told Larry that I was being encouraged to write a book about my life, and my experiences on 9/11. I asked if he would be willing to write the foreword for the book. The words were hardly out of my mouth when he emphatically said, "Yes, absolutely." Wow!

I did have one unusual interview request. A reporter from a national magazine, which I won't name, asked if I could wear the suit I was wearing on 9/11 for a photo to accompany his story. I thought that was ridiculous, and besides, my dust-caked suit was at the cleaners, to see if it could be salvaged. "In that case, I'm not interested." *Click!* Thank goodness and good riddance.

"Why did I survive this catastrophe?" I asked myself—and God, to be honest. I knew that asking why wouldn't really help, but my questions reminded me to trust God and his purposes for my life. The attack was a senseless act, so there was no good "why" other than the terrorists were trying to disrupt the whole world.

Still, my mind was filled with what-ifs. The plane hit my Tower above the 78th floor, providing me the opportunity, harrowing as it was, to escape. Those on the topmost floors didn't have that opportunity—courage had nothing to do with it. But in Tower Two, the plane hit at around floor 82 and did immediate and significant damage down to floor 77. I heard stories of people getting hit by steel beams that flew through the air, others overcome by the dust cloud—but I ran away from the collapsing Tower and suffered only minor scratches and a mouthful of dust before finding shelter. What if things had gone differently?

It was hard to think about. I didn't want to dwell on it. I didn't have survivor's guilt, but it made me wonder: Was I saved for a purpose? And if so, was that purpose something besides selling computer backup systems?

My employer wanted me to go on as if nothing had changed, but something had fundamentally shifted in me. I didn't even know how to put it into words at the time. As news of my survival story began to spread, I began getting interview requests from the media. People wanted to hear the story of how Roselle and I fled Tower One just minutes before it collapsed.

Meanwhile, the higher-ups at Quantum wanted me to focus on work, to get back to "normal." At the time, most Americans wondered if that would ever be possible. Despite my questions about the meaning of what I was doing, I actually exceeded my sales goals for both the third and fourth quarters that year. But the six-figure salary and the career I'd worked so hard for? I wondered how these things fit into my purpose.

I wasn't sure how long people would be interested in my story. But I found I really enjoyed public speaking, and I wondered if I could make a career out of motivational speaking.

"Becoming a speaker would mean I could have more fun," I told Karen. "I would be selling philosophy and inspiration, rather than going through the craziness of selling computer hardware." We prayed about the decision—it was a little scary to think of giving up a full-time salary and job security to be self-employed.

In addition, I was worried about how this traumatic event might impact Roselle. I called GDB and spoke to trainer Terry Barrett. "Do you think there will be any long-term effects for Roselle?"

"Well, did anything threaten her directly? Was she struck by anything that would cause her fear?" I answered no to both questions.

"Dogs don't do 'what if.' So long as nothing threatened her and you continue to behave like nothing happened to her, she will be totally fine." Terry was absolutely right.

---

When guide dogs go through their early training, their trainers expose them to all sorts of situations. They want them to be able to handle walking on different surfaces, from shiny tile floors to city sewer grates. They expose them to various distractions and situations to be sure that they don't get scared or lose focus. This slow and careful process of desensitizing the dogs builds their courage so they can do their job of dealing with obstacles and distractions.

However, one thing they try to avoid with puppies in training is "trigger-stacking." That is, giving the dog too much to handle at once—for example, noise, uneven surfaces, and another dog barking, all at once. That can overload the dog, causing stress and fear.

One week after 9/11, letters containing anthrax were mailed to media outlets and two senators, Tom Daschle and Patrick Leahy. Five people died, and seventeen others were infected. These crimes, on the heels of a terrorist attack, put Americans on edge. Everything felt out of control. Talk about trigger-stacking.

Since Karen and I lived in New Jersey, ten miles from the post office that several of the anthrax letters came through, we were nervous and opened our mail cautiously. We wondered if the terrorists would strike again. We, like all Americans, but especially New Yorkers, lived with a quiet dread. It was a time of fear, and of reevaluating our lives. What really mattered to us? Life was short, and fragile; anything could happen. We talked about wanting to move back to

California to be closer to Karen's family. We just didn't know how we could make that happen.

—————

During the time between September 11, 2001, and that final interview with Larry King in 2006, our lives changed dramatically. As Joanne predicted, I was asked to do hundreds of interviews. Karen and I talked about all this notoriety. She asked what I thought of all this visibility.

"First," I said, "Roselle has turned into quite the ham on camera."

Roselle quickly learned how to look straight into any lens that came her way. She was calm and very poised. I am sure she usually did much better than I did. Still, if my visibility would help people move on from September 11, if it would help educate people about blindness and help people better understand what a guide dog was all about, then it was worth doing.

I had my first speaking opportunity two weeks later. A pastor called and asked me to give a brief talk at an outdoor church service he was arranging to celebrate the lives of everyone from New Jersey who perished that day. Six thousand people attended.

In early October I was invited to speak at a guide dog event in Vancouver, British Columbia. Karen, Roselle, and I went to Liberty Airport in Newark to fly to Vancouver. Very few planes were flying yet. Karen said the airport was quite eerie, both due to the small crowds and, as she described, the young kids (who were probably in their late teens or early twenties) in the National Guard toting machine guns. The next morning, October 7, we went down to breakfast at the hotel. The television in the restaurant was on and caught Karen's attention.

"Mike, I think we are at war."

"What?"

"I think we have invaded Afghanistan." She began telling me what she was seeing.

So here we were in a foreign country, and overnight our homeland had gone to war. What a strange feeling it was.

We stayed in Canada for most of that week. Roselle clearly was in her element, taking all the accolades she could get and exhibiting no fear or concern at all. She surely put things in perspective for Karen and me, and in part because of her, we felt calm.

———

In late October, I received a call from Debra Barnes at Guide Dogs for the Blind, asking me to come to California in early December to speak at the annual GDB holiday fundraising luncheon. Both Karen and I were thrilled to do this, especially since we decided to surprise her parents in Southern California with a visit before going up the coast. The four of us—Karen, Linnie, Roselle, and me—arrived in California very early on Karen's dad's birthday, December 1. We got to their house in San Clemente and rang the bell, waking them up. "Surprise!" They had no idea we were even coming to California, so it added to the fun.

Later that week we left to drive to San Rafael. On the way we stopped to visit Cherie Jones, who had retired from The International Walk to Emmaus and who now was the pastor of Atascadero United Methodist Church. Cherie had two adopted rescue greyhounds who quickly made friends with Linnie and Roselle. We sat on Cherie's deck and watched the dogs nosing around the large yard. Suddenly the two greyhounds took off running full tilt with Roselle and Linnie in pursuit. It only took a few steps before our dogs were totally left in the dust. They came back up on the deck, tails between their legs, and their heads hanging down as if to say, "What just happened?"

At GDB I met the new executive director, Bob Phillips. We hit it off immediately. During one of our conversations, he asked me about my future plans.

"Karen and I would love to return to California." He said he might have to think about that.

The luncheon was quite successful. Before leaving for New Jersey, Debra told me that GDB planned to have a float in the 2002 Tournament of Roses Parade and they wanted me and Roselle to ride on the float. Wow! California twice in one month. A sign.

The night before the parade, Bob told me that he wanted to offer me a job as the national public affairs director/spokesperson for the school. Without hesitating, I said yes. I believe God guides us and answers prayers by putting circumstances in our path. It's up to us to listen and respond. Just as I was considering becoming a motivational speaker full time, Bob's job offer landed in my lap.

Bob told me that I would be working for Debra Barnes in the development/fundraising arm of the school. I also wanted to continue to speak. We agreed to set up a process where I would work full time promoting the school, as well as taking advantage of speaking opportunities which also brought money to the school. It was the best of both worlds, and after praying and talking about it, Karen and I knew it was the right choice. I began working for GDB on January 15, 2002.

Karen stayed in New Jersey until we found a house seven miles from the school and began modifying it for Karen. We moved into our new wheelchair-accessible home in Novato, California, at the end of June 2002. God absolutely provides.

Roselle took everything in stride and loved our new digs. On the other hand, Linnie's health declined further. In early July 2002, when I was representing GBD at the national convention of the National Federation of the Blind, Karen called and tearfully said that Linnie had crossed the rainbow bridge. I was sad that I wasn't able to be there, and that Karen had to do all the work, but at least Linnie wasn't suffering anymore.

It didn't take us long to decide that moving back to California was the right thing to do. I believe God guides us using our circumstances. Just as I pay attention to the subtle cues that my dogs use to guide my steps, so I must also listen to God to know the best path. This was clearly God saying, "Fear not, for I am with you."

When we're all alone and not sure which way to go, fear can grow. But knowing and listening to God banishes the isolation that can lead to blinding fear. Guide dogs know that listening to the Master keeps you safe and helps you to be brave because you know you're not alone.

I saw several circumstances coming together and steering me in a new direction—my questions about my purpose, the influx of speaking requests, and now this new job. It would be a change and a leap of faith, but I could see it was the right thing to do.

---

Roselle, Karen, and I stood in the early spring sunshine at Ground Zero, six months after 9/11. Being there, knowing there was just a gaping hole in the ground where two buildings had once stood, brought back difficult memories of that day. But the day wasn't about me—it was about Roselle.

She was being honored by The People's Dispensary for Sick Animals (PDSA), a British charity organization, along with Salty, another guide dog, and his person, Omar Rivera, and a search and rescue German shepherd, Appollo. PDSA often honored dogs for heroism in wartime. Roselle, Salty, and Appollo received the Dickin Medal (named for the organization's founder, Maria Dickin) on March 5, 2002, for their heroic efforts on 9/11. Roselle seemed mostly unimpressed by the medal and the reception afterward at the British Consulate.

This was the first of many awards Roselle would win. She was later honored by the Heroes of Hartz by the Hartz Mountain Corporation, the American Kennel Club, the British Guide Dogs Association, and The Little Rock Foundation, among others. Her name was read into the Congressional Record to recognize her service.

---

When you travel as much as I did for work, unexpected situations are inevitable. You might end up in a situation where you feel apprehensive or afraid. In those moments, I learned just how important trust and teamwork were. Roselle and I had been through hell—that we'd survived gave us more courage to handle other challenges. We knew we could trust each other, that we could work together as a team when we faced things that might have made us afraid.

That's not to say you should seek out exceptionally frightening situations to build your bravery. But when difficult things happen, try to see them as opportunities to build your trust in your team, in God, in yourself. God had promised to take care of me, and I believed him.

Two years after 9/11, Roselle and I visited the Guide Dogs for the Blind campus in Gresham, Oregon, where we met with students and donors, and I delivered a few lectures. I stayed in an apartment about two miles from the school. When I arrived, I unpacked my suitcase and fed Roselle, then decided to go and get some dinner at a nearby restaurant.

We walked to the restaurant, and I enjoyed a delicious meal. After I paid the bill, the two of us walked out the door, and I signaled Roselle to turn to the left. "Forward," I told her confidently. We walked about a block, then turned down a side street. After walking several blocks, I turned again, expecting to find the campus apartment building. But as I approached, I could tell the entrance was completely different. I stopped.

*The building I'm staying in has steps in front. This just has a flat sidewalk and a double door. This is not my apartment building. Hmm.*

Roselle sat by my side as I felt panic rising in my chest. What had I done? I was wandering in a strange city at nine at night, with no one but my guide dog with me. I had no idea where I was, and no clue how to get back to the apartment.

My fear in that moment was real. I took a deep breath. *Just breathe, Mike. You've faced far bigger challenges than this one.*

I'd been practicing mindfulness in calm moments for years at that point. I took a few minutes to let my mindfulness muscle memory kick in. Sometimes the first step toward being brave is to simply pause.

"Wait a minute," I said to Roselle. "We can figure this out." I wasn't sure yet how I would figure it out, but telling myself that I could solve my problem was an essential first step to managing my fear. I thought about the route I'd taken, retracing my steps mentally.

*Alright, think about what you can control*, I told myself, remembering the guidance God gave me on 9/11. I had to think about the resources I had. I had Roselle, but the neighborhood was just as unfamiliar to her as it was to me. While I couldn't just tell her to find our way, I knew she would help me make it there safely if I figured out the right way to go. I made myself consider my options: Flag down a passing car to ask directions? Try to find my way back to the restaurant and start again? I knew if I panicked, Roselle would feel my fear, which wouldn't help her do her job of guiding.

I retraced my steps back to the restaurant. "Here we are, Roselle. Let's try again."

We walked again, turning left, then right, then down another block, until . . . "Um, Roselle? I don't think this is right." She sat quietly beside me, waiting for my next command. She didn't know this city any more than I did. She could guide me down the sidewalk but couldn't read street signs any better than I could.

*This is not good. Okay, Mike. Be mindful. Take it slow. You may not have ever been to Gresham before, but you've been out of your comfort zone before. Focus on what you can control. Feel the fear, then use it to figure out your next step. Leverage it.*

*God, I know you're with me. Show me the way.*

The night was getting cool. I held Roselle's leash and harness in my left hand and put my right hand into my jacket pocket. *Wait, what's this?* My fingers connected with a small, flat rectangular object at the bottom of my pocket.

"Roselle! We're saved!" *Thank you, God.* It was the GPS device that I'd recently purchased—and thankfully, I had it in my pocket.

Slowly, using the GPS, Roselle and I found our way back to the apartment. As we got closer, I felt Roselle pick up her pace as she recognized landmarks (and probably smells), telling me I was on the right track. I was immensely thankful to finally put my key in the door lock and go inside.

Did I feel afraid at that moment, lost in an unfamiliar city at night? Yes. But what enabled me to think and figure out the answer to my dilemma? I would argue that it was my regular habit of practicing mindfulness, of being present. Of connecting with God, training myself to be aware of him.

What if I didn't happen to have that GPS with me? (I realize it sounds a little like the old television show *MacGyver* to just happen to have a tool that could help me in my pocket.)

My fear did not disappear when I found the GPS in my pocket. I still had to use it to navigate. But my fear had started to ease before that when I slowed down and carefully thought through my options.

I could have gone back to the restaurant and made a phone call. I could have flagged down a passing car. The point is, my problem was solvable, and knowing that enabled me to be brave and figure out the exact solution that would help me. Fear says, "Oh no! I don't know what to do!" but courage says, "I don't know what to do yet and I feel afraid, but I can figure it out." Regardless of what solution I chose, they all began with being mindful, and moving forward despite my fear.

You cannot practice mindfulness in a moment of fear unless you've practiced it in a moment of calm. Mindfulness is like a fire drill. No one actually sets a building on fire to conduct a fire drill. Instead, supervisors go over safety procedures when everyone is calm and attentive, then practice evacuating quickly and safely when things are calm and there's no danger.

Mindfulness is a workout for your thoughts and emotions. Just as a runner or athlete learns to control his body through training, you can train yourself to control your mind, and therefore, your fear. You may feel afraid, but by being mindful, rather than mindless, you can respond in a way that is productive and leverages that fear into right action.

Often, our fear has to do with things that happened in the past (which we can't change), or things that might happen in the future

**Guide dogs know that listening to the Master keeps you safe.**

(which we can't control). After 9/11, I could have let fear win. I could have flinched every time I heard an airplane overhead. Instead, I focused on what had actually happened: Roselle and I had been brave. We had made our way out of the Tower and to safety. We could handle difficult situations. We knew we could do hard things because we had done them before.

When our mind goes to the past or future, it's obviously not in the present, and it's not much help. But by practicing mindfulness, we can learn to redirect our minds to the present moment, where we can calmly figure out our next step.

———

Roselle was our only dog at that time, since we had lost Linnie. Karen and I knew we had room in our hearts and home for another canine, but Roselle was still strong and healthy. So in 2002, we let Guide Dogs know we'd be willing to foster dogs. When people who had a guide dog wanted to travel without their dog, for whatever reason, they could contact Guide Dogs and volunteers would care for the dogs in their home. Karen and I often welcomed a dog for a few days or a week at a time. Foster care was fun, but it still wasn't like having a permanent addition to the family. Oh, make no mistake, God was watching and had a plan.

In early 2003, one of the school veterinarians called me. "Mike, we have a senior dog who needs a long-term foster home. Her name is Panama. She was just returned to us by a family who said they couldn't take care of her anymore. She may be a bit of a challenge, as she is twelve, has arthritis, and is deaf. You said you would be willing to take a geriatric dog, and so here we are. Would you come meet Panama and then talk with Karen about this?"

"Sure." I walked from my office at Guide Dogs to the kennel, where I met Panama, a timid golden retriever. She wouldn't approach me, even when I called her. A day later, Karen came to Guide Dogs headquarters to meet her.

"When she got back to San Rafael, she was just a mess," Dr. Dietrick told us. "Filthy, dirty. Arthritic. And totally unresponsive—we think she's deaf. We dropped a Webster's dictionary on the floor next to her and she didn't even flinch."

"What's that big lump on her back?" Karen asked.

"We think it's probably an infected cyst; we'll take a look at it. She may have ringworm as well. We'll make sure she is up-to-date on all her shots and any treatment she needs. Would you be willing to take her until we can find her a permanent home?"

"Of course we will," Karen said. "Right, Mike?"

I smiled. I loved Karen's big heart for animals—especially ones that seemed to have been through difficult situations.

"Sure."

Panama had not made the cut in guide dog training. The only reason given on her record was "temperament." It takes a very special personality and temperament to make it as a guide dog. The dogs must be highly aware, but not easily distracted. They must be friendly but focused. They must be obedient, but also be able to know when to be disobedient (as we discussed in earlier chapters) to protect their handlers. It's not surprising that only 50 percent make the grade.

We took Panama home in February 2003. She wasn't interested in playing with Roselle, but Roselle seemed to understand that she needed to be gentler with this new dog.

Panama (we called her Pammy) needed time to build trust. We simply tried to love on her, but she was often wary or just unresponsive. The vet determined she did not have ringworm and was able to drain the cyst to get rid of the lump on her back. He did think she had slow-moving cancer but that she'd die from old age before the cancer took her.

Panama seemed to carry trauma with her. We realized she wasn't totally deaf, just hard of hearing. I spent a lot of time just talking to her. She began to respond to us when we spoke or called her. She'd look at us when we'd speak gently (but quite loudly) to her.

Eventually, she allowed us to pet and reassure her. For quite a while, she was afraid to take walks with us. She was stubborn at times—if she didn't want to do something, she let us know in no uncertain terms. At first, Panama was pretty leery of Karen's wheelchair. But Karen would sit near her and just talk in a soothing voice. After a while, Pammy allowed Karen to pet her for a moment.

Panama eventually grew accustomed to the wheelchair, and she would go for a walk with Karen. Most of the time she did fairly well, but remained skittish around other people.

While we couldn't be sure, we suspected Pammy had been abused at some point in her life. She'd sometimes whine, but she never barked. It was almost as if she was afraid to use her voice.

She was particularly terrified of our garage. When we tried to take her through it, she would shake and whine and refuse to move. She'd plant her feet and not budge. We wondered if she'd been locked in a garage or had been abused in a garage. She was adamant about it: She was not going into that garage.

If we wanted to take Pammy anywhere, Karen would back the van out of the garage, and I'd take her out the front door of the house. Her nervousness didn't subside in the van. She'd shake and whine.

We knew Panama needed a permanent home, so in July 2003, we adopted her as a member of our family. We even let her sleep on our bed sometimes—something I wouldn't let any of my guide dogs even consider.

A month later, we were getting ready to drive to the GDB campus in Boring, Oregon, for "Fun Day." This event was for puppy raisers to show off their dogs to people, and I was involved in the festivities.

"Almost ready to go?" Karen asked.

"Let me get the suitcase in the van. Then you can back it out. We'll load up the dogs and be on our way."

I picked up my suitcase and opened the door from the house to the garage. I heard the scramble of toenails on the kitchen's tile floor and felt a dog rush past me, almost knocking me over. "Roselle?"

"I don't believe it," Karen said, wheeling into the garage. "It's

Pammy!" She had raced through the garage and jumped into the open van.

I set my suitcase in the back of the van, then went to the side where Panama was sitting on the floor of the van, panting. I petted and praised her. "What a brave girl, Panama. You're here in the van. Good dog!"

This fearful canine senior citizen trusted us enough and had bonded with us so much that she didn't want to be left behind. Panama was willing to overcome her fear to make sure she got to be with us.

Trust and teamwork are essential to overcoming fear, and Panama illustrated that so well. We built her trust through kindness, care, and love. As the Bible says, "Perfect love casts out fear."

It took some time, but we didn't rush her. She'd learned fear, and now she was beginning to unlearn it. The day she ran out and jumped into that van showed me the power of building trust and teamwork, and how it helps you to be brave.

After that breakthrough in the garage, Panama continued to take daily steps of courage. She'd initiate interaction with us or with Roselle. She'd come when we called her. It was as if the hard shell she'd built to protect herself was slowly melting away.

Panama never indicated that she wasn't willing to be a loving dog. Despite her trauma she was never aggressive or mean. She was just a fearful dog until we showed her that we could be trusted.

We bent some of the rules for Panama to help her bond with us. When we'd be eating dinner, she would come up and put her nose under Karen's arm and push. Karen would stop eating and pet her. Eventually, she'd start doing the same with me. We never fed her from the table, but if she asked for affection we lavished it on her. It was all about being as supportive as we could be for this dog.

———

In 2003, Roselle and I were invited to travel to New Zealand for three weeks to help raise funds for the Royal New Zealand Foundation of the Blind (now known as Blind Low Vision NZ) and the local guide dog school.

I was fearful about the trip. While I flew frequently, I had never taken such a long flight, much less with a guide dog. How would Roselle handle flying for nearly twenty-four hours without a potty break and without much water or food?

I consulted GDB trainers and some other guide dog users who had taken long flights. Everyone recommended not to feed or give Roselle water much at all before departure. Even so, I had not done this before.

"Well, God, I trust your teachings and gifts." In early May 2003, we flew from San Francisco to Los Angeles, where we would catch a direct nonstop flight to New Zealand. There was time to take Roselle out for a relief break before boarding the New Zealand flight. But wouldn't you know it? Roselle did nothing during her break.

I gave her a few pieces of kibble and a little ice during the flight, but I kept everything to a minimum. When we reached New Zealand and I was able to get Roselle outside, she wasn't even desperate. She handled everything beautifully! I'm glad I didn't panic and fear too much. Faith does work.

---

In 2004, I was invited to be the speaker on a weeklong Alaskan cruise for guide dog users and their dogs. Karen and I planned to bring Roselle along. Just before the cruise in March, I took Roselle to the GDB vets for her annual physical. Her blood test results were quite unexpected.

"Mike, her platelet levels are very low," Dr. Dietrick said. After some further tests, he gave me a diagnosis: "Roselle has immune-mediated thrombocytopenia (IMT). It's an autoimmune blood disorder. Essentially, antiplatelet antibodies are attacking her blood platelets, which is impacting her kidney function. I have no idea what's causing it."

"On 9/11, Roselle and I both were exposed to a huge dust cloud when the Tower collapsed," I said. "We inhaled a lot of dust and debris, probably some toxic fumes. Who knows what was in that dust cloud? I felt like I was drowning in it. Could that be what has caused this?"

"It's possible," he said. "There's really no way to test for the cause, especially now, three years later. But I'd like to put her on medication for her kidneys, so that she can continue working. But you'll need to monitor her closely. If she starts acting fatigued, she may need to retire. I advise having Roselle stay home instead of going on the cruise."

As I listened, I felt a little dizzy. The vet kept talking, but it was as if I was hearing him from far away. I struggled to clear my brain. *Retire? Roselle? Kidney function?*

I tried to argue with myself. *Okay, you have had plenty of experience with having to retire guide dogs. None of them works forever or lives forever. But Roselle—she's one in a million. I've never had a dog like her. I'm not ready to say goodbye. We'll treat this. We'll help her get better.*

So, Roselle stayed home, and I fulfilled my speaking obligation. As happened when Linnie got sick in 1999, I used a cane on the trip. Twenty-one other travelers brought their guide dogs on the cruise, but Karen and I had to go dogless. I checked in with the GDB staff as often as I could, since their veterinarian staff was conducting regular blood workups on Roselle. Her platelet count continued to drop and reached a low of 10,000 platelets per microliter of blood. The normal count should be around 250,000 platelets per microliter of blood. Yes, I was worried, but I knew this was out of my control. Roselle was in the best place and in the best hands possible, including the hands of God.

By week's end when we returned, Roselle's platelet count had stabilized and slowly began to improve. She was put on an immuno-suppressant to help keep her body from attacking her blood platelets. Once she got on the medication, Roselle improved. She continued to work and guide. In fact, in 2005, we traveled to Korea with some of my colleagues at Guide Dogs for the Blind. A guide dog school there had developed a relationship with our organization, and we were learning from each other. Ultimately, they wanted to broaden the canine gene pool by interbreeding dogs from Korea with US guide dogs. Our visit was part of a goodwill tour, and I gave a speech about my experiences and the importance of teamwork.

Korea was not the end of Roselle's world travels. In October of 2006 she and I were invited to Japan to speak at a conference sponsored by the Hokkaido Guide Dogs for the Blind Association. As always, Roselle took everything in stride. We flew to Japan on a Thursday and returned to California on Sunday, then immediately traveled to San Diego for a GDB donor-hosted event. Roselle made new friends everywhere she went and was chipper as ever. Clearly, the meds she was on were still allowing her to perform at peak efficiency.

---

In 2006, another dog came into our life. Fantasia came to our home as part of Guide Dogs for the Blind's "breeder keeper" program. Though she was not a guide dog, she taught us many valuable lessons about how to live with courage. Though she technically belonged to GDB, she lived with us when she wasn't at the school being a mother.

Like other breeder dogs, Fantasia started out in guide dog training. However, when her trainers noticed that this gentle yellow Lab was unusually bright and eager to please, they shifted her into the breeding program in the hopes that she would produce litters that shared these same traits. She produced thirty-one puppies, half of which became guide dogs. A few others entered the GDB breeder program.

We'd wanted to welcome one of these dogs into our home for a while, not only because Karen wanted a well-trained dog to serve as a friend and companion, but also because we wanted to help the school produce the kind of top-notch guide dogs I had greatly benefited from over the years.

I remember the first time we met Fantasia in January of that year when we made our breeder keeper visit. When we arrived, Marina, the director of the breeder program, pulled us aside and said, "I think we have a dog that will work perfectly for you!"

We were scheduled to meet four different dogs, one at a time. In a conspiratorial tone, Marina whispered, "I'm not going to tell you which one it is, because I don't want to prejudice you against the others. They're all wonderful dogs. But I really do think she'd be a perfect match."

Marina brought Fantasia into the room first and unhooked the leash from Fantasia's collar. Fantasia looked at Karen, sitting quietly in her wheelchair, quickly walked over and climbed up onto the footrests, then placed her front legs on Karen's lap. The yellow Lab licked Karen's face enthusiastically.

"Well, hi there," Karen said, a little surprised. She stroked Fantasia's soft ears, then hugged her. Fantasia wiggled happily. It was love at first sight.

"That's what I thought might happen!" cried Marina joyfully.

"Wow, she's something, isn't she?" said Karen. "Oh, Mike, she's beautiful. She's perfect!"

"She sure is," Marina said.

I stood next to Karen's chair, reached over and petted Fantasia. "Welcome to the family, Fantasia," I said. Fantasia nosed me for a second, then turned her attention back to Karen. We thought we had a say in picking out a dog—it turned out that the dog was picking us out, and there was clearly no debate about it in Fantasia's mind!

Karen had found her dog, and Fantasia had found her person and her home.

We did meet the other dogs. But we quickly realized none of them would work well with Karen. All three hung back, seemingly puzzled by or even afraid of Karen's wheelchair. Although none of the dogs had probably ever seen a wheelchair before, Fantasia somehow accepted it without batting an eye, and fearlessly climbed up to greet Karen. She somehow knew this was her person, and if she came in a chair instead of on two feet, that was perfectly fine with her.

———

From Day 1, Fantasia was at Karen's side. She would walk calmly next to Karen as she wheeled herself around the house, down the block, at the grocery store, or anywhere else Karen went. When Karen was at the sewing machine and she dropped her scissors or a piece of fabric, Fantasia would gently retrieve it and place it in Karen's open hand.

A dog and their person build a relationship of trust over time. Fantasia trusted Karen, who gave her consistent care and attention, and praised her when she responded. But just as important, Karen trusted Fantasia. She realized over time that Fantasia's intuition and instincts to protect and guide her were always spot on. Fantasia anticipated what Karen needed and provided it.

For example, Karen sometimes struggled with anxiety. When she felt overwhelmed, Fantasia would come up to Karen's chair and put her front paws on Karen's lap. Karen didn't have to ask Fantasia to do that—Fantasia sensed it. That gesture of attentive love reminded Karen to take a deep breath, pet her dog, notice her own feelings of fear or anxiety, and to remind herself: *I'm not alone. I'm loved.*

As a breeder dog, Fantasia had not gone through the full training as a guide dog, much less as a service dog for someone with any kind of disability. She was so attuned to Karen, though, that she worked herself into that role.

Fantasia also simply picked up fetching (a rather advanced skill) on her own, showing how much she understood Karen and how eager she was to help her. Every day I thanked God that Karen had this incredible dog on her team.

While I never let my guide dogs sleep in our bed, Fantasia knew she was special. She slept in between us at night. Karen and I used to joke that "Tasia took her half of the bed out of the middle."

And my word, was that dog smart! One day, Fantasia was up on our bed chewing on a bone, when suddenly she dropped the bone, jumped down from the bed, and ran out of the room. A few minutes later she returned and jumped back up on the bed.

"What a clever girl!" Karen exclaimed.

"Why clever?" I asked. "What happened?"

"She's just so smart," she said, her voice full of love and admiration. "She was trying to chew on her bone, but it kept slipping out of her paws, so she went and got her Goughnut and is using it to hold the bone in place, so it won't slide away!" (For the uninitiated, a Goughnut is a hard rubber doughnut-shaped chew toy with a hole in the middle that Fantasia somehow concluded would be a perfect anchor for a slippery bone.)

"Well, that is clever! Good girl!" I praised Fantasia, scratching our brilliant pup behind her ears.

Fantasia, Roselle, and Panama got along well, with Fantasia and Roselle playing gently with Panama, mindful of her age. It's as if the two of them also knew that they had to carefully build trust with Panama to help her overcome her fear. In late 2006, Panama became so weak she couldn't stand up, and soon after she passed away. We were glad that we had given her a safe home and a family (both human and canine) that helped her live her best life.

———

In 2007, during a routine blood workup, the results showed some of Roselle's kidney values were changing. "It's time to retire her," Dr. Dietrick said. We knew this was coming. On March 7, 2007, Roselle retired in a ceremony at Guide Dogs for the Blind. The entire staff attended. Even TV and newspaper reporters covered the event. An imprint of her paw was stamped into the cement in front of the administration building. In August, Roselle received her highest honor. In a special meeting for Guide Dogs for the Blind's board of directors, her name was retired forever. Typically, the organization repeats guide dog names over and over, but that wouldn't be the case for Roselle. There would only be one—my loyal and amazing friend. Her name was the first Guide Dogs' name to be retired.

Roselle lived with us in her retirement. Her energy level stayed high, and she continued to love to play tug whenever she could find a victim.

It was time again for me to meet a new teammate. What I didn't know was that my next guide dog—Meryl—would teach me lessons about fear that I totally didn't expect.

## Guidance from the Word

*Forget the former things;*
    *do not dwell on the past.*
*See, I am doing a new thing!*
    *Now it springs up; do you not perceive it?*
*I am making a way in the wilderness*
    *and streams in the wasteland.*

**ISAIAH 43:18-19**

## Prayer for Courage

God, I want to listen to you. When I feel afraid, remind me to stop, breathe, and listen for your voice of reassurance.

# 8

# MERYL

## Rest rejuvenates our courage

I think of a balanced dog as one that
is comfortable in his own skin. It is a
dog that gets along with other dogs
and people equally well . . . that isn't
handicapped by behavioral issues like
fear, anxiety, or obsession.

**CESAR MILLAN**

**I HAVE SAID BEFORE THAT GUIDING** is very stressful for a dog
because they always want to get it right and they take their jobs
extremely seriously. I have also observed that every dog has its own
personality, just like us humans. A guide dog ensures that the team of
handler and dog walk safely, remaining engaged as long as the harness
is on. They must be vigilant and focused.

I have been fortunate to have received my guide dogs from a
school that has always looked for ways to maintain and improve training techniques. Could Squire or Holland have done the work on
September 11 that Roselle did? Possibly, but I do believe Roselle was
all the better for improved methods of training that GDB created
over the years. Of course, GDB is not the only school that constantly
perpetuates training enhancements. All good schools do it. My 2006

trip to Japan was an example of ways schools throughout the world come together to compare and improve.

Make no mistake, dogs do focus, but they also need time to relax. My dogs love it when they get to rest, rejuvenate, and visit when the harness is removed. Some take the process to an extreme. You haven't lived until you see a guide dog in a school with hundreds of young children who want their turn at petting. Some of my dogs, including Roselle, have discovered that simply spreading their bodies out on the floor as much as they can gets the most attention. They absolutely enjoy children. I have never, and would never, want a dog that was tense or nervous around children, even a crowd of them.

We could learn a lot from this kind of dog personality. We all need to learn how to relax more and go with the flow. "Don't worry about what you can't control" is such an invaluable but difficult lesson to learn and put into practice, and it really is essential to being brave. Those who do learn and discover the power of taking a break and relaxing are all the better for it. They tend to do better in all aspects of their lives. Again, this is as much true for dogs as it is for people. I know this from personal experience.

When Roselle retired, we welcomed Meryl, a female yellow Lab, into our home and I heartily welcomed her to my team. At first, she seemed to get along fine with Roselle and Fantasia. Our house was a bit chaotic with three dogs. Karen had her hands full caring for two dogs when Meryl and I traveled, which we did frequently.

Because I was working for Guide Dogs for the Blind at the time, I had one-on-one sessions with a trainer, which permitted us to customize our training and preparations. At night Meryl and I would go home, which gave her the opportunity to more quickly become accustomed to our home life.

Even with this slightly different training regimen, I was still part of a regular class. I planned to attend the graduation ceremony with

Meryl for that class, which was scheduled for a Saturday in early April. But that week I had a speaking engagement scheduled out of town. I was supposed to fly home with Meryl Friday and attend the graduation on Saturday.

Our return flight went through Dallas, and as often happens at that time of year, there were thunderstorms rolling through about the same time as our flight.

As soon as we got off our connecting flight, I knew we had only a brief window to make our connecting flight to San Francisco. I quickly asked the agent at the gate I was leaving to call our connecting gate to let them know we were coming. She assured me she would do so.

I grabbed my rollerboard suitcase in one hand, and Meryl's harness and leash in the other, and we jogged through the Dallas Fort Worth airport. When I got to the gate for my flight to San Francisco, however, the door had just closed, and they would not let me board.

"I'm so sorry, sir," the gate agent said. "We can't reopen the door. The plane is backing away from the jet bridge now."

"I told them to call and let you know I was coming," I said. "I'm an executive platinum member!" She was apparently unimpressed with my frequent-flier status.

"I'm sorry, sir, we didn't receive any call about your connection. I can get you on a flight first thing tomorrow morning. Here's your boarding pass. That flight will depart out of gate C15, three gates down the hall."

I sighed.

"Is there anywhere I can take my dog to relieve herself?"

"Hmm. You can go outside through the front of the terminal," she said. "But security closed at 10:00 p.m., so you wouldn't be able to get back in."

It was nearly midnight. I walked to my gate and found a chair.

*I need to stay calm. Thankfully, Meryl hasn't had food or much water. I sure hope her capacity for holding it is as legendary as Roselle's. I guess I'll find out! If I keep her calm and quiet, she's less likely to have an accident.*

I sat down and Meryl lay by my feet. I slipped off her harness but held her leash. I took the strap that I keep around my suitcase and wrapped it around my wrist, so that I'd feel if someone tried to take it while I dozed.

"Let's try to get a little sleep, Meryl. Good dog."

Was I nervous sleeping in an airport? Not really. However, I wasn't happy about missing my flight and having to sleep in an airport, especially with a new guide dog who relieved herself just before we boarded our first flight, but now wouldn't be able to go outside until we reached San Francisco. I didn't sleep well, sitting up in a chair, a dog leash in one hand, my suitcase strap in the other, but I did manage to nap. I actually didn't feel scared, in part because I knew that DFW has security guards, but also because I had my dog with me. I wasn't alone. Even though Meryl was relatively new to me, I could tell she was focused and did her job very well. I think Meryl got more sleep than I did.

The next morning, we caught our flight to San Francisco. Immediately after disembarking, I found the animal relief area for Meryl. While she held everything in all night, I observed that she was quite pleased to have a chance to relieve. "Good dog, Meryl. We dodged a bullet, didn't we?"

We boarded our favorite Marin Airporter bus and made it to San Rafael in time to attend the graduation. Karen met us there. We were looking forward to a great partnership with a new dog, who'd already shown her ability to face challenges.

Meryl settled right in both at home and in all aspects of work. Karen noticed that Meryl paid extra attention to me and didn't interact much with Fantasia and Roselle. In less than a year, however, Meryl's behavior shifted. She became even more focused on me. It may seem strange, but she was too vigilant. She was always on. She would not relax. Her "off switch" didn't seem to work. She somehow forgot that when the harness comes off, it's playtime. She had a type A personality and couldn't leave work at the office, so to speak. What was Meryl's problem?

Fear.

Her concern and vigilance escalated into anxiety that affected her ability to guide. She seemed worried about me all the time. She had become, in the words of Cesar Millan, "unbalanced."

One evening, Karen and I sat on the couch, listening to an audiobook. Roselle and Fantasia slept on the floor while Meryl sat attentively beside the couch, occasionally nosing me.

"It's okay, Meryl. Go lie down." She whined but refused to leave my side.

"You just went out, you had your dinner, your water bowl's over there. Take a break."

"It's almost like she's guarding you," Karen said. "Like she's on alert."

"It seems like this dog can't relax. She's getting more anxious every day."

"Maybe you can get her to play with Roselle and Fantasia," Karen suggested. "Maybe that will distract her and get her to relax."

"Great idea." I went to the toy box and grabbed the Booda Bone. Roselle and Fantasia immediately got up.

"Here we go. Meryl, come." She immediately came to my side—but didn't seem interested in the toy.

The other two dogs pranced around us as I tried to get Meryl to engage in a little game of tug-of-war. She refused, and when Roselle and Fantasia bumped into her playfully, I heard a growl and a snap of teeth.

"Meryl, no!" Karen said. "Mike, she just snapped at Fantasia."

I dropped the tug bone, and Roselle and Fantasia grabbed it, immediately jumping into their favorite game, ignoring the fact that Meryl wasn't joining in. As I walked back to the couch Meryl hovered against my left leg—in her guiding position, except she wasn't in harness. I sat down and she sat in front of me. "Meryl, you have to play nice," I said as I petted her.

"It's like she doesn't want to play at all," Karen said. "She's looking over her shoulder like she's worried."

---

I didn't know how to help Meryl relax. Finally in July 2008 I called Brian Francis, the head of graduate services at GDB. When program graduates or their dogs run into any problems or issues, he and his team address them. Since we lived seven miles from GDB, Brian came to our house to see what was going on. Meryl was shaking as I buckled the harness and snapped on her leash, something that Brian saw firsthand.

"Hmm. This is odd behavior, for sure. But I'd like to see how she does in public," he said. "Let's drive over to the grocery store in town."

We got in Brian's car, and the problems worsened immediately.

"Hooooowwwwwoo!" Meryl howled piteously from the back seat. I reached back to pet her, to try to calm her, but she shook, whined, and would not stop howling, no matter what I did.

*This is not normal. Something is going on with this dog's mental health. I swear she's having a panic attack.*

"Well, this is rather concerning," Brian deadpanned.

At the grocery store, Brian walked a few steps behind Meryl and me through the aisles. Meryl walked beside me, but kept her head down, panting like crazy. She walked tentatively, not guiding or even paying attention to me, just walking along looking scared.

"Mike, I have to agree with you. This isn't right. She seems terrified. How long has she been like this?"

"She's been like this for a few weeks. It's so strange. In certain situations, she actually seems to be having some sort of panic attack. It's like she can never relax."

"Mike, based on what you've told me and what I'm seeing, I think Meryl needs a career change. This isn't good for her or for you."

Things got worse after that. Meryl went from always wanting to guide and sticking to me like glue, to the point where she became

Guide dogs know that when the harness comes off, it's playtime. They seem to intuitively know that taking time to play and relax allows them to perform better and more bravely when the harness is on.

totally afraid of guiding. She lost her ability to focus on the work because she never took her focus off work. She guided from a place of fear, rather than confidence. Eventually, she was so overloaded with anxiety that she wasn't able to guide at all.

Meryl was my sixth guide dog, but I'd never seen behavior like hers. It turned out that her nervous behavior stemmed from stress which was amplified by her workaholic personality. Somehow, the trainers had not detected this tendency when she'd gone through training. She'd seemed extremely competent and smart—which she was. But because she couldn't relax, fear got the upper hand.

This is something that can happen with guide dogs and even with humans. After graduating, some dogs end up not settling in as expected. This group is very small, but such dogs do exist. I simply never thought I would work with a dog that was literally blinded by fear.

So we began the process of looking for another dog and making plans to retire Meryl. She eventually went to live with her puppy raisers in Nevada. Once she realized she didn't need to guide anyone, and could just be a dog, she did much better.

If you find yourself feeling like Meryl, maybe you need to evaluate. Are you working too hard? Have you taken on too much, or are you in a job that doesn't suit you? Has fear blinded you or taken over your life?

It's possible that I wasn't the right person for Meryl. My demands for her as a guide were pretty heavy. I traveled frequently to speak about my experiences on 9/11, in addition to working full-time for GDB. My other dogs had handled the job just fine, but maybe it was too much for her.

When I first got Meryl, she knew her job and did it well. The trainers at GBD knew me and my lifestyle when they placed her with me, and she showed no signs of any problems until almost a year later. Just as with people, stress can be a cumulative thing for dogs.

I've met people who've had the same problem—people who work

all the time, who don't take time to play or rest. So what happens? Their marriage dies; their relationships suffer; they may turn to drinking and other addictions they think will ease the stress. But it only makes things worse. They eventually burn out or become less effective at their job. They may suffer from chronic anxiety like Meryl did.

Humans—and dogs—need to disconnect and unwind. Downtime is as important as sleep in order to function well. No one has to teach puppies to play—they do it naturally. But sometimes, anxiety can take over.

Our culture lauds workaholic types. They're admired for their focus, rewarded for their drive. But I wonder if people who can never unplug might actually be motivated by fear. Maybe deep down, they fear failure, or that they won't have enough resources. Maybe like Meryl, they feel hyper-responsible for the people around them, always needing to keep their guard up.

When you are willing to disconnect and to slow down, you are given an opportunity to examine your own motives, to think about what you're doing and why you are doing it. Taking a break forces you to trust that everything will be okay, even if you aren't working or micromanaging things. In a way, rest affirms your trust in God.

Guide dogs know that when the harness comes off, it's playtime. They seem to intuitively know that taking time to play and relax allows them to perform better and more bravely when the harness is on. Rest rejuvenates courage.

---

The average American is exposed to as many as 10,000 advertisements per day. Per day! And many of those ads that bombard us from our phones, our computers, television, and radio are designed to subtly tap into our fear. It's hard to turn off the noise, to get away from the constant barrage of information and pitches.

All of us have developed ways of ignoring ads that don't interest us—or do we really? Advertisers know that in order to keep you from scrolling past or ignoring their messages, they have to create a sense of urgency. Fear does that really well. In fact, advertisers purposely use "fear appeal" as a marketing strategy.

> Fear appeal in advertising is a strategy used that provides the audience with a persuasive message that emphasizes a serious threat or harm that might come to them if they do not do what is asked of them in the advertisement. This tactic is often used by companies that want their audience to engage in a potential behavior, usually buying their product.

Even if an advertisement is not specifically fear-based, it often plays on our fear of missing out or tries to create a sense of discontent. Our old car doesn't have Bluetooth connectivity or heated seats—we need a new one. We'd be happier and more attractive if we bought this makeup, this toothpaste, those shoes, that designer handbag.

When we're surrounded by so many messages, low-grade fear often becomes the dominant emotion in our lives. Like Meryl, we live with constant anxiety. And beyond advertising, other voices in our lives create fear. Just watch the news—this awful thing is happening—it's scary. Even the weather report is overly dramatic, just to get you to pay attention. "Oh no! It's going to be dangerously hot (or cold)!"

But seriously: Step back and notice the messages that come your way all day every day. How many of them, whether subtly or overtly, stir up a bit of fear?

The first thing is to become aware of these messages and how they impact you. Cultivate self-awareness: Are these messages true? Are they trying to make me feel fear? Is there a credible threat to my safety, or is this just a manipulation tactic?

---

You've probably found yourself in a situation where you were worried and afraid. Your mind spins, yet you go nowhere. But by beginning with self-awareness and self-care, you can take control of your fear.

An oft-quoted verse tells us to "take every thought captive" (2 Corinthians 10:5, ESV). I love how *The Message* renders that verse:

> *We use our powerful God-tools for smashing warped philosophies, tearing down barriers erected against the truth of God, fitting every loose thought and emotion and impulse into the structure of life shaped by Christ.*

With God's help, we can see "warped philosophies" (i.e., lies and manipulation) for what they are, and begin to change our "loose thought[s]" (i.e., fear) into more rational and trustworthy truths. I love the idea of "smashing warped philosophies." Our fear-soaked world needs that now, doesn't it? We all need it—and we can't do it on our own. We need God to empower us to be brave. But as this verse reminds us, we have "powerful God-tools."

You may even need to visualize giving the situation to God, handing it to him like a package for safekeeping. Tell yourself, "I'll let God handle it for now, and I'll revisit it tomorrow. Get a good night's sleep, then pick it back up in the morning." Give yourself some time to think about your fear. *Why am I afraid? Where does it come from? Is this fear based in reality or am I making it worse by imagining terrible outcomes? Am I being triggered because of past mistakes or bad experiences?*

As you try to answer these questions—even if you only stop for a fraction of a second—you are taking control of your thoughts, your responses, and your actions instead of allowing fear to do so. It may not be totally resolved immediately, but this is an important step to keep fear from blinding you.

In late 2008, after Meryl retired and moved back in with her puppy raisers, a sweet yellow Lab named Africa became my guide dog. Now we had three dogs in the house again—Roselle, Fantasia, and Africa. Karen and I were especially excited to welcome Africa because she was Fantasia's daughter. I think Fantasia was just as excited!

Roselle, on the other hand, seemed a bit skeptical at first. Although she had retired, she still wanted to be the guide dog. She liked being in charge.

Because we had Meryl for such a short time, and since we lived so close to GDB, we did in-home training with Africa. Trainers from GBD came out, and we worked in various places (our house, the neighborhood, on public transit, at the store, and lots of trips to San Francisco, Oakland, and Berkeley).

When you have other animals in the house, it's usually best to introduce them on neutral ground initially. We used the same strategy we'd used when we introduced Roselle to Linnie—we had Roselle and Africa meet in the garage.

I knew Roselle would warm up to Africa if we played with the tug bone. I also wanted to be sure that Africa knew how to play. I gave Africa one end of the rope, and I started tugging on the other end. Roselle just watched us at first, still suspicious about this newcomer. Then I called Roselle and gave her the other end of the rope, and I kept hold of the middle. We all tugged, and then I let go and let the two of them continue their tugging. Before long, Fantasia joined in the fun, and the three yellow Labs remained inseparable from then on.

I felt joy and relief to see that Africa had no problem playing and romping around. She became a very brave guide dog, in part because she knew how to take a break and play. But there was much more she taught me.

## Guidance from the Word

*We demolish arguments and every pretension that sets itself up against the knowledge of God, and we take captive every thought to make it obedient to Christ.*

**2 CORINTHIANS 10:5**

## Prayer for Courage

God, I sometimes struggle to take a break and relax, and it makes me anxious. Help me to take a break, to play or rest today.

# 9

# AFRICA
## Faith drives out fear

Faith is a place of mystery,
where we find the courage
to believe in what we
cannot see.

**BRENÉ BROWN**

**IF MERYL HAD TROUBLE KNOWING** how to play, Africa had the opposite problem. When the harness was on, she did a great job guiding and staying focused. But when she was not working, that sweet and affectionate yellow Lab sometimes got into trouble. She was so mischievous that Linda, a friend of Karen's, teased that my dog's name was actually "Africa NO!" because that's how we seemed to address her most often.

For some reason, this dog thought paper was the tastiest treat she could find. She once even ate a five-dollar bill (Karen found the last bit of it in her mouth)! She did keep us on our toes as far as keeping clutter, especially paper, out of reach—though she would sometimes grab papers off the counter or my desk. More than once, she grabbed the end of the toilet paper in the bathroom and carried it in her mouth, spooling out toilet paper across the house. I didn't appreciate her "TP-ing" our living room!

Africa came into our home and our hearts at an interesting time—a time that was a little scary for me. In 2007, our country was sliding into a recession. In March 2008, I was told by the new CEO at Guide Dogs for the Blind that she was phasing out my job as national public affairs director because she felt the position was not helping the organization. This CEO came to the organization in late 2007, after Bob Phillips retired and, for the first time in the organization's history, laid off employees. While they technically offered me a different position, it would require that I give up my speaking and take a pay cut. I declined.

It was a difficult transition. Obviously, I disagreed with their decision, but I felt I needed to step out in faith. On July 1, 2008, I started The Michael Hingson Group, Inc., a consulting and speaking business. I continued to travel and speak to not only organizations connected with blindness, but business groups, civic organizations, and more.

So by the time Africa became my guide dog in November of 2008, I was self-employed. My first attempt at launching and running my own business years before had not ended well—we nearly ended up bankrupt! I did feel positive about this new venture, having had over six years of speaking experience already while at Guide Dogs for the Blind. Karen and I both felt that starting our own business was the right thing to do.

All of us have core fears, and one of mine is around finances. Will we have enough? Perhaps you struggle with this fear as well—I think most people worry about money, at least once in a while. For me as a blind person, this fear has a second layer. I believe blind people can do anything sighted people can do. My life has shown that I'm actually capable of doing just that. But I often feel my own success is not just about me, but about proving to the world that blind people deserve opportunities that are often denied them. Because our culture equates financial success with competence, my worries about money are tangled up with my fear that people will discriminate against me because I am blind. And that fear is based on reality: I have faced discrimination my whole life, and part of my boldness is a response to needing to overcome the prejudice that others have against not just blind people, but anyone with any sort of disability.

My consulting and speaking career provided me with an opportunity to face those fears and walk boldly forward. In that season my faith in God deepened. I needed God to provide—and God did! Little did I know the amazing ways in which God would guide me. When we trust, and God provides, our faith grows. And with it, our courage.

For example, on Christmas Eve 2008, I received a wonderful and unexpected gift when my phone rang early, about 7 a.m.

"Mike, it's Marc Maurer."

"Dr. Maurer! How are you? Merry Christmas."

"Merry Christmas to you too. I won't keep you long. I do have an opportunity I wanted to let you know about. You, of course, remember Ray Kurzweil—you worked for him and sold the Kurzweil Data Entry Machine. Remember how he always predicted that there would be a smaller version of the reading machine someday? Well, someday is here. He's been working for years to develop a mobile reader. It's about the size of a Palm Pilot. Are you familiar with those?"

"Sure." A Palm Pilot wasn't accessible to a blind person in those days because the technology to read screens and voice text was still in its infancy. But I was being given the opportunity to help take the next step even from the Palm Pilot product.

"Ray and the NFB are introducing the next generation of reading technology. This mobile reader combines the Symbian operating system on a Nokia cellular phone with a camera that can scan and read pages," Dr. Maurer explained. "It uses voice technology provided by two alternative screen reading programs that run on Symbian. It's called the KNFB Reader Mobile. I'd like you to take charge of selling these systems—taking the components, putting them together, writing an instruction manual, and selling the product. You already have a selling business in place, so I think this is a good project for the Michael Hingson Group to undertake."

"Wow, really? That sounds like a very interesting opportunity."

At the time, voice technology on phones was in its infancy. But the KNFB mobile reader was cutting edge for 2008, and God provided a great opportunity to use my skills in technology and sales to bring full circle the relationships I'd built on my first job out of college.

Rather than being an employee of Kurzweil Education Systems, or the manufacturer, I'd be the integrator of the system and sell it through my company. And I'd be the primary seller of the KNFB Reader Mobile in the United States. I knew the value of having a text reader that would fit in my pocket—it was an absolute game changer. But I didn't know how many people would be willing to spend $1,800 to buy one.

My job was to do all the things that I knew how to do, which was to help the team get people excited, present every year at the NFB national convention and, of course, assemble and sell the product. But it was a risk. And it was a risk for me because I hadn't been directly involved in the development of the product, setting up distribution, or how it was going to be sold.

What a wonderful Christmas present! Karen's and my minds kicked into high gear. First, prayers and thanks to God. Then, of course, we began to strategize about how we would sell the system. Kurzweil already had engaged some dealers from within the blindness community, but they weren't really moving the product. The KNFB Reader Mobile was only one of their products, and from an assistive technology viewpoint, it was a complex device. I think this is why Ray Kurzweil and Marc Maurer approached me. I would devote the proper time to the technology, and I already understood it and knew its value.

Any time you introduce new technology, people are a bit suspicious and, dare I say it, fearful. Kurzweil and the NFB needed my tech savviness and my sales experience to take this amazing technology and get it to users who would find it life-changing—they just didn't know it yet.

The company proposed I would buy the three components—phone, reading software, and screen reading software. I would load software onto the phone to make it talk, do the initial setup, and make sure that it read right and was fully tested. Along the way I created a manual detailing how to operate the system I'd assembled, walking users through everything from turning on the phone to getting it to scan and read documents. Then I put it all together as a product, boxed it up, and labeled and shipped it out. Karen did the labeling and shipping. It was a complete integration process from beginning to end. I recruited blind people from within the NFB who were willing to become KNFB Reader Mobile dealers and we were off to the races.

And so, six months after starting the Michael Hingson Group, I added this job as a systems integrator and salesperson to my work as a keynote speaker and consultant. God provided income through that venture for about four years—until the technology developed to the point where the same functions could be done via an app on the latest tech gadget in 2012—the iPhone. That was an abrupt change, as the product I was selling became obsolete quite quickly. It was scary.

Still, I felt like God was guiding my steps. Karen and I both felt that call from Marc Maurer, whom I'd known since college, was a blessing from God. It was the perfect next step, but like any step, it didn't last forever. But by that point in my life, I'd realized that God had a pretty great track record in my life and that I could trust my next step to him. Which is exactly what happened.

I went back into speaking full-time. Make no mistake, I had sought speaking opportunities while integrating and selling the KNFB Reader Mobile, but in 2012 speaking became my sole full-time venture again. Now I had much better technology to help read printed content, and I installed one of the apps on my iPhone, which was great. Today I have apps on my phone that read the screen and

**Guide dogs know that faith in your Master drives out fear.**

allow me to read and send text messages and emails, surf the web, and even order lunch!

I've learned through the years not to worry about the stuff that I don't have control over. It doesn't mean I'm not aware of it. That reminder, which God gave to me and Roselle on the streets of Manhattan that fateful Tuesday morning, proved true over and over again. And it may very well be that God provides opportunities to help me control things that I didn't think I had control over, like getting a job or other things that come along.

Africa never worried—she was playful and mischievous, even a little naughty sometimes. But she had faith in me, and when the harness was on she guided very capably and bravely. Guide dogs know that faith in your Master drives out fear. If you have trust in your teammate (and isn't that what faith really is?), you don't have to worry or fear.

---

All of my dogs traveled with me. When I'd fly from New York to California, for example, my dogs had to handle a relatively longer flight. I knew how to help them be successful, to fly calmly and safely, training them about how to have good manners on a plane, but also preparing them by limiting their food and water intake before and during the flight to prevent accidents.

When Africa became my guide dog, training had evolved considerably. A great addition to the training was the use of clickers. When the dog did what you asked, you immediately clicked the small handheld clicker, then rewarded them with a bit of kibble.

So the first time I took Africa on a plane, I set her up for success.

"Any passengers needing assistance may board now," the gate attendant announced. Africa and I made our way to the podium. I'd learned that it was best to board early when I could, to allow my dog to get situated and for the sake of the other passengers.

We walked down the Jetway and into the plane. But instead of turning right to head to our seat, I signaled Africa to turn left. She peeked in the cockpit.

"Well, hello, who do we have here?" I heard the pilot say.

"I'm Mike, and this is my guide dog, Africa. We just thought we'd say hello before we find our seats. She just wants you to know she's here. She's ready to fly or do whatever you need her to do if the need arises." Of course, what was happening at the time was that the crew was making friends with Africa, who loved the experience.

"Welcome aboard, Africa," the pilot said. "I'm Samantha, your captain. And this is Bob, your first officer. We'll do everything we can to give you a smooth, safe flight."

"Thank you," I said. Africa and I made our way down the aisle to our seat. I put my suitcase in the overhead bin, then detached the handle from Africa's harness, so she could more easily slip under the seat in front of me.

"Africa, sit," I said, positioning her in front of my seat. As soon as she obeyed, I clicked the clicker in my hand and gave her a kibble from a pouch attached to my belt, then sat down.

"Down," I told her, and as she did, I gently guided her rear end under the seat so her head was on my feet.

"Good girl," I said, clicking and rewarding her right away. Africa loved the attention and treats and was always eager to please. One thing GDB had done in the early 2000s was to adopt a new harness model with a removable handle. Before Africa went under the seat I removed the handle and I slid it into the seat-back pocket.

Some people think putting the dog under the seat is too restraining. But anyone who's seen a dog nestle into a small, cozy space will realize that the dog feels safest under the seat, and in fact, is safer there. In case of turbulence, they're safely constrained. Africa took to flying right away and was very happy under the seat in front of me, where I could reach down and pet her or offer her an ice chip or a piece of kibble at any time.

In guide dog training, they sometimes have airplane or bus seats set up in the classroom to allow the dogs to practice what riding on a plane, train, or bus will be like. But a plane with all its smells, the changes in cabin pressure, the movement (and occasional bumps), the people, and distractions is a much more challenging environment. Africa was very obedient—she knew she was working and behaved perfectly. Well, most of the time.

In 2010, Africa and I traveled to the Netherlands at the invitation of KNGF Geleidehonden, also known as the Royal Dutch Guide Dog Foundation, to speak at their 75th anniversary celebration.

This was Africa's first international trip. How would she handle the stress of a ten-hour flight? She'd done shorter trips, but not a long-haul international one.

KNGF had kindly paid for me to travel by business class. After we boarded, I got Africa tucked in under the seat, as usual. She promptly took a nap. Once we reached cruising altitude, I tipped my seat back, delighted to find that it fully reclined. I started to doze off.

*Thump.* I suddenly found myself with a weighted Labrador blanket stretched out on top of me. Africa nuzzled my neck and rested her head on my chest. Soon we were both snoozing our way to Amsterdam.

"Good dog, Africa," I said, stroking her back for a minute before letting myself drift off again. Other passengers laughed, but no one had a camera to get a shot of the two of us.

I was thankful for Africa's reassuring presence—maybe she sensed that I needed some comfort and courage. I was going to a strange country, a place I'd never been. I didn't speak Dutch. I am quite adept at navigating airports, but how would it be in a country where I might not be able to ask people for directions? I think Africa sensed my concern and wanted to reassure me by cuddling with me. Either that or she just wanted to take advantage of the perks of business class! Ultimately, although I was somewhat fearful, I didn't overly worry. I had already traveled alone to Japan and elsewhere. I knew we could do this.

When we arrived, one of the people from the guide dog school had arranged to meet me at the gate, and guided Africa and me through the airport. It all worked out fine. When I was growing up in Palmdale, I never thought I would travel the world. But the courage I'd learned by exploring on foot and by bike served me no matter where I went. We had a wonderful time in the Netherlands, as well as a terrific flight back. Africa clearly loved the entire experience. I didn't need to worry about any future travel abroad.

Guess what? Two years later we flew to Japan.

⸺

As early as 2002, when Roselle received an award from the American Kennel Club, people had been suggesting I write a book. I had conversations with people in publishing, but they didn't quite get what I wanted to communicate. One suggested, because of my experience in the business world, that it be a book more oriented to motivating and educating business leaders. But I wanted to write a more general story that would help a wider audience understand blindness—how it really wasn't a handicap, just a difference. I wanted to tell the story not just of 9/11, but of my life.

I really wasn't sure how to go about writing a book, but I started making notes. It was one thing to tell my story in a forty-minute speech. Writing a book seemed more involved. I amassed a sizable collection of notes and had faith that God would guide me to the next step.

In 2010, a writer named Susy Flory contacted me. She was writing a book called *Dog Tales*, a collection of inspiring stories about dogs. She had heard about Roselle and me and wanted to include our 9/11 story in the book. I agreed and told her the details of our experience.

"Wow, Mike," she said. "That is an amazing story. Have you ever thought of writing your own book?"

"Well, I would like to, but I'm a scientist and a salesman. I need someone to help me write it."

There was a long pause. (Susy later told me she got goose bumps when I said I needed a writer.)

"Would you be interested in collaborating with me to write it?" she asked.

"Well, how does that work, exactly?" I asked.

Long story short, Susy and I began a series of conversations and created a book proposal. Not long after that, with the help of her agent, Chip MacGregor (who also became my agent), we signed a contract with Thomas Nelson, the largest Christian publisher in the United States, to write a book!

For a year, Susy came to my home once a week to interview me. She'd write chapters based on our conversations, send them to me to review, revise, and add more content. Each time Susy visited, Africa, Roselle, and Fantasia would greet her enthusiastically. We'd drink tea and talk not only about 9/11, but about how my parents taught me that being blind was an inconvenience but was nothing to be afraid of.

While we were writing *Thunder Dog*, Roselle continued to slow down. The IMT impacted her energy, and her blood levels continued to drop. She sometimes suffered from back pain and was having a hard time standing up. Once she was up, she still loved her daily walks.

In the summer of 2011, Karen and I planned a trip to visit her parents. Our friends David and Louise Wilson, who were the breeder keepers for Roselle's father, Sievert, agreed to take care of Roselle while we were gone. But a few days before we were to come home, I got a phone call.

"Mike, it's Louise."

"Hey, Louise, how are you? Is everything okay?"

"Roselle is having a tough time. She started vomiting blood and her paws were starting to swell up. We took her to the Pet Emergency and Specialty Center (PESC) since Dr. Codington's office is closed for the weekend."

"Good call. What did they say?"

"It's not looking good, Mike. They recommended we leave her there for observation. Of course, it's up to you, but you might want to consider letting her go. Roselle is just not responding to much at all."

"Louise, I appreciate that," I said, fighting tears. "I think we'll cut the trip short and come home as soon as we can."

Africa, Fantasia, Karen, and I made it back to Novato on Sunday night, and we went straight to the vet. If it really was time to let her cross the rainbow bridge, we wanted to let the dogs say goodbye as well.

Roselle's feet were swollen, she was lethargic, and she seemed to be in pain. I petted her and she feebly licked my hand once, then put her head back down. The vet at PESC told us some of her immune medical conditions had returned, and that the vomiting blood might possibly indicate other issues as well.

"Poor baby," Karen said. "I hate to see her suffer, Mike. It's time."

The PESC staff was kind. They made Roselle comfortable and then gave her a sedative injection. She fell asleep but was still breathing, so after a while they gave her a second injection, and she was gone. Africa and Fantasia came up and sniffed her body. They were brave—they didn't whine or cry, but I was still thankful for their presence. I'm certain they understood what was going on and they knew they had to let her go, like we had done.

Roselle passed on June 26, 2011, and on August 2, 2011, *Thunder Dog: The Story of a Blind Man, His Guide Dog, and the Triumph of Trust at Ground Zero* was officially released. And, yes, Larry King was true to his word and wrote the foreword.

---

In July 2010, I spoke at the national convention of the National Federation of the Blind, telling the audience about the upcoming book and how it would help the world understand that blind people were capable of anything. At the 2011 convention we had advance copies we could sell.

Early in the afternoon of August 11, 2011, Karen and I were at home when I got a phone call from my Thomas Nelson editor, Bryan Norman. "I have something to tell you. You need to sit down for this."

"What is it?" I asked.

"Please sit down."

"Well, Karen is sitting. Does that count?"

"You need to sit, too, for this."

"Okay, I'm sitting."

The next thing I heard was, "In its first week out *Thunder Dog* made it to the *New York Times* Bestseller list!" It remained on the list for 13 weeks and still sells well today. My surprise quickly gave way to gratitude. *God, thank you.*

Being an author brought more opportunities to speak and travel. Africa and I did our best to educate people about blindness, guide dogs, and the powerful bond of trust that blind people share with their dogs. I spoke a lot about courage and trust, but the book itself was a memoir of my life and the events of 9/11. So while I was no longer selling the KNFB Reader Mobile, God provided other opportunities to grow my speaking business. I knew I eventually wanted to write another book, showing people how they could apply to their own lives the principles about dealing with fear that I'd learned over the years with my dogs.

*Thunder Dog* was translated into many languages. In 2012, when the book was published in Japan, I was invited to spend two weeks there. My previous visit to Japan with Roselle had only been for four days. But because Africa had already traveled with me internationally, I felt confident that whatever happened, I could deal with it.

It was a great trip, and it was amazing to be there with Africa beside me at the podium for every speech. One special highlight was riding the bullet train from Tokyo to Hiroshima. Despite going 200 miles per hour, the train moves so smoothly that you couldn't really tell how fast you were going.

I was thankful that Karen had Fantasia at home to keep her company and look after her. Little did I know just how important it would be for Karen to have her service dog beside her.

## Guidance from the Word

*For we live by faith, not by sight.*

**2 CORINTHIANS 5:7**

## Prayer for Courage

God, help me to live by faith, to walk beside you and trust you to guide me and show me the way.

# 10

# FANTASIA

## Your instincts will protect you

This may be the primary purpose of dogs: to restore our sense of wonder and to help us maintain it, to make us consider that we should trust our intuition as they trust theirs, and to help us realize that a thing known intuitively can be as real as anything known by material experience.

**DEAN KOONTZ**

**I STOOD IN OUR BEDROOM,** packing for yet another business trip. I walked into the closet, where hangers holding a suitcoat, shirt, pants, and matching tie hung. Karen and I always sorted shirts, ties, and suits together, hanging an entire outfit on one hanger after getting clothes back from the cleaners, which made it easy to pack. When you're traveling several times a month, you learn shortcuts. Another packing (and dressing) hack: only buy one color socks. They always match.

Then I heard Karen coughing . . . again.

"I really think you need to go to urgent care," I told her. "This respiratory thing doesn't seem to be clearing up."

"It's just a cold. I'll rest up while you're gone, and I'll be fine." I knew Karen didn't ignore problems when it came to her health. Still,

I worried. *Should I contact the National Federation of the Blind and tell them I can't come to the National Washington Seminar this year?*

Fantasia was doing her best to comfort Karen, putting her front paws into Karen's lap. "Don't worry, girl," Karen said, stroking her. "You're such a good dog."

*Maybe she's right*, I thought, as I continued to pack my suitcase. I understood her aversion to hospitals and doctors. But she didn't seem to be getting over this "cold."

"Did you remember . . . ?" Karen asked, teasing.

"Yes, I have underwear," I said, grinning.

The underwear was a private joke between us. When we were first married, we'd taken a "familiarization" trip to Hawaii. Karen would check out facilities on-site in her travel agent role so she could make informed recommendations to her clients. On this trip, after checking into our hotel, I discovered that I had packed everything I needed—except underwear. So before we could relax and enjoy the tropical paradise, we "familiarized" ourselves with a department store in downtown Honolulu.

*If she's feeling well enough to joke around, maybe she'll be okay. Maybe.*

I zipped my suitcase shut as Karen turned her wheelchair around to head to the kitchen and start dinner, Fantasia beside her.

By this time, Fantasia had been Karen's service dog and near-constant companion for eight years. *Surely*, I reasoned, *Fantasia will take good care of Karen while I am away.* She had, after all, been extra attentive to Karen over the past several days, always staying within arm's reach, and often resting her chin on Karen's leg. "I swear," Karen remarked at one point, "the way Tasia's clinging to me and looking at you, you would think she's afraid that if she so much as blinks, I'm going to disappear!"

*Yes, she'll be fine*, I reassured myself. *Still, I'll ask her friends to check on her while I'm gone.*

Africa and I arrived at the Federation's National Center in Baltimore on Friday afternoon, meeting up with more than five hundred leaders from around the country. We discussed pending legislation and services available to blind people around the country, and prepared for meetings we would have with legislators at the seminar in DC that would begin Monday.

When I called home on Saturday morning, Karen's voice was almost unrecognizable.

"You don't sound good," I said, no longer able to keep the worry out of my voice. "You sound like you're completely out of breath. Please, I'm begging you . . . go get this checked out."

"I'll be fine," she croaked. "I've got my nurse, Fantasia, here. Poor thing slept with her head on my chest all night." Tasia had never draped herself across Karen like that before.

After we hung up, I reached down and scratched Africa's ears. "I'm worried about her, girl," I said, once again second-guessing my decision to leave. Africa nudged my leg with her nose, almost as if to say, "I understand."

The more I thought about Karen's description of Fantasia's behavior, it made sense. Tasia always seemed to know what Karen needed before Karen even did. It confirms what so many studies have discovered about dogs.

According to the American Kennel Club, a dog's powerful sense of smell can detect subtle changes in a person's body. Our scent often changes when we are ill.

> The human body is a complex cocktail of chemicals that gives off odors our dogs can easily detect. . . . So, dogs know a person's individual smell and when illness changes that smell, dogs can notice that, too.

Fantasia likely noticed a change in Karen's body chemistry, in her breathing and heart rate. She knew something was off, but couldn't tell us, other than to be more attentive than usual, if that were even possible.

I adored Karen, and it gave me great comfort to know that Tasia did, too, and was always looking out for my wife and wanted to protect her. Africa and I shared a similar bond—when a dog is your teammate and not just a pet, the connection feels and is amazing. They look to you for leadership and seem to derive a certain joy from doing what you ask.

I stroked Africa's ears, grateful for her comforting nuzzle on my hand.

"But your mama is there, and she's taking good care of her," I said, trying to convince myself.

Whenever I feel afraid, my first instinct is to stop and pay attention. To remind myself that God is always with me. I closed my eyes. *God, I trust you. Please protect her.*

Echoing my own concern, Africa rested her head on my knee and whimpered slightly. "You know what, girl?" I said, reaching for the phone. "I think it's time to get your mama a little help. Maybe Karen will listen to her sister."

Karen's sister, Vicki, was an ICU and CCU nurse. If anyone could convince Karen to get to a doctor, it would be her.

"I'm really concerned, Vicki. Can you call Karen?"

As soon as we hung up, Vicki called Karen, and it didn't take her long to assess the situation. "You need to go to Kaiser Hospital now. Don't fool around with this, Karen. Call an ambulance immediately, or I'm going to call one for you."

Karen made arrangements for her longtime friend Judy to watch Fantasia and then called for an ambulance to transport her to the hospital.

Meanwhile, in Baltimore, I had to try to put aside my worry and get through the work we had to do to prepare for the seminar. I was prepared to cut the trip short at a moment's notice if Karen got worse.

"Mike, how's Karen?" asked Dr. Maurer, who was still the president of the National Federation of the Blind.

"Well, she went to the hospital just now," I said. "She says it's bronchitis, but it seems more serious than that. Frankly, I'm worried about her."

"Of course you are," he said. "Does she have someone with her?"

"No," I said, realizing how awful that sounded. Vicki had told me she and her husband, John, could make the eight-hour drive to Novato from their home in Southern California if we needed them to. But we were waiting to see what the doctors said.

"Do they know what's wrong?" he asked.

"Not yet, but I hope the doctors can figure it out. I'm torn. I wonder if I should go home—but I'm not sure there's anything I could do to help."

"Well, keep us posted," he said. "If you need to cut this trip short, you just let us know. Your wife's well-being is what matters."

That Saturday afternoon I sat in a meeting, absently petting Africa's ears as I tried to listen to what was going on. Africa should have been lying on the floor under the table, but she somehow sensed I needed comfort and courage, which she offered via her cold nose and gentle nuzzles.

My body was in Baltimore; my heart was in a hospital in California. I imagined myself at Karen's bedside, holding her hand. I tried to visualize us in God's light, with his care and love surrounding us. Africa, as if eavesdropping on my prayers, laid her head on my knee and whined ever so quietly.

*God, protect Karen. Heal her. I know you have the power to heal and protect us. Give me courage. Direct my steps and actions. I know with you all things are possible.*

I felt a gentle wave of peace steal over me, a deeper awareness of God's presence. I knew I could trust him to watch over my wife.

On Sunday morning, I called Karen. "Mike, I'm scared," she confided. "It's getting worse." She was gasping for breath, sounding as if she had just climbed several flights of stairs.

*I shouldn't have left. I should have noticed Fantasia's signals that something wasn't right.* But I wanted to ease Karen's fears—I was very aware of how afraid she was. And now my fears were growing as well.

"Don't worry," I told her. "We'll get through this. You're going to get good care at the hospital."

"I don't know if that's true." Her voice rose slightly, as she fought to control her emotions. "The doctors aren't listening to me. They keep saying I have the flu."

"This is not the flu," she told anyone who would listen.

Karen was on the verge of tears. It didn't help that Fantasia was at our house with Judy, instead of by Karen's side.

"Okay, listen. I'm going to call the doctor."

"Tell them it's not the flu," she croaked.

"Hang in there, and I'll call you tonight. I love you, and I'm praying for you."

Karen's voice had been terribly weak. I immediately dialed the hospital's main number.

After being transferred countless times, I left a message for her doctor, who called me back that afternoon.

"Karen has double pneumonia and ARDS—acute respiratory distress syndrome, Mr. Hingson. We're going to have to intubate her to help her breathe."

"You're putting her on a ventilator?"

"Yes, it's really our only option," he said. "We'll keep you posted."

On Monday morning, Vicki called to let me know what was happening. She was now in critical care nurse mode and had been calling the hospital nonstop for information. "Mike, they put Karen on a ventilator, but she keeps trying to pull the tube out. They're going to have to sedate her. John and I are driving up there now. You should probably come home too."

In the office in Baltimore, I sat down and reached instinctively for Africa, steadying myself. My hand was shaking slightly and Africa licked it gently. She somehow knew, as dogs do, that I needed a comforting touch.

"What do you mean—sedate her?" I asked.

"Pneumonia can progress very rapidly, and that's what happened. The doctors are going to put her in a medically induced coma to force air into her lungs to begin to clear them," Vicki explained.

"A coma?!" My throat constricted. I forced myself to concentrate, to breathe, to listen to Vicki's words, even though they made me want to panic. *Why did I think going to DC was a good plan? Fantasia tried to show us that something wasn't right. That this was more than "just a cold."*

I wanted nothing more than to rush to Karen's side.

Africa pressed her head against my knee, feeling my sadness and fear and trying to reassure me with her physical presence. That gentle pressure brought me back to the moment.

"Okay," I said slowly. "I'm going to change my flight and get home as fast as I can."

I don't believe in dwelling on negative thoughts—or what-ifs or should-haves—but I wrestled with regret.

I immediately called the airline to book the next available flight from Baltimore to San Francisco. "God, please protect her," I prayed, while I sat on hold with the airlines as they rebooked my flight. Despite my fears, I envisioned my dear wife in the light of God's love and healing.

Africa and I boarded the plane around 2:00 p.m. I found my seat and she curled up under the seat in front of me. I tried to act calm, but anxiety gnawed at me, like a dog with a bone. Africa kept reaching up with her nose to touch my knees or hands, reassuring me with her gentle touch.

*God, thank you for Africa. I need your peace and presence right now. I'm not looking for easy answers, God, just reassurance that you're with me. What if my sweet Karen dies? How will I manage without her?*

As the plane took off, tears welled in my eyes. I put my head in my hands.

When we got to cruising altitude, I felt a gentle hand on my shoulder. It was one of the flight attendants. "Sir, are you alright? Can I get you anything? Some water?"

I struggled to regain my composure, unable to speak. "Is everything okay, sir?" he asked.

"Not really," I blurted out, suddenly glad to have someone to share this burden with. "My wife went into the hospital on Saturday and now she's in an induced coma. I'm going back home to be with her."

"I'm so sorry to hear that. If there is anything at all you need, just let me or one of the other flight attendants know."

His kindness was an answer to my prayers, even though it made me tear up even more. To this day it is hard to describe how much I appreciated his comments. I think God sent the right person to talk to me just then.

I took a deep breath and refocused. I imagined myself gathering up those fears in my hands and handing them to God. I sensed God reminding me to just let go and trust him.

Prayer for me is talking *with* God and being aware of God's presence. I don't ever go into the "Why is this happening to me" mindset with God. That is not the way God operates. In that moment—that life-and-death situation for Karen—I trusted that he was with us.

I sat on the plane, my feet resting against Africa's body, just putting the whole situation in God's hands.

Once again, I took a deep breath. *Karen's in a coma and on a ventilator. She can't breathe for herself. But I trust God.*

From the airport, Africa and I took the Marin Airporter shuttle, that dropped us off at a stop near our home. We had been on the go since receiving the devastating news of Karen's condition that morning, leading to a five-and-a-half-hour plane ride, an hour-and-a-half bus ride, and a three-mile cab ride to our house. It had been a very long day, and I'd been running on adrenaline and tears.

Fantasia bounded toward us as I opened the door, then immediately ran past me, apparently looking for Karen. I dropped my suitcase and sighed, finally feeling the exhaustion that had been building all day. Fantasia circled us, obviously agitated.

"She's been like that all day," Judy told me. "She's been patrolling the house. I think she's looking for Karen."

Fantasia sniffed Africa, me, and my luggage carefully, but then resumed her restless pacing. She walked to Karen's office, then the bedroom, then back to me, nudging my hand gently.

"I know, Fantasia." She whined quietly, then resumed making the rounds from kitchen to office to bedroom and back.

I believe we underestimate the intelligence of dogs, the power of their instincts, the knowledge that they have. A lot of people would have said that Fantasia was just being restless, but I knew she was looking for Karen, that she sensed my distress, and that she was displaying her own stress and fear.

I sat down in a chair in the living room. "Fantasia, come," I called. She padded across the floor and sat in front of me. She rested her head on my knee, and I stroked her head and scratched her gently behind the ears. "It's going to be okay," I said, comforting myself as much as her. Africa joined us and we all just sat and prayed in our own ways. I worked to stay calm for Karen, for myself, and for both pups.

My iPhone interrupted our reverie. "John and Vicki Levario," the phone intoned. I grabbed it.

"Hi, Vicki," I said. "Where are you and what's happening?"

"We're on our way to your house from the hospital," Vicki said.

"Have they given you a prognosis?" I struggled to keep the worry from my voice.

"Mike, I have to tell you, it doesn't look good. Honestly, she may not come out of this. You must face that possibility."

"Thanks a lot, Vicki. That's a really comforting way to welcome me home," I said, my exhaustion and worry giving way to frustration and a bit of sarcastic humor. This wasn't Vicki's fault and so I tried to stay as light as I could with her. For a nurse, Vicki didn't have the kind of bedside manner I would have preferred at that moment. "I refuse to give up hope. Karen is a fighter."

"You need to be prepared for it," Vicki said. "I want you to be realistic." I knew that Vicki guards her emotions, so her clinical approach to this conversation was just a way of coping with her own fear.

"I am realistic," I argued, feeling suddenly very fatigued. "I think I can be realistic and positive at the same time." I wanted to be brave and keep a positive attitude toward Karen. I felt frustrated and scared but didn't want to talk about it. My head ached.

When Vicki and John arrived, we ordered food to be delivered and discussed Karen's situation while we ate.

After an hour, I was ready to excuse myself. "I'm exhausted. It's been a long day."

"Of course," Vicki said. "You should get some sleep. We'll pick you up at about eight to go to the hospital."

I could see through Vicki's brusqueness—I think she felt more afraid than I did. She knew how serious Karen's situation was, and she was trying to prepare me for the worst. I suppose it's sometimes hard to find that balance between facing reality and providing comfort.

———

The next morning, Vicki and John arrived bright and early as promised. Africa and I were ready to go.

"I think it would be best to leave the dogs at home until we get a sense of what her situation is," Vicki told me. Although I often argue with Vicki, I decided to relent for the present. The fewer distractions, the better. We left the dogs with Judy and drove to Kaiser.

At the hospital, we went straight to Karen's room in the ICU.

John pulled a chair next to the bed. "Sit here, Mike."

I touched the bed. "Where's her hand?" I asked.

"She's got it on her chest," Vicki said. I reached across and gently took Karen's hand, which was completely limp. I could feel an IV taped to it, so I held it very gently.

**Guide dogs (and service dogs) rely on their instincts to keep themselves and the people around them safe.**

"Can she hear what we're saying?" I asked. Sometimes, having a nurse for a sister-in-law can be helpful.

"You know, they really don't know," Vicki said. "But you should try talking to her, because maybe she can hear, or at least sense you. Don't assume she can't."

For a moment, I was silent, struggling to put my swirling feelings into words.

"Karen, honey, it's me," I said. "I came home early to be with you, and Vicki and John are here too. We're going to help you get through this. You're going to be okay. We're here for you."

I forced myself to smile at her. "You know," I continued, "there are easier ways to get our attention. I hope you are smiling inside and that you hear me."

I couldn't think of anything else to say, and if I had, I wouldn't have been able to choke out much more anyway. John stood behind me with his hand on my shoulder. I was thankful for his reassuring presence.

A while later, Karen's doctor stopped in.

"Hello, Mr. Hingson, I'm Karen's doctor," he said, shaking my hand. "Could I have a word with you out in the hall?"

I was pretty sure I didn't want to hear what I knew he was about to say.

"Karen's condition is very serious," he said. "As I told you on the phone, she has double pneumonia and ARDS. We've induced the coma so that we can pump oxygen into her lungs with the ventilator."

"Why did you guys think it was the flu for so long?" I asked. "It seems like we wasted precious time."

"When she arrived, there was no evidence of pneumonia," he said. "She only had bronchitis. What you need to understand is that pneumonia can happen within a matter of just a few hours. Your wife's lungs were clear when she got here on Saturday. But Sunday, her lungs filled up with fluid, to the point where they are 90 percent occluded. This took place in a hurry and we had to act fast."

I stood in the hospital hallway, full of medical staff rushing around, but I couldn't hear them. My own lungs felt tight, as if they, too, were filling, like I was drowning. *I wonder if this is what Karen felt like—suddenly unable to breathe? God, help me.*

He paused, and I turned to go back into Karen's room. He touched my forearm. "I must tell you, Mr. Hingson, that about 40 percent of people in your wife's condition don't come out of it. This is very serious."

My gut clenched, and I struggled to draw a breath. People talk about how fear triggers a fight-or-flight response. But before that reaction, we're in "freeze" mode. I was underwater, but not even kicking toward the surface. Drowning, and unable to move. But then my body and heart suddenly went from frozen to fight mode.

*I am not going to give up! The doctors are wrong! I have to believe that she'll get better. I have to be strong for her. She needs me, and I need her.*

"Well, that means that 60 percent do make it," I said quickly. "Right?"

He sighed quietly. "Mr. Hingson," he began, then he stopped and was silent for a moment. *I need her. Make her better. Make her well.* Finally, he spoke again, quietly.

"Yes, that's true. And we'll do everything we can to make sure she's in that 60 percent."

"Thank you," I said. I stood outside the doorway to Karen's room. Inside, Vicki spoke quietly. "Karen, it's Vicki. We're all here, and we're going to do everything we can to help you get well."

*If only Fantasia could be here. I know the healing power of a dog's presence, the comfort they bring. If Karen could just be with Fantasia . . .*

I heard the doctor starting to walk away. "Um, doctor?"

"Yes?" He paused.

"My wife has a service dog at home. I wonder if I can bring Fantasia in to visit. She's very well trained and I think it might somehow help Karen."

I'm allowed to bring my guide dogs anywhere, but I wasn't sure what the hospital protocol was for a service dog to visit a person in a coma. Service dogs are trained to do what their humans cannot do for themselves. Technically, a person in a coma can't really be assisted by a service dog. Or can they?

"You know, I think that would be alright," he said. "Let me make a phone call, but it will probably be okay."

———

A few days later, Vicki and I brought Fantasia to the hospital. Her nails clicked on the slick tile floors. As we got closer to Karen's room, Fantasia's pace picked up.

"I think she must be able to smell Karen," Vicki observed. "She's so alert right now."

As we walked into Karen's room, Fantasia looked around, sniffing carefully. She'd never been in a hospital before with so many strange sights, sounds, and smells. I sat down on the chair beside Karen's bed, stroking my wife's back with one hand, holding Fantasia's leash with the other. Fantasia poked at Karen with her nose, assessing the situation. The distractions of the busy hospital faded and for both Fantasia and me, nothing mattered but Karen.

"What a sweet dog," said a nurse who had come into the room to check Karen's vitals. Fantasia wagged and said hello to the nurse, but then quickly turned her attention back to Karen.

When the nurse had completed her tasks, I said, "Would it be alright if I invite Fantasia to go up on the bed? She sleeps with us at home, and I think it might comfort both Karen and Fantasia to be close together for a few minutes."

The nurse hesitated for only a minute. "You know what? Go ahead."

I patted the bed, and Fantasia very gently put her front paws on the bed and climbed up, moving so slowly she barely disturbed the sheets.

"What a good dog," the nurse said as she watched Fantasia carefully position herself next to Karen.

"Good dog, Fantasia," Vicki said. "Mike, I'm so glad we brought her."

*Me too. God, please. Use Fantasia to reach Karen, to help heal her.*
"Karen, Fantasia's here, lying beside you," I said, holding her hand, which was still limp. "She's worried about you like we all are. We're gonna take care of you, and Tasia is here to help you." As the ventilator whooshed, Fantasia sighed quietly. I knew she understood what was going on and was purposefully trying to help.

I ran my hands along Fantasia's back, feeling how she had snuggled up close to Karen. My heart swelled with gratitude for the dog that loved my wife.

*God, surround Karen with your light and love. Let her feel your strength and courage through me, through Fantasia. Let me feel that courage too.* I imagined God's love wrapping around Karen like a soft blanket.

After about fifteen minutes, Vicki said, "Mike, we should probably go. We'll come back tomorrow."

"Fantasia, come. Good girl," I said, inviting her off the bed. She calmly stood and turned tightly on the bed, careful not to step on Karen, then jumped lightly to the floor. "Time to go home."

---

"Good morning, Mike," Karen's nurse greeted me from the nurses' station. I had visited the hospital every day for two weeks, so I had gotten to know the staff. Vicki and John had returned home, so Judy had been driving me to the hospital.

"Good news," the nurse said. "We're easing Karen off the sedation. Her lungs are clear."

I almost ran into Karen's room and immediately grabbed my wife's hand. It was still limp. To me it seemed as if she was still in a coma.

I sat at her bedside, hoping for some sort of response. But there was none. The beeps and sounds of hospital machines provided a backdrop I was growing weary of.

Her doctor came into the room.

"Doc, is she going to come out of this?"

"Yes," he said. "We think so. We'd like to see it happen more rapidly, but we believe she'll recover. It is just that everyone reacts differently to being on propofol for a long period. However, she's been on the ventilator for a long time. We may need to do a tracheotomy if she doesn't come around within the next day or two."

"Wait—you *think* so? But the nurse said her lungs have cleared."

"Her condition has improved dramatically, but she's not out of the woods yet. We're doing everything we can, but some patients take a while to wake up from a medically induced coma."

*God, help!* I breathed. In that moment, I felt God's presence lifting me, reassuring me.

As it turned out, they did have to do a tracheostomy. A person can only be intubated and on a ventilator for so long. I tried to trust that the doctors knew what they were doing, but all I wanted was for my wife to wake up, and to come home.

---

A few days later, when Africa and I were at Karen's bedside, I filled her in on what had happened at the Washington Seminar. "Hey, honey, my colleagues said that even without me there, they were able to get a lot done. They told me they met with four different congressmen, and they think they'll get some key legislation into committees."

I rambled on about my work and what was going on at home, sharing mundane things in hopes she would hear me.

"Everyone has been asking about you," I said. "Your friend Tom Painter has called several times. Judy has been to see you several times already. When you wake up, she and Nancy will come visit. Africa is here with me, lying under your bed. She's been a very good dog when she visits. And don't worry, I've got lots of support. Friends have been giving me rides to the hospital and even bringing meals over."

Two days later I brought Fantasia to the hospital again, as I had done several times over the two-week period. This time she simply sat beside the bed, her snout resting on Karen's arm, as if holding a vigil. I held Karen's other hand.

"I love you. I can't wait for you to come home," I said as I squeezed her hand.

Almost imperceptibly, Karen squeezed back.

"Nurse!" Fantasia jumped.

"Yes?"

"I think I just felt her squeeze my hand," I said, nearly in tears.

The nurse came in and took hold of Karen's other wrist, feeling her pulse. "Her pulse is a little elevated. Karen, can you hear me?" Karen's fingers moved just slightly.

"That's an excellent sign," she said. "Sometimes it just takes a while to come off propofol. I'm sure you'll see progress over the next few days."

It turned out to be slow progress, over a couple of weeks, not days. One day I had Vicki on the phone, trying to get Karen, who was still groggy, to talk.

"Do you know where you are?" Vicki asked.

"Jail," she mouthed, referring to the fact that her arms had been restrained to keep her from pulling out her IV and trach tube. I laughed. That was my feisty Karen!

---

A little over a month after she first went into the hospital, I wheeled Karen into the house. Judy walked behind me carrying flowers that some of Karen's quilting friends had sent to the hospital.

"Welcome home!" Judy's granddaughter, Toni, who worked for us at the time, greeted Karen.

Fantasia's body wriggled in excitement as she circled Karen's chair. Africa followed Fantasia, wagging. I felt just as excited as the dogs. As soon as Karen's chair rolled to a stop in the living room, Tasia put her front paws in Karen's lap, licking her face and wagging her tail. She started to climb up onto the wheelchair, but then backed off.

She seemed to realize that Karen wasn't as strong as before. I think she sensed that what Karen used to welcome—a Labrador lapdog—would cause her mom to wince in pain right now.

"Good girl, Tasia," Karen murmured as she stroked her dog's soft ears. "I missed you, girl." For the rest of the day, Tasia stayed as close as she could to Karen's side, occasionally carefully putting her front paws up on Karen's lap to check in, give her a kiss on the cheek, and get a reciprocal hug from Karen.

That night, Fantasia lay in bed between us as we held hands and prayed "thank you" to God. We knew there was still more recovery time ahead, but God had protected and healed Karen—and we just felt incredibly grateful.

Karen doesn't remember Fantasia's hospital visits at all. But I believe that Fantasia gave Karen strength in those moments. I know it helped me. Fantasia was Karen's constant companion and protector. Their bond grew tighter each day. I knew that her presence comforted Karen, even if Karen was not conscious of or even aware of it. And Karen also drew courage and healing from our prayers. I felt comforted and inspired seeing this dog do her job to help and strengthen Karen by doing what she could not do for herself.

Karen's full recovery took several months. We realized that we could trust God to be with us in those challenging times.

Ironically, fear is sometimes a gift to help us find the path to courage. If you've ever played *Trivial Pursuit*, you know that the first answer that comes to mind—your first impulse, your first instinct—is often the right answer but you often ignore that impulse and give the wrong answer. Similarly, our first instincts in each situation can protect us.

Guide dogs (and service dogs like Fantasia) rely on their instincts to keep themselves and the people around them safe. But sometimes we don't listen to our intuition because it feels like fear or apprehension. When I thought I shouldn't leave when Karen was sick, I should have listened to that and stayed, rather than dismissing my fears. That winter, Karen and I realized that sometimes you need to trust your God-given intuition—and your dog.

---

After Karen's hospitalization, our family convinced us to move closer to them in Southern California so that they could help if Karen had more issues. After some soul-searching and looking around, we found a piece of property to purchase in Victorville, a small town a few hours north of San Diego. It was a vacant lot in an unincorporated area called Spring Valley Lake. Our niece, Tracy, and her husband, Charlie, lived there. Unfortunately, we could not build until we secured a construction loan, and once we did, we had to have our home built. We desired to build a home that would be accessible for Karen right from the outset. In our last home, we'd spent $150,000 to modify an existing structure. It made more sense, both from an accessibility standpoint and a financial one, to design inclusion from the beginning. In the meantime, we moved into an apartment across town which was accessible enough that Karen and I could both make it work. We moved there in early July 2014.

In January 2015 we had taken up volunteering one day a week in Tracy's classroom. Tracy was a kindergarten teacher and loved the extra help. One day as we came back to our apartment we noticed that our next-door neighbor was moving. Actually, he wasn't there, but two women were moving out all his furniture.

While I went into our apartment to drop off some things and greet Africa and Fantasia, Karen went over to the neighbor's place to find out what was going on. When I came over, Karen told me that the neighbor's wife had died the month before and he decided to move to an assisted living facility.

We knew our neighbors had a cat, so Karen asked about the future of the kitty. One of the women said the widower had instructed them to take the cat to the pound.

"Absolutely not!" Karen said. We knew that taking the cat to the pound would most likely mean the cat would be euthanized. We didn't want a cat in our small apartment with two dogs, but we said we would take the cat and find her a home.

Then I made the mistake of asking the cat's name. "Stitch." Immediately I knew that this cat would not be going anywhere but into our home. Since Karen had been a quilter since 1994, do you think she would pass up a cat named Stitch? We did ask how this cat behaved around dogs and were assured that Stitch loved dogs, so we took her.

Well, it was not a love affair at first. As soon as Stitch came into our apartment and the two dogs saw her, they approached her with curiosity, but friendliness. Stitch would have none of it. It took several days, but eventually détente did rule, and Stitch has been with us ever since. She has decided that all our dogs are—as far as dogs go—okay and peaceful.

On December 17, 2016, Karen and I, with Fantasia, Africa, and Stitch moved into our new house in Victorville, California.

---

"Mike, can you help me?" Karen asked. I was brushing my teeth as we got ready for bed.

"Sure, what do you need?"

"I don't know why, but my arms are just really feeling weak. I'm going to need some help getting from the chair into bed."

Karen had always been strong and able to get herself in and out of bed, but in 2017, that and other routine tasks began to become more difficult for her. Her body just hurt.

It seemed like every day she experienced more pain, more fatigue. Something wasn't right. Eventually I convinced her that she wasn't "just tired" and should see our doctor. After some tests, he referred her to a rheumatologist.

Long story short, Karen was diagnosed with rheumatoid arthritis. RA is an autoimmune disease, in which a person's immune system malfunctions, attacking healthy cells. It manifests differently in different people, but it most often inflames the joints.

By the time we finally got that diagnosis, her condition had worsened. It was exceedingly difficult to get her in and out of bed or into the car, and her joints were increasingly painful and stiff. We purchased a new van with a mechanism that permitted Karen to drive her wheelchair right into the driver's space and lock it into place. (The driver's seat was, of course, removed.)

To help with Karen's debilitating pain she was put on a regimen of medications, including a monthly infusion administered intravenously at the doctor's office. This treatment caused her pain to greatly subside, to the point where she could drive as before, but she still needed more help around the house with things like getting in and out of bed. We secured the services of a caregiver named Courtney who helped Karen for an hour a day, getting her out of bed in the morning and starting her day, so I could work in the mornings. I was the caregiver the rest of the time, but mostly I was needed only when we went to bed.

This diagnosis was scary because RA is degenerative. The infusions helped manage the pain, but they would not cure the disease. I was still traveling a lot and thankful for our caregiver. I was thankful for God's guidance in moving us to Victorville, near Karen's niece Tracy.

Our dogs and Stitch took it all in stride. Africa and Fantasia both stayed very attentive to Karen. Of course, Fantasia always stayed by Karen's side and snuggled up with her on the bed whenever she could. She knew her person was struggling, and she wanted to do all she could to ease her pain.

———

That same year, I noticed Africa was also starting to slow down. I knew that the waiting list for guide dogs was long, often a year or more. So as soon as I saw signs of Africa getting older—walking slower, sometimes struggling a bit to get up after she'd been lying down—I notified Guide Dogs for the Blind right away, telling them I would need to retire my sweet mischievous guide. Not only was Africa moving slower, but she was not seeing well at night. I had experienced this with my other guides as they grew older, so I recognized the signs.

Even so, Africa and I continued to travel. We flew all over the United States and to Canada, even in the dead of winter. Africa was a trouper and loved it all. We had the opportunity to visit elementary schools several times, which Africa loved. Of course, all the children wanted to pet her. After our talks, I'd take off Africa's harness and then invite everyone up to visit.

The teachers tried valiantly to keep the kids in line. It didn't work. For Africa's part, she soon discovered that if she would lie down and spread out her body as much as she could—the law of maximizing petting potential—she could get that much more attention. She soaked it up, loving every minute. Children loved her and she loved each and every one of them. I think that even children who were scared of dogs overcame their fear because Africa was so sweet and approachable. She was not afraid of them, even when they swarmed around to pet her all at once, and they in turn knew they could trust her.

Many dogs would be overwhelmed or even fearful of being mobbed by children eager to pet them. I'd often hear the teachers say things like "My dog could never behave like that" or "My dog would freak out." Not Africa. While guide dogs are typically more highly trained than most dogs, I firmly believe her handling these situations so calmly was in large part because of the faith and trust she and I had in each other.

At each event, when I removed her harness, Africa knew she was going to be surrounded by an enthusiastic and energetic crowd. But it never bothered her because she was looking to me and I was calm. I trusted the teachers and, even more importantly, I trusted Africa.

Yes, I also trusted the children to behave, and they did. In all, it was a rewarding and fun time for all. The trust and lack of fear Africa and I had was, I think, the biggest contributor to the success we had in the classrooms. Lest you think Africa was the exception, Roselle also had met lots of children, with no problem. Our relationships, trust, and lack of fear make the difference.

That summer I got a call from GDB saying I had a choice: I could go to the Oregon campus in February 2018 to get a new dog or I could wait until June and go to San Rafael where I had gotten all my other guide dogs. I chose Oregon, mostly because I was curious to see how and if the training process differed from the main campus. And I would be matched with a dog about four months sooner, which would be helpful.

Africa retired that same February. Because I was traveling a lot then, we thought Karen would have a challenge dealing with two dogs, especially since Fantasia was getting to a geriatric stage. And even though she was older, Africa was still known as "Africa NO!" and hadn't given up her mischievous streak, especially her taste for eating paper. She went to live with Bill and Peggy Sproul, her puppy raisers in San Marcos, a suburb of San Diego. We knew the Sprouls would give her a great home. She lived with them for about two years and passed away in 2020.

Once again, I looked forward to meeting a new canine partner.

## Guidance from the Word

*Trust in the LORD with all your heart*
*and lean not on your own understanding;*
*in all your ways submit to him,*
*and he will make your paths straight.*

**PROVERBS 3:5-6**

## Prayer for Courage

God, help me to pay attention to the ways
you guide me—through my thoughts,
intuition, imagination, and the people and
animals around me. Help me to trust you
when I feel afraid.

# 11

# ALAMO

## Forward gets you unstuck

This may be the primary purpose of
dogs: to You will not "get over" the
loss of a loved one; you will learn
to live with it. You will heal and you
will rebuild yourself around the loss
you have suffered. You will be whole
again but you will never be the same.
Nor should you be the same.

**ELISABETH KÜBLER-ROSS**

**IN 2018, TWO DAYS AFTER AFRICA** went to live with her puppy
raisers, I flew to Oregon in February to visit the GBD campus in
the aptly named Boring, Oregon—a small town outside of Portland.
While that part of the country doesn't typically have harsh winters,
there was so much snow that we weren't able to walk around outside
with the dogs nearly as much as we normally would. I remembered
my adventures in Boston and Iowa with Holland all those years ago
and felt thankful we didn't have to navigate icy sidewalks!

On February 12, I was introduced to a gentle and affectionate
black Labrador named Alamo, my first black Lab. We completed
the training and graduated on February 24--my birthday. What a
wonderful birthday present!

Alamo and Fantasia hit it off right away. Stitch, for her part, displayed her usual disdain for a new dog in the house, but within a few days she begrudgingly accepted Alamo and life got back to normal. Despite the fact that he weighs about sixty pounds, Alamo loves to jump in my lap (or even other people's laps—he's not picky) for cuddles and petting. He's a very affectionate dog and likes to be close to me. If he's in my office with me and I get up to walk into the kitchen, he calmly follows me.

This behavior isn't fear-driven like Meryl's had been. He just loves company and wants to be where I am.

Alamo handled travel fearlessly, which I appreciated because I was frequently on the road. I was traveling to speak, but also working for AIRA, which stood for Artificial Intelligence Remote Assistance. Back in 2015, right after Karen had been in the hospital, I received an email from a man named Larry Bock, the financial backer for AIRA.

In its first iteration, this product combined a cell phone app with Google Glass, which was a pair of glasses which included a video camera. (Google Glasses are no longer sold, for a number of reasons.) A blind person could don the Google Glasses and talk to a live operator on their phone. The operator could see what the Google Glass camera was recording in real time and describe it to the blind person over the phone.

Eventually, the product just became a phone app. However, recently another company, Envision, developed a relationship with Google and began providing the Google Glass Enterprise, as well as AIRA, support. I began using this new system in 2022 and still use it today.

The technology is incredibly useful—especially when navigating unfamiliar places like airports or a city you've never visited. An AIRA agent can read signs for you, tell you which gate you're at in an airport, tell you when your Lyft, Uber, or taxi is pulling up to the curb. It's a great tool. You can also use it with just your phone, since phones have built-in cameras. You could wear your phone on a lanyard around your neck and talk to the AIRA agent who would describe whatever is in front of you as you make your way through the world. AIRA and the Envision team have a technology that does much more than providing a travel tool. This technology can be used to read food labels, signs, and virtually any print. And there is even a way for an AIRA agent to be connected with a person's computer to assist in reading and handling inaccessible materials.

At the beginning, Larry Bock and Suman Kanuganti, who developed the product together, had their office in San Diego and told me they wanted my help in making the world more aware of their new product. So I met with them and agreed to help them on a volunteer basis.

Early in 2016 I took Suman to the NFB headquarters in Baltimore and showed the product to the new NFB president, Mark Riccobono. That led to AIRA coming to the national convention in 2016, again accompanied by Alamo and me. After a lot of conversations and questions from skeptical blind people, they began to take orders for AIRA at the convention.

In 2017, AIRA hired me. For a while I was in sales, then I helped them start the Do More Foundation, which was a nonprofit focused on getting AIRA to people who needed it but couldn't afford it.

I worked for them until October 2019. Having that technology, which I still use today, was a game changer. Yes, I still needed my dog to guide me, but since she can't read signs any better than I can, it's great to have a set of eyes that I can call up at a moment's notice.

I've never been afraid of traveling through airports, as there are literally helpful staff people every few feet, available to answer questions. Over the years I've become intimately familiar with many of them.

But having the AIRA technology available when needed helps me to be even more bold and courageous. It's especially helpful when navigating a strange city or shopping.

Using tools that help provide us with information can help us prepare and be aware, and therefore help us to be brave.

On one business trip, Alamo and I boarded a plane, and as I sometimes do, I signaled him to turn left as we boarded to say hello to the captain.

"Well, hello there," the captain said. "Who have we here?"

"This is Alamo, my guide dog."

"Oh hello, Alamo," he said. "Are you a good boy?"

I slipped off Alamo's harness so he could greet the pilot and copilot. They must have been quite enthusiastic in petting and fussing over him, because in a minute or two, Alamo jumped into the pilot's lap. We all laughed and one of the flight attendants even took a photo. Alamo seemed to understand that his job is not only to guide me but to be an ambassador for all guide dogs and make friends wherever he goes.

Alamo and I continued work for AIRA as well as traveling to speak and consult. Karen did our bookkeeping, and we really worked to pay down some credit card debt we'd accumulated. Paying that off really brought me peace of mind. My fears about money were being turned into courage. I realized that God had taken care of me all these years, and I could trust him.

My gig with AIRA and their foundation ended in 2019, when they had to cut costs with a round of layoffs. But I was able to continue speaking. Alamo and I traveled to Canada once in 2019 to speak at an event put on by several churches in British Columbia.

There was another milestone that year: Karen's longtime companion, Fantasia, passed away. As with our other senior dogs, Fantasia began really slowing down. She also developed a tumor on the left side of her mouth. The day came when she couldn't even stand easily and walk. We knew it was time. Karen was sad, but grateful for the memories of her wonderful dog. Tasia will always be missed. Like Roselle, she was one in a million.

Of course, Karen and I had each other. But now we had only one dog, Alamo, and one cat, Stitch. Stitch ran the whole house as a cat will. She even developed the habit of insisting on being petted and rubbed while she ate her food. (Or should I say, she trained me to pet her while she enjoyed her food? That might be more accurate.)

---

In March of 2020, I was invited to speak in New York City. With connecting flights, the trip took twelve hours, and Alamo handled it beautifully.

After my speaking commitment was finished, I was scheduled to fly home at 5:00 p.m. on March 6. But we were hearing news about a strange virus that had begun spreading around the world and had now hit New York City. Because Karen is immunocompromised, I was always vigilant about protecting her (and myself). I changed my flight to get home earlier. I escaped New York City at 7:30 a.m. on March 6, just in time as it turned out. I just wanted to get home. About a week later, New York City shut down completely.

And soon, so did the rest of the country. Suddenly, my speaking career hit the brakes. While there were some opportunities that switched to an online format, most of the people who had booked me as a speaker decided to postpone until we knew more. Of course, at the time, we wondered if this lockdown would last a month or two. Who knew that it would actually be two years, not two months, before life even started to get back to normal, and that our country was entering a time of almost unprecedented fear and confusion.

One thing that concerned me was how well Alamo would do during the pandemic. He would not get in nearly as much walking and travel. Even so, Alamo did not and has not forgotten any of his training. He is an extremely bright dog who has had the benefits of good training at GDB. I feel most blessed. Alamo, I think, came along at the exact right time.

In the years since 9/11, it seems we've become more fearful as a society. In part, that makes sense: school shootings and police violence feel like they're commonplace. The coronavirus pandemic took our fear to a new level—in part because we weren't sure what to be afraid of and what not to be. The level of trust in our society and each other plummeted. Fears and conspiracy theories abounded and spread like wildfire on social media. We are still dealing with the fall-out, and mistrust in the government and in one another still marks many of our interactions.

Many of these theories are not only false, but they are fear-based. But fear is a strong motivator, and so the lies proliferate.

During the pandemic, many people began working remotely. While there are advantages to that, it became difficult for some people to put boundaries on their work time. Like Meryl, they were always "on." They may have felt isolated and disconnected, yet still tethered electronically to their jobs. The boundaries between work and "not work" blurred significantly for many people. Their work was always right there at the kitchen table, so they couldn't disconnect. The anxiety that is often a part of our work permeated all, or most, of our time.

Because of Karen's health issues, we were careful during the pandemic—careful but not fearful. There's a difference: One is empowering, the other is debilitating. You can be wise and cautious without being fearful. Neither of us ever contracted Covid.

When I first felt called to write a book on overcoming and con-trolling fear, I had no idea that I'd write it during a global pandemic when so many people gave into fear and chose not to think calmly. A case study on responding to fear unfolded before us each week on the news: first reports of a deadly unknown virus in China, then news of people dying around the globe, then a growing number of cases and deaths in the United States. Soon, that fearful situation became even more fraught with political divisions.

Some people felt afraid of the virus, others were suspicious or downright afraid of the vaccines developed to battle the virus. Campaigns of misinformation meant to manipulate and play on people's fear made things worse.

This bled over into the political arena. Wearing a mask, or not, became not just a health issue, but a political one. The fearmongering became so intense—not just about the pandemic but about countless other issues, including the integrity of our elections, that things got to the point where people so distrusted the government and our democracy that some of them attacked the US Capitol in an effort to overturn the election. I believe at the heart of the political mistrust and anger, if we dig deep enough, is fear.

All of my dogs have at times felt fear—it's a normal human and canine emotion. But their training and temperament almost always enabled my dogs, including Alamo, to use their fear to help them avoid problems and figure out the best way forward. Fear can immobilize us, and in those moments when we feel stuck, we would do well to remember the most essential guide dog command: "Forward." Guide dogs know that fear is a gift—if we use it properly. It keeps us from engaging in risky behavior and enables us to flee or fight when threatened.

Fear keeps us from engaging in risky behavior and enables us to flee or fight when threatened. Fear of the virus actually protected people because it inspired them to wear masks, wash their hands, stay home when they felt sick, and get vaccinated. The pandemic frightened people at the beginning because it was caused by something that we can't even see or feel on our bodies until it's too late.

I found myself comparing the pandemic to another catastrophe: my experience in the World Trade Center years ago.

The events of 9/11 impacted those of us in the Tower in a different way than those who watched it unfold on their TV screens or read it in the newspaper. It caused fear for people around the world, but not in the same way. New Yorkers experienced it differently than people in say, Kansas.

However, the pandemic impacted everyone—no matter where they were in the world. Everyone suddenly had to face their own terror-filled experience. They needed a way to deal with their fear.

Being brave means embracing change and learning from it. Instead of complaining, we can reframe change as progress. We can move forward. Because of the pandemic, we have educated the world about disease prevention, we've learned about how vulnerable we are, and we've developed science to help us cope. We need to take control of the things we can and let go of the rest.

You can make fear a powerful positive tool in your life. You can use fear to heighten your senses, to become more aware of what's around you. You can use it to better prepare for unexpected situations. That preparation will help you develop a mindset that enables you to move forward despite your fear. To turn your fear into courage.

God allows us to choose how we deal with challenges. His power, light, and strength are available. Do we invoke the power of God to do the things that we need to do? Do we tap into the power that God gave us?

How do you deal with things like a family member's illness? Or an auto accident? Or maybe as your own health is declining later in life? Do you blame God? Do you cower in fear? I hope that as you've read this book, you've learned that when something unexpected happens, we can't blame God, other people, or even ourselves.

I decided to continue with my life, including attempting to spread humor when I could. I always loved to tease the TSA people when I went through airports. For example, I would get up to the security desk and the TSA agent would ask me, "May I have your ID, please?" My response, "Don't I look like me?" most always got a laugh.

In June 2021 I needed to go to the bank. Karen drove but stayed in the car. It was a short trip, so I left Alamo at home. I went in, masked as I chose to be whenever I went outside our home, and walked up to the teller as always. All the people at this branch knew me. The teller greeted me and then I said, "Don't you think it is interesting that nowadays someone can walk into a bank wearing a mask, walk up to the counter, and then (at this point I raised up my cane) say this is a stickup?" She burst out laughing. Word quickly spread around the bank, and the manager came up to me and said that none of them had had such a good laugh in quite a while. See how easy it is to lower fear and bring sanity, for a bit, back into the world?

―――――――

In late 2020, I heard about accessiBe, a company that helps other businesses make their websites accessible to people with a variety of disabilities, including blindness.

I've always been an advocate for accessibility. Having a wife who has spent her life in a wheelchair has provided all too many experiences with the obstacles and discrimination that persons with all types of disabilities encounter.

So accessiBe's software product, and company goals, intrigued me. With my technical background and my experience in sales, I considered joining their partner program, where you could sell accessiBe and earn a commission. It appealed to me because I could do it from the safety and comfort of my own home.

I spoke to the technical people and developers at the company, and I liked what I saw. But then I got a call from the owner of the company.

"Michael, my name is Shir Ekerling. I'm the president of accessiBe. I understand you're interested in our partner program."

"Yes, it seems like a great opportunity for someone like me, because I have a background in selling technology."

"We've heard of you, and we're excited that you want to work with us, but we don't want you to be a partner. We want you to join the company."

"Really? I didn't know that was an option. What role do you think I could fill in your company?"

"We're thinking about creating a position that would focus on educating people about what we do. You'd interface with our customers, but also educate the public and us internally about accessibility for people with disabilities. You'd help people understand how our product enhances website access not just for blind people but for persons with disabilities."

"Mr. Ekerling, I'm flattered by your offer. I'd like to talk to my wife about it. Can I get back to you in a day or two?"

I took a day to think, pray, and talk to Karen about it. I did my due diligence and paid attention to my instincts and imagination, which I believe is how God guides us. We decided to move forward. I called him the next morning.

"Mr. Ekerling, I accept. Let's create the position. I propose the title of chief vision officer with an appropriate salary."

———

In January 2021, the position and title were mine. I tried to stay open, curious, and ready to learn as much as I could. Because the pandemic was still going strong, I felt that a job I could do from home was truly a sign of God's protection and provision.

I joined with a lot of confidence. But early on, I started getting a lot of pushback from people outside of the company. They would question the technology's effectiveness, or even accuse the company of lying about what it does.

This negativity came from a small group of people—people who are afraid of something different that had come along that can enhance what they do, make life better for blind people by doing a scalable process of making websites accessible. The most adamant critics are manual coders who say the only way to make a website accessible is to insert manual code and charge thousands of dollars to do it. And when these programmers say it doesn't work, it's because they are afraid. They're afraid this new technology will replace manual coders. Also, there are those who are afraid of the concept of artificial intelligence. Sound familiar?

But I'd been dealing with people's fear-based resistance to technology for years—from the time I sold CAD systems, to blind people's resistance to tools like AIRA. As Karen had reminded me years ago,

I knew how to sell by turning perceived liabilities into assets. I knew all those experiences made me the right person for this job.

One of my responsibilities at accessiBe was hosting a weekly podcast called "Unstoppable Mindset: Where Inclusion, Diversity, and the Unexpected Meet." I love it, and I get to interview all kinds of fascinating people. I believe I absolutely made the right decision. Hosting a podcast each week feels like a smart next step on my journey as a speaker. The podcast has become so popular that in August of last year we began producing two episodes a week.

On the podcast, I interview a variety of people—some with disabilities, many without. They all demonstrate an unstoppable mindset in one way or another. In most cases, my guests have faced adversity or challenge, and have prevailed against it. In other words, they have experienced fear, and yet they have not let their fear blind them.

As we put the finishing touches on this book, I had the opportunity to test my courage in a way that I would not have chosen nor one I expected.

In July 2022, Karen developed a wound from a pressure sore—an unfortunately common risk for wheelchair-bound folks. Josie Reynoso, one of her caregivers, noticed it and suggested Karen go to the doctor. Karen thought it would heal up on its own.

Of course, it didn't. One morning, Karen complained of having the chills. I called 911 and the EMTs came and checked her out.

She was running a low-grade fever. "If you start feeling worse, you should probably go to the hospital," they said.

The wound became infected, and eventually went all the way down to her hip bone. At the end of July, two weeks after I first called 911, she was feeling worse and went into the hospital. They put her on antibiotics and treated the wound, but she was there for about a month.

When she returned home on August 28, she was quite weak, and she had little appetite. I remember meals where she'd have one

**Fear is a gift—if we use it properly.**

bite of steak, or a few sips of soup, then say she wasn't hungry. The wound began to heal, but other issues arose, causing her much pain and fatigue.

Karen had to stop her monthly infusions for rheumatoid arthritis, treatments that relieved pain by suppressing her immune system. RA causes the immune system to kick into overdrive, so that the body is fighting itself, so to speak. But she needed her immune system to fight the infected wound. So as her medical treatment was adjusted to try to heal the pressure sore wound, her level of pain and discomfort rose substantially. Through September and October, she spent most of her time in bed, not moving much and not eating a great deal. In fact, she ate less and less as the days went by.

One day, Josie was sitting at Karen's bedside, trying to entice her to eat some soup. I stood in the hallway, listening to their conversation.

"I'm just not hungry," Karen said. "I'm just so tired. Josie, am I dying?"

"Karen, we're going to do everything we can to help you to get better," Josie said. "Can I get you something else to eat if you don't want soup? It will make you stronger."

"No, thank you. I think I'll just rest for a while."

I walked into the living room and sat on the sofa. For nearly forty years, Karen and I had been a team. She's in a wheelchair; I'm blind. I'm her legs; she's my eyes. *God, we need each other*, I prayed. *I'm worried that she's giving up. I don't know how to help her. I need you, God. Show me how to move forward.*

I'd often sit with Karen and talk with her. Of course, Alamo would come with me. We had a hospital bed at home, and it was too high for Alamo to jump on, but he would come and nose Karen's arm or shoulder, as if to say, "Hey there, are you doing alright? Need anything?" She'd reach over and pet him, and it seemed to comfort both of them.

While Alamo typically followed me around, if I left Karen's room, he'd often linger, lying beside her bed as if keeping watch. He knew she was struggling, and I think he just offered the gift of his presence—which Karen appreciated. Still, I could see her slipping away.

"Mike," she said one evening. "I don't know whether I'm going to . . . live or not."

I swallowed hard. My chest felt tight, my throat constricted. I didn't know either. I forced myself to take a deep breath, to pray. *God, give me the right words. Let me feel your strength and comfort, so that I can give it to Karen.*

"Sweetheart, you're going to do your best, and we're going to help you. You can do this. We'll get through it."

She just sighed. I felt afraid—it was almost like she was giving up. *I'm not ready to lose my life partner. I want her to fight this. Where is my feisty, funny, sarcastic Karen? What if she does die? How will I live alone? She handles so much of the details of our lives. She brings so much life and joy into our home. What will I do without her?*

While Karen grew weaker from August through October, I had the opportunity to relearn how to do more of the work to maintain the house, Karen, and myself without her active participation. There was a lot I'd taken for granted—things that just happened because Karen managed them.

Thankfully, we had Josie as well as Dolores Neria, who had been taking care of Karen for a while. And Jeannette, our housekeeper, who had been with us since we moved to Victorville, came in every week to clean and do laundry.

But clearly, I had to step in to accomplish tasks normally Karen or both of us would do together. I had to figure out how to handle our finances, which Karen had done most of. Josie began to help with that and with running my business—taking care of administrative details that Karen had once helped me with. I felt sad and overwhelmed, yet grateful to have Josie on my team.

In early November, Karen really hadn't improved. The first Sunday in November, we sat in our bedroom—she on the hospital bed, I on my bed. We listened to the audio version of *Fool's Paradise*, a Jesse Stone detective story by Robert B. Parker. We read the whole book, but Karen didn't say much. Stitch sat on her lap, and she absently petted her. I wondered if she even heard the story—I barely was able to pay attention myself.

*We've been through a lot, but I've never seen her like this. I love her so much, but I wish I could motivate her to fight this. I'm preparing for the worst, but I'm still scared. How does a person live alone?*

I remembered 2014, when Karen had been in that medically induced coma, and how she'd always been a survivor, a fighter. How she'd been an advocate for herself, for other people with disabilities. She'd built a business around providing travel opportunities for people who might not otherwise be able to travel. Alamo lay on the floor between the beds—he seemed to know his presence was the best thing he could give both of us at that moment.

———

"Good morning, Mike," Josie called as she came into the house the next morning. "How's our girl?"

"I'm worried about her, Josie," I said. "She won't eat; she's very lethargic."

Josie walked into the bedroom.

"Karen, how are you?" she asked.

"Okay, I guess," Karen said, her voice weak and raspy.

Josie didn't mince words. Karen was obviously unwell, and Josie knew she had to take action.

"Well, you don't look very good. You're going to the hospital," Josie told her. "Mike, call 911. Karen needs to see a doctor."

The ambulance transported her to St. Mary's Hospital. Josie and I drove there and got her admitted.

Once again, I found myself sitting beside my wife in a hospital, praying for her. Alamo and I would talk to her, but after a couple of days, she really didn't talk. She would nod her head if I asked a question, but that was about it.

I was at home on Friday afternoon when the doctor called.

"I just wanted to let you know that we've put Karen on life support," he said. "She's on a ventilator and is receiving medication intravenously. We're doing all we can."

I sat down, and Alamo immediately came to my side, nosing my hand. "Is she going to make it?" I asked.

"We're doing all we can," he repeated. "We'll keep you apprised."

I ended the call and sat there, stroking Alamo's ears. I let the tears fall. "I'm afraid I'm going to lose her, Alamo," I said. Stitch came up and sat in my lap, requesting petting, offering comfort in her own way. Memories of the last forty years with Karen flooded over me—from our trips when she ran the travel agency to 9/11 to our ordinary routines, like ordering Jersey Mike's sandwiches for lunch every Tuesday. And the dogs—all the dogs that had been part of our family through the years. I remembered Karen walking both Roselle and Fantasia in her power wheelchair at the same time, racing along the sidewalk. I remembered Fantasia climbing onto Karen's hospital bed to offer a solace that only a dog can.

That evening, the ICU nurse called.

"Mr. Hingson, you really should come over to the hospital. She's not going to be able to stay on life support for long."

I was silent for a moment, processing this. Even though I'd been watching her decline, my throat felt tight, and I fought back tears. *God, really? You're going to take her from me? I'm not ready to lose her. I need more time, just a little more time. She's my life. She's my world.*

I swallowed and forced myself to answer the ICU nurse.

"I know her sister will want to be there to say goodbye," I told her. "Is it possible to keep her on life support until tomorrow?"

"Yes," she said. "That's a good idea."

I called Vicki to give her the latest update, and she said that she and John would meet us at the hospital at 10:00 a.m. the next day. I called Tracy, Vicki's daughter, and also gave her the news. She said that she and her husband, Charlie, would also come.

The next morning our housekeeper Jeannette drove us to the hospital. She and I walked through the hospital with Alamo by my side to Karen's room, an odd sense of déjà vu enveloping me. We arrived in Karen's room and I stood by her bedside.

I touched the bed. "Where's her hand?"

"She's got it on her chest," Vicki said. I reached across and gently took Karen's hand, which was completely limp. I could feel an IV taped to it, so I held it very gently.

"I'm here, Karen," I said. But then I couldn't say more. This time, the story was going to be different.

The doctor walked in. "I'm so sorry," he said. "We did all we could. But here's the situation. A person cannot stay on life support indefinitely. If we take her off life support, she will pass. If we don't, she'll be here for a few days and then pass."

I swallowed hard, sitting with one hand on Alamo's head, the other holding my wife's hand. Jeannette put her hand on my shoulder, attempting to comfort me, I suppose. But I didn't feel comforted. I felt exhausted and sad. I needed another voice in the conversation. My brother-in-law, Gary.

"Vicki, have you talked to Gary?" I asked.

"Yes, I spoke with him last night," she said. Because he lives in Idaho, he couldn't be there with us.

"I'd like to talk to him," I said. Vicki dialed her brother's number and handed me the phone.

I filled him in on the latest details, the decision we were facing.

"You know," Gary said, "she's probably already made the transition. So I agree that it would be best to let her go."

I'd never thought of it that way—that Karen's body was being kept alive, but perhaps her soul had already moved on. And that's what this was: not an ending, but a transition. *God, thank you for Gary. Thank you for speaking through him, giving him those words that are helping me to let go. To trust you.*

After I hung up, I handed Vicki her phone. "Vicki, you know, well, what do you think?"

"Well, I think so," she said. Neither of us could speak directly, but we understood what we were deciding. It was the right thing, but it was unfathomable.

At 11:25 a.m., they stopped the meds. The doctors kept her on a ventilator because they said they didn't want her to suffer or for us to see her suffer, which she would have. We listened as Karen's heartbeat gradually slowed.

I sat beside her, holding her hand. "Karen, I love you. Alamo and I are right here, and we're going to be okay. It's okay to let go—I will miss you so much but I'm going to keep moving forward, I promise." Tears rolled down my cheeks. Alamo sat up and pressed his body against my leg, as if he were trying to hold me up.

At about 12:15 p.m., Karen's heart stopped beating. Fifteen days before we would have celebrated our fortieth wedding anniversary, I said goodbye to my best friend.

Despite my "preparation" for losing Karen, it is difficult to actually face the fact that I am now alone. Some days, in that space between sleeping and waking, I roll over and reach for the other side of the bed. It's only when I find it empty that I remember, and it hits me afresh: She's really gone.

I think this would be true for anyone who loses someone who has been a part of a life team for so long, but that doesn't make it any easier. How do I go on? How do I take over handling all the financial and other aspects of our business that Karen did so well? How do I live alone?

When someone dies, people often talk about the need to grieve, and then move on. But I don't ever say I'm going to move on without Karen. Rather, the question is, how are we going to move forward? It's not moving on because I don't ever want to forget Karen. It's moving forward.

I haven't lost Karen. She's in a different place. She didn't desert me—although there's moments when I feel the emptiness without her. Her body didn't keep up with her spirit. Her body wasn't able to continue. That's okay. But I know that she is around. And I love to tell people that if I don't behave, I'm going to hear about it. So that helps keep me on the straight and narrow. I feel her presence, I know she's there, every day.

So, fear? Yes. There would be something amiss if I did not experience fear in this tragedy. But the fear need not be blinding. When grief threatens to turn into fear, I remind myself that I have forty years of team knowledge I can apply to help me move forward. I have lessons from the joys and the challenging times to help me go on. I have Alamo and Stitch to guide and comfort me.

Most of all, I simply have forty years of memories of a life with Karen. Bottom line: I choose not to allow fear, depression, and the unknown to overwhelm me. And that is what this whole book is about. For me, writing this book is personal and I hope what Keri Wyatt Kent and I have offered you will teach you not to live by fear, but by faith, trust, and by confidence.

I want to share with you one final item that is helping me move forward after a life with Karen. I published the following on Facebook, my personal blog at www.michaelhingson.com, and on some lists right after Karen passed. It sums up my feelings about Karen and it demonstrates how I choose to deal with whatever comes from now on.

In April 1972 I attended my first meeting of the Orange County chapter of the National Federation of the Blind. It was an adventure, and I chose to explore this new and different world. Through the federation I have been involved in many adventures and am certain there will be more.

In 1976 I began an 18-month assignment from the president of the National Federation of the Blind, Dr. Kenneth Jernigan, to help Dr. Ray Kurzweil bring his dream of a reading machine for blind people to fruition.

I think my greatest adventure was not, however, directly related to the NFB. Oh, a Federationist started me down an unexpected road when, in January of 1982, he introduced me to a woman, Karen Ashurst. Little did I know that day what would happen. Suffice it to say that Karen and I were married on November 27, 1982.

Karen and I began to share not only NFB adventures but many others as well. Probably many of you are familiar with what must be the most significant one, when I escaped from Tower One of the World Trade Center on September 11, 2001. In 2011, *Thunder Dog: The Story of a Blind Man, His Guide Dog and the Triumph of Trust* was published. Some of you did not know Karen directly, but if you read *Thunder Dog*, you did get to meet and know her.

Yesterday, November 12, 2022, just 15 days before we would have celebrated our 40th wedding anniversary, Karen passed away. Her passing was somewhat expected, but not so soon. She discovered a wound, probably from a pressure sore, in late July. Yes, a pressure sore as Karen is a paraplegic and has been in a wheelchair her entire life. As I love to say, she reads, and I push. Anyway, the sore eventually required her to go to the hospital.

She returned home on August 28 with a healing wound, but with an extremely diminished appetite and a great deal of pain. Karen has suffered from Rheumatoid Arthritis since January of 2017. She has been receiving infusions of medications to diminish the RA, but those infusions seriously lower her immune system. She had to stop the infusions in August while in the hospital. This was because lowering her immune system further could result in more wound infections. The other side of the coin is that it caused Karen excruciating pain. Over the past three months the pain took its toll as her appetite diminished and she couldn't even swallow much food.

This past Monday, we put her back in the hospital. Over this week her strength and stamina dropped precipitously. Yesterday, at the suggestion of her doctors with agreement from Karen's sister, a retired CCU and ICU nurse, we stopped life support.

I write this long message as I know many of you had some contact and knowledge of Karen. I want everyone to know fully about her, what happened to her and what happens now. I intend to continue to be active where I can. I will not stop moving forward as that would be an insult to Karen and all our 40-year marriage meant to both of us. I will continue to travel and speak. I will continue my work with accessiBe. I will work as I can to support the NFB. Most of all, I will have and treasure 40 years of memories with Karen. Life goes on and it is what I intend to do as well.

God bless you, Karen. You always are and will be at the forefront of my mind and heart. You will always be my guiding light and shining star. For all of us here on Earth, let's continue to move forward and grow until the entire world understands and believes that "disability" does not mean inability, but rather such is just a characteristic.

Thanks for reading. If you knew Karen and are saddened by this message, don't be. Instead renew your conviction for equality for all of us. I know Karen today is, as the founder of the National Federation of the Blind, Dr. Jacobus tenBroek, would say, 'Within the grace of God.'

Best Regards,
Michael Hingson

---

The first and most important command a guide dog learns is "Forward." The dog steps forward first, on command, and the handler walks beside him. Often, the way to turn your fear into courage is to simply go forward. Prepare as best you can, let God guide you, trust your instincts, and just keep moving through the challenges.

What does it mean to be brave? At the heart of it, I believe it is a decision: to acknowledge and feel fear, but then use your fear to fuel right action.

Since the age of fourteen, I've walked through my life with eight different guide dogs. Each of them has taught me something about being brave and controlling fear. You've met my dogs in these pages and seen how they taught me to overcome fear and live my best life, as well as helping them to live their best lives too.

Whether you have a dog or not, I hope that some of the tools we've explored in this book will help you to be brave and confident, even in situations where you feel afraid.

As I said, I am not moving on after Karen's death; I am moving forward.

I hope my stories of teamwork remind you to seek out friendships and relationships that inspire you to be brave. Your friends, family, and spouse—they need you, and you need them.

In addition to relationships with other people, we can also find courage by connecting with God. Now that Karen is not here physically, I lean on God more than ever, if such is possible. God invites us to let go of fear and walk by faith—to be ever increasingly aware of God, who is in you and with you and able to guide you and give you strength. Cultivating mindful awareness of God is, in my opinion, the most effective way to avoid being blinded by fear.

How do you get to that inner sanctuary? That's what I did as I walked down the stairs in the World Trade Center. And that's what I do regularly. I take time at the end of each day to cultivate mindfulness by stopping and thinking about my day—what went well and what I could have done better, how I'm feeling, and where I was aware of God. This simple practice may not even be related to a fear you are facing, but it strengthens your mind and soul, and that helps you to connect with the light within you. In other words, to be brave.

## Guidance from the Word

*The righteous cry out, and the LORD hears them;*
*he delivers them from all their troubles.*
*The LORD is close to the brokenhearted*
*and saves those who are crushed in spirit.*

**PSALM 34:17-18**

## Prayer for Courage

God, grant me the serenity to accept the things
I cannot change,
the courage to change the things I can,
and the wisdom to know the difference.

# EPILOGUE

**WE ALL ARE CONSTANTLY BOMBARDED** by phrases like "Change is all around us" or "We have to get back to normal" and "But for the grace of God . . ." If change is all around us and we are constantly experiencing it, why do we hate it so much and complain about it? What is "normal" anyway, and if we get back to normal then what happened to change? And embracing the mindset of "but for the grace of God" tends to separate us from almost anything we find unacceptably different. "Within the grace of God" is more appropriate, I think, and is explained well in the appendix included in this book. In *Live like a Guide Dog*, I hope you have seen that not only is change all around us, but we can be and are part of that change. When we adopt a more positive attitude, we move forward and grow.

Speaking of moving forward, as the pandemic subsides, my travel and speaking engagements have picked up again. Now, in addition to the other things I have talked about for the past twenty-one-and-a-half years, I speak on controlling fear and moving forward. If my life with Karen, and in fact, if my whole life means anything, it is that growing and moving forward are parts of my psyche. I don't just "move forward" without a reason, but moving forward and learning not to be afraid of that is to me, and now I hope for you, important.

With Karen's passing I have realized I can either wallow in sadness or I can continue to live. I choose the latter. Talk about change: It is now just me, Alamo, and Stitch in the house. Lonely? Sure, but I know Karen would not want me to be constantly sad and unhappy. So, I am choosing to be active mentally and physically.

Karen's caregivers, Josie and Dolores, now help me, especially Josie, who assists me with paperwork, reaching out to speakers' bureaus, crafting speaking proposals, and even making sure Stitch is happy. If you need a speaker and want to talk to me about speaking at an event, please email speaker@michaelhingson.com. I'd love to hear from you.

AccessiBe keeps me quite busy too. In fact, in August 2023, at the end of last summer, Alamo and I made our first and very productive trip to accessiBe's offices in Israel. Alamo traveled like a trouper, and as usual, he was the hit of the trip. AccessiBe's and my Unstoppable Mindset podcast now is released two times a week, which helps keep me busy.

In addition to speaking, I also am beginning to write more. Please keep an eye on my blog at www.michaelhingson.com to see what I create.

I firmly believe God has opened doors for me to enter. My job is to love the adventure and go through the doors. I hope you will come along.

# The Courtesy Rules of Blindness

**WHEN YOU MEET ME,** don't be ill at ease. It will help both of us if you remember these simple points of courtesy:

1. I'm an ordinary person, who happens to be blind. You can talk to me as you would anyone else—no need to raise your voice. If you have a question, please address me directly rather than asking my companion.
2. I may use a long white cane or a guide dog to walk independently. If I use a guide dog, please don't pet, feed, or play with my dog without my permission. If I'm in an unfamiliar place, I may ask you for directions or assistance. Please don't grab my arm, my cane, or my dog. If I need to and if you don't mind, I'll ask to take your arm just above the elbow and keep a half step behind to anticipate curbs and steps.
3. When I am in a room, I like to know who else is there. Please speak or introduce yourself when you enter.
4. Please keep in mind that a door left partially open, particularly to an overhead cabinet or a car, is a potential hazard to me.
5. I do not have trouble with ordinary table skills. At meals, I can serve myself and pass items to other diners, so please

don't reach over or past me. Just let me know what's being offered and I'll take it from there.

6. There is no need to avoid words like "see" or "look." I use them too—for example, I watch television.

7. Blindness is just the loss of sight. My sense of smell, touch, and/or hearing did not improve when I became blind. I simply rely on them more than you might and, therefore, may gather more information through those senses than you do.

8. If I'm your houseguest, there is no need to be extra attentive or to move any furniture; I'll use my cane and other senses to find things or I will ask for your help.

9. I'll discuss blindness with you if you're curious, but feel free to talk to me about anything that interests you. I have as many other interests as you do.

In all 50 states, the law requires drivers to yield the right of way when they see my extended white cane or guide dog. Only the blind may legally carry white canes. Normally I can hear the sound of traffic and will behave like any other pedestrian. If you drive a hybrid or electric vehicle, I may not hear your car approach, so exercise caution and use the horn if needed. You see more blind persons today walking alone, not because there are more of us, but because we have learned to make our own way.

# Within the Grace of God

*The following are excerpts from a speech given on July 1, 1956, by Professor Jacobus tenBroek, then-president of the National Federation of the Blind at their annual convention. Although there has been progress on the issues Dr. tenBroek addressed nearly seventy years ago, there is still a lot of work to be done within the sighted community to change how the blind are perceived and accepted in society. He begins by lauding the efforts of the NFB since its founding in 1940.*

**[WE ARE] AN ORGANIZATION** with purposes as irrepressible as the aspiration of men to be free, with far-flung activities and accomplishments, with the solid adherence and participation of rank-and-file members, and with the selfless devotion of an ever-increasing array of able and distinguished leaders.

We have seen the action and the forces of action. We have also seen the reaction and the forces of reaction. There is perhaps no stronger testimony to our developing prestige and influence as the nationwide movement and organization of the blind than the scope and intensity of the attacks upon us. These attacks are not new. They have persisted from the very beginning. They have ranged from unspeakable, whispering campaigns against the character and integrity of the leaders of the Federation to public disparagement of its goals and structure. Now, however, the attacks have taken on a new bitterness and violence.

Whence come these attacks? What is the motivation behind them? Are they personal? Are they institutional? Are they based on policy differences as to ends as well as to means? What is the pattern of action and reaction for the future? Is such conflict unavoidable? To what degree is reconciliation possible?

It is to an analysis of these problems and to an answer to these questions that I should like to direct your attention tonight.

Let me begin by giving you a purely hypothetical and very fanciful situation. Imagine that somewhere in the world there exists a civilization in which the people without hair—the bald—are looked down upon and rigidly set apart from everyone else by virtue of their distinguishing physical characteristic.

If you can accept this fantasy for a moment, it is clear that at least two kinds of organization would come into being dedicated to serve the interests of these unfortunate folk. First, I suggest, there would appear a group of non-bald persons drawn together out of sympathy for the sorry condition of this rejected minority: in short, a benevolent society with a charitable purpose and a protective role.

At first, all of the members of this society would be volunteers, doing the work on their free time and out of the goodness of their hearts. Later, paid employees would be added who would earn their livelihood out of the work, and who would gradually assume a position of dominance.

This society would, I believe, have the field pretty much to itself for a rather long time. In the course of years, it would virtually eliminate cruel and unusual punishment of the bald, furnish them many services and finally create enclaves and retreats within which the hairless might escape embarrassing contact with normal society and even find a measure of satisfaction and spiritual reward in the performance of simple tasks not seriously competitive with the ordinary pursuits of the larger community.

The consequence of this good work would, I venture to say, be a regular flow of contributions by the community, an acceptance by the community of the charitable foundation as the authentic interpreter of the needs of those unfortunate and inarticulate souls afflicted with baldness, an increasing veneration for the charitable foundation, and a general endorsement of its principles, and—gradually but irresistibly—the growth of a humanitarian awareness that the bald suffer their condition through no fault of their own and accordingly that they should be sponsored, protected, tolerated, and permitted to practice, under suitable supervision and control, what few uncomplicated trades patient training may reveal them able to perform.

Eventually, a great number of charitable organizations would be established in the field of work for the bald. They or some of them would join together in a common association which might well be entitled the American Association of Workers for the Bald. Step by step, upon the published "Proceedings" of their annual meetings, carefully edited to eliminate the views of the outspoken bald, they would aspire to climb to professional status. As a part of their self-assigned roles as interpreters and protectors of the bald, they or some of them, would sooner or later undertake to lay down "criteria" and "standards" for all service programs for the bald to be "a manual of guidance for those responsible for operating the programs. . . ."

These, then, would be the assumptions and the ends to which the charitable organizations for the bald would tirelessly and success-fully exert themselves. They would petition the community through both public and private enterprise to support these purposes, and their appeals would dramatize them through a subtle invocation of the sympathetic and compassionate traits of human nature. Sooner or later, some of them, in order to drive competitors out of business, garner favor with the public and to give color of legitimacy to their own methods would issue what they would unabashedly call a code of fundraising ethics.

All this presumably would take much time; but before too many generations had passed I expect that most if not all of these objectives would have come to fruition, and there would appear to be an end to the problem of the bald.

Unfortunately, however, there seem always to be those who persist in questioning established institutions and revered traditions; and in my improbable fable, at some point well along in the story, there would appear a small band of irascible individuals—a little group of willful men—bent on exposing and tearing down the whole laborious and impressive structure of humanitarianism and progress. Incredibly and ironically, these malcontents would emerge from the very ranks of the bald themselves.

At first I suspect that they would pass unheard and almost unnoticed; but eventually their numbers would increase and their dissent become too insistent to be easily ignored. What they would be saying, as I make it out, is something like this:

"You have said that we are different because we are bald, and that this difference marks us as inferior. But we do not agree with certain Biblical parables that possession of hair is an index of strength, certainly not that it is a measure either of virtue or of ability. Owing to your prejudice and perhaps your guilt—because you do not like to look upon us—you have barred us from the normal affairs of the community and shunted us aside as if we were pariahs.

But we carry no contagion and present no danger, except as you define our condition as unclean and make of our physical defect a stigma. In your misguided benevolence you have taken us off the streets and provided shelters where we might avoid the pitiless gaze of the non-bald and the embarrassment of their contact. But what we wish chiefly is to be back on the streets, with access to all the avenues of ordinary commerce and activity. We do not want your pity, since there need be no occasion for it; and it is not we who suffer embarrassment in company with those whom we deem our fellows and our equals. You have been kind to us, and if we were animals we should perhaps be content with that; but our road to hell has been paved with your good intentions."

One of the leaders of the bald doubtless would rise to say: "We do not want compassion, we want understanding; we do not want tolerance, we want acceptance; we do not want charity, we want opportunity; we do not want dependency, we want independence. You have given us much, but you have withheld more; you have withheld those values which we prize above all else, exactly as you do: personal liberty, dignity, privacy, opportunity, and—most of all—equality. But if it is not in your power, or consistent with your premises, to see these things as our goals, be assured that it is within our power and consistent with our self-knowledge to demand them and to press for their attainment. For we know by hard experience what you do not know, or have not wished to recognize: that given the opportunity we are your equals; that as a group we are no better and no worse than you—being in fact a random sample of yourselves. We are your doubles, whether the yardstick be intellectual or physical or psychological or occupational.

"Our goals, in short, are these: we wish to be liberated, not out of society but into it; we covet independence, not in order to be distinct but in order to be equal. We are aware that these goals, like the humane objectives you have labored so long to accomplish, will require much time and effort and wisdom to bring into being. But the painful truth must be proclaimed that your purposes are not our purposes; we do not share your cherished assumptions of the nature of baldness and will not endure the handicap you have placed upon it.

"And so we have formed our own organization, in order to speak for ourselves from the experience which we alone have known and can interpret. We bear no malice and seek no special favors, beyond the right and opportunity to join society as equal partners and members in good standing of the great enterprise that is our nation and our common cause."

End of fable. Is this fable simply a fanciful story or is it a parable? Some will say, I have no doubt, that I have not presented the case of the blind—that there is no parallel and therefore no parable. For one thing, is it not surely ridiculous to imagine that any civilized society could so baldly misinterpret the character of those who are not blessed with hair on their heads? It may be! But civilized society has always so misinterpreted the character of those who lack sight in their eyes; and on a basis of that misinterpretation has created the handicap of blindness. You and I know that blind people are simply people who cannot see; society believes that they are people shorn of the capacity to live normal, useful, productive lives and that belief has largely tended to make them so.

For another thing, did the fable accurately portray the attitudes of at least some of the agencies for the blind? Are their goals really so different from the goals of the blind themselves? Do they actually arrogate to themselves the roles of interpreter and protector, ascribing to their clients characteristics of abnormality and dependency? To answer these questions and to demonstrate the bona fides of the parable, I shall let some agency leaders speak for themselves in the form of seven recent quotations:

Quotation number one uttered by an agency psychiatrist: "All visible deformities require special study. Blindness is a visible deformity and all blind persons follow a pattern of dependency." That one hardly requires any elucidation to make its meaning plain.

Quotation number two uttered by the author of a well-known volume upon the blind for which the American Association of Workers for the Blind conferred upon him a well-known award: "With many persons, there was an expectation in the establishment of the early schools . . . that the blind in general would thereby be rendered capable of earning their own support—a view that even at the present is shared in some quarters. It would have been much better if such a hope had never been entertained, or if it had existed in a greatly modified form. A limited acquaintance of a practical nature with the blind as a whole and their capabilities has usually been sufficient to demonstrate the weakness of this conception." That one also speaks adequately for itself.

Quotation number three uttered by a well-known blind agency

head: "After he is once trained and placed, the average disabled person can fend for himself. In the case of the blind, it has been found necessary to set up a special state service agency which will supply them not only rehabilitation training but other services for the rest of their lives." The agencies "keep in constant contact with them as long as they live." So the blind are unique among the handicapped in that, no matter how well-adjusted, trained and placed, they require lifelong supervision by the agencies.

Quotation number four uttered by another well-known blind agency head: "The operation of the vending stand program, we feel, necessitates maintaining a close control by the Federal Government through the licensing agency with respect to both equipment and stock, as well as the actual supervision of the operation of each individual stand. It is therefore our belief that the program would fail if the blind stand managers were permitted to operate without control." This is, of course, just the specific application of the general doctrine of the incompetence of the blind expressed in the previous quotation. Blind businessmen are incapable of operating an independent business. The agencies must supervise and control the stock, equipment, and the business operation.

Quotation number five, first sentence of the Code of Ethics (so-called) of the American Association of Workers for the Blind: "The operations of all agencies for the blind entail a high degree of responsibility because of the element of public trusteeship and protection of the blind involved in services to the blind." The use of the word "protection" makes it plain that the trusteeship here referred to is of the same kind as that existing under the United Nations Trusteeship Council—that is, custody and control of underprivileged, backward, and dependent peoples.

Quotation number six uttered by still another well-known blind agency head: "To dance and sing, to play and act, to swim, bowl, and roller skate, to work creatively in clay, wood, aluminum or tin, to make dresses, to join in group readings or discussions, to have entertainments and parties, to engage in many other activities of one's choosing—this is to fill the life of anyone with the things that make life worth living." Are these the things that make life worth living for you? Only the benevolent keeper of an asylum could make this remark—only a person who views blindness as a tragedy which can be somewhat mitigated by little touches of kindness and service to help pass the idle hours but which cannot be overcome. Some of these things may be accessories to a life well filled with other things— a home, a job, and the rights and responsibilities of citizenship, for example.

Quotation number seven uttered by still another head of a blind agency: "A job, a home, and the right to be a citizen, will come to the blind in that generation when each and every blind person is a living advertisement of his ability and capacity to accept the privileges and responsibilities of citizenship. Then we professionals will have no problem of interpretation because the blind will no longer need us to speak for them, and we, like primitive segregation, will die away as an instrument which society will include only in its historical records." "A job, a home, and the right to be a citizen," are not now either the possessions or the rights of the blind—they will only come to the blind in a future generation! A generation, moreover, which will never come to the sighted since it is one in which "each and every blind person" will live up to some golden rule far beyond the human potential. In that never-to-be-expected age, the leaders of the agencies for the blind will no longer discharge their present function of "interpretation," because the blind will then be able to speak for themselves.

Whatever else can be said about these quotations, no one can say that these agency leaders lack candor. They have stated their views with the utmost explicitness.

Moreover, these are not isolated instances of a disappearing attitude, a vestigial remainder of a forgotten era. Such expressions are not confined to those here quoted. Many other statements of the same force and character could be produced; and the evidence that the deed has been suited to the word is abundant.

At long last, we now know that we must finally lay to rest the pious platitude and the hopeful conjecture that the blind themselves and the agencies for the blind are really all working towards the same objectives and differ only as to means for achieving them. I would that it were so. We are not in agreement as to objectives although we frequently disagree as to means as well.

The frankly avowed purposes and the practices of the agencies tend in the direction of continued segregation along vocational and other lines. The blind would move vigorously in the direction of increasing integration, of orienting, counseling, and training the blind towards competitive occupations and placing them therein, towards a job, a home, and normal community activities and relations. The agencies, by their words and their acts, tend to sanctify and reinforce those semi-conscious stereotypes and prejudicial attitudes which have always plagued the condition of the physically disabled and the socially deprived. We, by our words and acts, would weaken them and gradually blot them out altogether. Their statements assert and their operations presuppose a need for continuous, hovering surveillance of the sightless—in recreation, occupation, and congregation—virtually from cradle to grave. We deny that any such need exists and refute the premise of necessary dependency and incompetence on which it is based.

Their philosophy derives from and still reflects the philanthropic outlook and ethical uplift of those Friendly Visitors of a previous century whose self-appointed mission was to guide their less fortunate neighbors to personal salvation through a combination of material charity and moral edification. We believe that the problems of the blind are at least as much social as personal and that a broad frontal attack on public misconceptions and existing program arrangements for the blind is best calculated to achieve desirable results. We believe, moreover, that it is worthwhile inquiring into the rationale of any activity which takes as its psychological premise the double-barreled dogma that those deprived of sight are deprived also of judgment and common sense, and that therefore what they need above all else is to be adjusted to their inferior station through the wise ministrations of an elite corps of neurosis-free custodians.

The agency leaders say, and apparently believe, that the blind are not entitled to the privileges and responsibilities of citizenship or to full membership in society betokened by such attributes of normal life as a home and a job. This can only be predicated on the proposition that the blind are not only abnormal and inferior, but they are so abnormal and inferior that they are not even persons. We believe that blind people are precisely as normal as other people are, being in fact a cross-section of the rest of the community in every respect except that they cannot see. But were this not so, their abnormality would not strip them of their personality.

The Constitution of the United States declares that all persons born in the United States or naturalized are citizens. There is nothing in the Constitution or in the Gloss upon it which says that this section shall not apply to persons who are blind. If born in the United States or naturalized, whether before or after blindness, blind persons are citizens of the United States now and are now, not merely in some future generation, possessed of the right to be citizens and share the privileges, immunities, and responsibilities of that status. Moreover, the bounty of the Constitution extends to all persons, whether citizens or not, rights to freedom, equality, and individuality.

As citizens, then, or as persons, who happen to be deprived of one of their physical senses, we claim, under the broad protection of the Constitution, the right to life, personal freedom, personal security; the right to marry, have and rear children, and to maintain a home; and the right, so far as government can assure it, to that fair opportunity to earn a livelihood which will make these other rights possible and significant. We have the right freely to choose our fields of endeavor, unhindered by arbitrary, artificial or man-made impediments. All limitations on our opportunity, all restrictions on us based on irrelevant considerations of physical disability, are in conflict with our Constitutional right of equality and must be removed. Our access to the mainstreams of community life, the aspirations and achievements of each of us, are to be limited only by the skills, energy, talents, and abilities we individually bring to the opportunities equally open to all Americans.

Finally, we claim as our birthright, as our Constitutional guarantee and as an indivestible aspect of our nature the fundamental human right of self-expression, the right to speak for ourselves individually and collectively. Inseparably connected with this right is the right of common association. The principle of self-organization means self-guidance and self-control. To say that the blind can, should, and do lead the blind is only to say that they are their own counselors, that they stand on their own feet. In the control of their own lives, in the responsibility for their own programs, in the organized and consistent pursuit of objectives of their own choosing—in these alone lies the hope of the blind for economic independence, social integration, and emotional security.

What should the posture of the National Federation of the Blind be in the midst of these attacks and struggles. As the possessors of power, we must exercise it responsibly, impersonally, and with self-restraint. As a people's movement, we cannot allow others to deflect us from our course. We must apply our power and influence to achieve our legitimate goals. To this end, we must all exert ourselves to the utmost. Our opponents have history and outmoded concepts on their side. We have democracy and the future on ours.

For the sake of those who are now blind and those who hereafter will be blind—and for the sake of society at large—we cannot fail. If the National Federation of the Blind continues to be representative in its character, democratic in its procedures, open in its purposes, and loyal in its commitments—so long, that is, as the faith of the blind does not become blind faith—we have nothing to fear, no cause for apology and only achievement to look forward to. We may carry our program to the public with confidence and conviction—choosing the means of our expression with proper care but without calculation and appearing before the jury of all our peers not as salesmen but as spokesmen, not as hucksters but as petitioners for simple justice and the redress of unmerited grievances. We will have no need to substitute the advertisement for the article itself nor to prefer a dramatic act to an undramatic fact. If this is group pressure, it is group pressure in the right direction. If this involves playing politics, it is a game as old as democracy, with the stakes as high as human aspiration.

In the sixteenth century, John Bradford made a famous remark which has ever since been held up to us as a model of Christian humility and correct charity and which you saw reflected in the agency quotations I presented. Seeing a beggar in his rags creeping along a wall through a flash of lightning in a stormy night Bradford said, "But for the Grace of God, there go I."

Compassion was shown; pity was shown; charity was shown; humility was shown; there was even an acknowledgement that the relative positions of the two could and might have been switched. Yet despite the compassion, despite the pity, despite the charity, despite the humility, how insufferably arrogant!

There was still an unbridgeable gulf between Bradford and the beggar. They were not one but two. Whatever might have been, Bradford thought himself Bradford and the beggar a beggar—one high, the other low; one wise, the other misguided; one strong, the other weak; one virtuous, the other depraved.

We do not and cannot take the Bradford approach. It is not just that beggary is the badge of our past and is still all too often the present symbol of social attitudes towards us; although that is at least part of it. But in the broader sense, we are that beggar, and he is each of us. We are made in the same image and out of the same ingredients. We have the same weaknesses and strengths, the same feelings, emotions, and drives; and we are the product of the same social, economic, and other environmental forces. How much more consonant with the facts of individual and social life, how much more a part of a true humanity, to say instead: "There, within the Grace of God, do go I."

Me and Squire, both teenagers.

# PHOTO
# GALLERY

Enjoy some moments from my life over the years, and the dogs who have been my companions along the way.

HINGSON AND SQUIRE
Two friends take one of many walks together

## Palmdale youth completes school, gains guide dog

There will have been two important graduations in young Michael Hingson's life this year. Last month he was graduated from Sage School in Palmdale and this month from Guide Dogs for the Blind, Inc. in San Rafael, Calif. His diploma this month is in the form of a beautiful Golden retriever Guide Dog named Squire.

## Thorngate enters UCB guitar class

Warren Thorngate, 540 West Ave. J-9, will attend Andrea

The class of 11 students were formally presented their guide dogs on July 18 by the 4-H youngsters who raised them.

Michael, who lives with his parents at 38710 Stanridge Ave., Palmdale, was 14 on Feb. 24, and will enter his freshman year at Palmdale High in September. His older brother, Ellery, 16, will be a junior at the same school.

Blindness has never been a hindrance to this bright energetic young man. He has many interests, chief of which is short wave radio and electronics. He and his father, G. D. Hingson, have a receiver and two walkie-

Squire to his friends at home and said he is sure it will be far easier to go places now. He takes exceptional pride in care of Squire and grooms him meticulously every day.

Michael reads Grade 2 Braille but said he will probably need volunteer readers in high school this fall, as there aren't Braille books available in all of his subjects.

Guide Dogs for the Blind, Inc. is a non - profit school dedicated to providing guide dogs and four weeks training to deserving blind men and women throughout the 34 western states and Canada at no cost to them. The school is supported entirely by private contributions.

GOOD EATING
Double - corn sticks ma

Me and Squire making our media debut in the local paper.

Me and Klondike sitting with a Klondike admirer.

Roselle and Linnie playing tug-of-war.

Me and Karen, Christmas 1996.

Karen with Panama.

Roselle as a puppy.

With Roselle at Windows on the World restaurant in the World Trade Center.

Crossing a busy street with Roselle.

*Photo taken by Guide Dogs for the Blind in 2002.*

A sweet moment of connection
between Roselle and me.

Roselle wearing one of her many medals
for heroism.

Me and Roselle meeting Prime Minister Helen Clark
of New Zealand on a trip benefiting the Royal New
Zealand Foundation of the Blind and the local guide
dog school.

With Meryl and Roselle.

Africa was a hit with everyone when we visited schools!

Me and Africa.

Fantasia just after being pampered by her groomer—including getting a new scarf.

Me and Alamo making friends at
Edwards Air Force Base.

Alamo in class, wearing his
"puppy-in-training" vest.

Alamo takes to the skies and gets
a special invitation to check out
the cockpit.

Alamo thinking he's a lap dog.

I've been blessed to travel and speak all over the world to share messages of faith, perseverance, and hope.

# Acknowledgments

Books come to life through the work not of just one author but a team—most of them working behind the scenes. This book is no exception.

We want to thank the following people for their roles:

Susy Flory, who introduced us (Mike and Keri) and thought we might be a good team of writers. Thank you, Susy, for facilitating the connection, providing helpful feedback on an early draft, and cheering us on the whole way!

Sarah Atkinson, publisher at Tyndale Momentum, for believing in this project and gently but firmly guiding us toward making it the best it could be.

Bonne Steffen, our editor at Tyndale, for asking a lot of questions and fine-tuning all the details as we wrote, revised, and brought nine dogs to life in the pages of this book.

Steve Laube, our agent, for finding the right publisher and keeping us grounded all along the way.

Karen Hingson, Mike's wife of forty years, who passed away just as we finished the manuscript for *Live like a Guide Dog*. Karen was feisty and smart and a dog lover, which is a wonderful combination.

Scot Kent, Keri's husband of thirty-three years, who offered support and encouragement all along the journey, not just for this book but all the others that led to this one.

The people at Canine Companions who graciously allowed Keri to visit puppy training classes as part of our research, and the many people who shared their service and guide dog stories with us.

And Todd Jurek, a trainer at Guide Dogs for the Blind, who shared insights on guide dog training.

Michael Hingson and Keri Wyatt Kent

# Notes

page 9   *If you are going to make your kids tough:* https://www
         .youtube.com/watch?v=sgicbipMj4c.

page 66  *Mike never really proposed:* Michael Hingson and Susy Flory,
         *Thunder Dog: The True Story of a Blind Man, His Guide Dog,
         and the Triumph of Trust* (Nashville: Thomas Nelson, 2011), 147.

page 88  *"Come to me, all you who are weary":* Matthew 11:28, NIV.

page 91  *Although I did have a car:* Mike's car and driving days are
         mentioned in *Thunder Dog.* Hingson and Flory, *Thunder Dog,*
         107.

page 149 *"Fear not, for I am with you":* Isaiah 41:10, NKJV.

page 158 *"Perfect love casts out fear":* 1 John 4:18, NKJV.

page 175 *It's hard to turn off the noise:* "Digital marketing experts
         estimate that most Americans are exposed to around 4,000
         to 10,000 ads each day," Jon Simpson, "Finding Brand Success
         in the Digital World," Forbes Agency Council, August 25, 2017,
         https://www.forbes.com/sites/forbesagencycouncil/2017/08
         /25/finding-brand-success-in-the-digital-world/.

page 176 *Fear appeal in advertising is a strategy:* "Fear Appeal in
         Advertising," Rachel Jankielewicz, Study.com, updated
         June 2, 2022, https://study.com/learn/lesson/fear-appeal
         -theory-examples-what-is-fear-appeal-in-advertising.html.

page 197 **The human body is a complex cocktail of chemicals:** "Does My Dog Know If I'm Sick?," Stephanie Gibeault, MSc, CPDT. Published: Nov 03, 2022 . https://www.akc.org/expert-advice /advice/does-my-dog-know-if-im-sick/.

page 220 **However, recently another company, Envision:** See https:// www.letsenvision.com.

page 229 **In other words, they have experienced fear:** Want to listen to or learn more about the podcast? Please visit www .michaelhingson.com/podcast. If you have a story to tell, reach out, and we will talk about you being a guest.

# About the Authors

**MICHAEL HINGSON** is the *New York Times* bestselling author of *Thunder Dog*, the true story of how he and his guide dog Roselle escaped from Tower One on 9/11. An internationally acclaimed public speaker, he has addressed influential groups such as ExxonMobile, AT&T, FedEx, Rutgers University, Children's Hospital Los Angeles, and the American Red Cross. He is the chief vision officer for accessiBe, a company that creates products to make websites more accessible to people with disabilities, and is also the National Federation of the Blind's ambassador for its National Braille Literacy Campaign. Visit him at michaelhingson.com.

**KERI WYATT KENT** is the author of twelve books and the coauthor of a dozen more. She has collaborated with business leaders and pastors, including Rick Warren and Greg Hawkins. She has been published by Zondervan, InterVarsity Press, and Revell Books, among others. She is the founder of A Powerful Story, a company that provides collaborative writing, editing, and publishing services. She has spoken and led retreats at many churches around the United States. Keri and her husband, Scot, live in the Chicago area and have two grown children. You can learn more about Keri at keriwyattkent.com.